Digital Modeling of Appearance

Digital Modeling of Appearance

JULIE DORSEY

HOLLY RUSHMEIER

FRANÇIS SILLION

AMSTERDAM • BOSTON • HEIDELBERG • LONDON
NEW YORK • OXFORD • PARIS • SAN DIEGO
SAN FRANCISCO • SINGAPORE • SYDNEY • TOKYO

Morgan Kaufmann Publishers is an imprint of Elsevier

Publisher	Denise E. M. Penrose
Senior Acquisitions Editor	Tiffany Gasbarrini
Publishing Services Manager	George Morrison
Project Manager	Marilyn E. Rash
Marketing Manager	Ian Seager
Assistant Editors	Michele Cronin, Matthew Cater
Copyeditor	Jodie Allen
Proofreader	Daniel Stone
Indexer	Ted Laux
Cover Design	Molly Bigelow
Typesetting/Illustration Formatting	diacriTech
Interior/Cover Printer	1010 Printing International Ltd.

Morgan Kaufmann Publishers is an imprint of Elsevier.
30 Corporate Drive, Burlington, MA 01803-4255

This book is printed on acid-free paper.

Library of Congress Cataloging-in-Publication Data
Dorsey, Julie

Digital modeling of material appearance / Julie Dorsey, Holly Rushmeier, Francois Sillion.
    p. cm. — (The Morgan Kaufmann series in computer graphics)
Includes bibliographical references and index.

ISBN 978-0-12-221181-2 (alk. paper)

1. Computer graphics. 2. Visualization. 3. Image processing—Digital techniques.
I. Rushmeier, Holly E. II. Sillion, Francois X. III. Title.

T385.D6824 2007
006.6—dc22   2007036188

For information on all Morgan Kaufmann publications,
visit our Web site at *www.mkp.com* or *www.books.elsevier.com*

Printed and bound by CPI Group (UK) Ltd, Croydon, CR0 4YY

Transferred to Digital Print 2011

Contents

Acknowledgments

We would like to thank our colleagues, friends, and family for their comments and support while we wrote this book. In particular, Anne Pardoen provided invaluable moral support. We are grateful to our fellow researchers who gave their consent to have images from their works included here. Cyril Soler contributed several new illustrative images.

We were helped a great deal by comments and suggestions on draft versions by Russell Rushmeier and by anonymous reviewers. We benefited from the rich intellectual environments we work in at Yale and INRIA. We are indebted to Tiffany Gasbarrini, Michele Cronin, and the production team at Elsevier for their persistence and hard work in turning our early drafts into a polished publication.

Each of us spent several years early in our careers working at the Program of Computer Graphics at Cornell University. Our work, including this book, has been inspired by the vision and example of our mentors at Cornell, Professor Donald Greenberg and Professor Kenneth Torrance.

1 INTRODUCTION

Computer graphics systems are capable of generating imagery of stunning realism. For feature film and games, entire new visual worlds are created and synthetic scenes and characters are mixed seamlessly with recorded live action. Designers, architects, and engineers are able to visualize and evaluate product concepts in realistic settings. Historians and archaeologists are able to reconstruct a visual world of the past. The development of accurate digital models of material appearance has been an essential element in the building of this capability. This book presents the foundations of modeling material appearance.

Systems to generate realistic images are the result of efforts of three diverse communities: computer science researchers, software engineers, and artists and designers. Researchers have built mathematical models of materials based on many different disciplines. Computer scientists have adapted and expanded models of material light interaction that were originally developed in areas such as optics, biology, and various branches of engineering. Using these models, they have developed algorithms to efficiently capture different aspects of appearance. Software engineers have implemented these algorithms into systems that model an object's shape and illuminate its environment as well as material. Artists and designers use the various systems to produce visual output. The process is not just a one-way flow of information. To create what they envision, artists and designers often press systems and use them in ways not originally intended, as well as push software engineers and researchers to produce new and improved models and systems. Software engineers often enhance and expand the algorithms that come directly from researchers.

The result of this activity among the different communities involved in computer graphics has been a rich but disorganized body of work in the area of digital modeling of appearance. Many different classes of materials have been modeled, and many different classes of algorithms have been developed for computing the appearance of these materials. Some common material models are so complex that they require setting in excess of 50 parameters to obtain a particular look. Literally thousands of web sites directed at the full range of users; from hobbyists to professionals, are devoted to explaining how to achieve different effects. It is becoming increasingly difficult for individuals to learn what has been done, what can be done, and what needs to be done in the area of digital appearance modeling.

This book provides a common foundation for modeling appearance. This foundation is based on the physics of how light interacts with materials, how people perceive and specify appearance, and what the implications of encoding models are on a digital computer. While all communities are not going to explore each of these areas in equal depth, considering all of the issues will provide a basis for researchers and practitioners to more effectively interact.

Chapter 2 contains background information with a perspective on the major issues involved in materials modeling: the physics of light and human visual perception. These are broad topics and we describe the essentials that are needed to start modeling materials. First, we identify the three elements—shape, material, and incident light—that produce a visual image. Next, we identify the three major aspects of materials: spectral, directional, and spatial variations.

With this basic background outlined, we then consider different classes of materials in Chapter 3, Observation and Classification. For researchers and software engineers, it is essential to spend time looking at materials in the world before addressing mathematical, or any computational, considerations. We take as inspiration the training that artists have had in observation. However, in contrast to observation in art, the goal of the chapter is to observe, in a more technical framework, the way appearance is affected by how light rays reach the eye from a source.

Ultimately, to encode models on a digital computer, we need mathematical descriptions. In Chapter 4, Mathematical Terms, we define the basic terms, concepts, and notations used in describing light and materials. For many years, computer graphics systems used ad hoc descriptions of shades and lights making it difficult to compare and combine methods across different vocabularies, units, and scales. Successful realistic modeling was advanced by adopting the standard terms used by the illumination and radiative transfer communities. While understanding the definitions of radiance and reflectance can be challenging, it is the key to being able to understand material models.

Using basic mathematical terms, Chapter 5, General Material Models, presents the basic models for how materials scatter light. The chapter traces the development of the various named reflectance models (e.g., Phong, Blinn, Cook–Torrance, and Oren–Nayar) that appear in most graphics systems. It also puts in context more complex models that account for interference, diffraction, and volumetric scattering.

While many materials can be defined as simple combinations of the general material models, other materials require specific models of small-scale geometric structure and multiple spatially varying layers. Chapter 6, Specialized Material Models, provides a guide to these specific models, which have been published in diverse, more specialized, conference documents and journals, as well as in major conference—ACM, IEEE, and Eurographics—proceedings.

Whichever model is used for materials, we need some means to determine the parameters for it. In a design setting, parameters may be selected to achieve a particular effect. In many other cases, a model of a particular existing material that matches suitable benchmarks is needed. Chapter 7, Measurement, discusses the different techniques available for obtaining data for existing materials.

Materials have a temporal, as well as a spatial, dimension. Material appearance depends on the history of usage and environment and the basic chemical components and surface finish. Materials may be purposefully treated to achieve particular end results or may change as the result of natural aging or weathering. Chapter 8, Aging and Weathering, presents methods that either simulate temporal evolution of changes in materials or directly model the visual results of processed materials. This is still an emerging area of materials modeling, and open questions and issues are identified.

Chapter 9, Specifying and Encoding Appearance Descriptions, considers how various models are efficiently encoded, and how these models are presented to the user for modification. Representation in terms of different basis functions expose different types of controls to the user. Further, the chapter considers how material models are associated with shapes to specify complete object descriptions.

Finally, Chapter 10, Rendering Appearance, looks at how material models are integrated into complete systems for generating images. Different representations of models are used for different rendering approaches. Different models can be appropriate for offline and real-time systems.

This is the first comprehensive work on digital modeling of the appearance of materials. It is not a "how-to" book in the sense of providing a series of screenshots showing how to set parameters in a particular software system, or pseudocode for rendering a particular material. The book is meant to be a guide of how to decompose the appearance of materials so that they can be represented digitally. It identifies the basic appearance attributes of materials. In addition, the book presents definitions and principles that have been applied to modeling general classes of materials. Finally, the book is a guide to the range of material appearance effects that have been considered in computer graphics to date. For researchers, we hope the book helps to focus future work in this area. For practitioners, we hope the book provides a perspective to help make sense of the wide array of tools currently available.

2 BACKGROUND

"Material appearance" is the visual impression we have of a material. To model material appearance, we need to express, in the form of data and algorithms, everything needed to simulate how the material would look from any view, in any environment. Modeling materials is just one area of computer graphics, however, it is a complicated area that builds on models from a variety of other disciplines. In this chapter, we introduce some basic principles from other disciplines that we use as a starting point for modeling.

Modeling the appearance of an object's material gives us the capability to simulate what an object would look like. How the object will look depends on both physical and psychological phenomena. Light leaving an object that reaches our eye is the physical stimulus that allows us to see it. The connection between that stimulus and the idea that we form about the object is a complex result of the physiology of our eyes and the processing in our brains. The vehicle we use to present the simulation of an object is a two-dimensional image. In generating images from digital models, we want the display to produce a physical stimulus that will generate the same idea of how an object would appear if we had viewed it directly (Figure 2.1). To do this, we build on knowledge of the physics of light, human perception, and image formation.

The physics of light has been intensely studied for centuries. Our understanding of light has moved from the Greek's corpuscular theory, to Huygen's waves, to the theory of quantum electrodynamics, and continues to expand. In modeling appearance, our goal is not to incorporate the entire body of knowledge that has been accumulated.

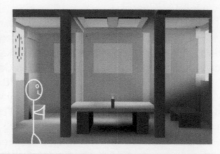

Figure 2.1: The light from a synthetic image should stimulate the same response as the light coming from viewing the real object.

It is generally not appropriate, or useful, to use the most low-level, detailed models of light that have been developed in physics. What we want to do is extract from what is known about light the models that are relevant to the human process of seeing an object.

Perception and the human mind have also been studied for centuries. Our understanding of how we form ideas about what we see is in a far more primitive state than our understanding of physical light. There have been a great deal of data collected for specific aspects of human vision and cognition, and many different models have been developed to explain these observations. As in the case of the physics of light, our goal is not to try to incorporate all of the models that have been formed for vision and cognition. Unlike physics, however, this is not because these models are not relevant to our goal. The problem is that in the field of psychology there is no comprehensive model that can reliably combine even a substantial subset of these individual observations.

We can observe, however, how we describe our impressions of objects. We refer to objects as being, for instance, "shiny red," "mottled gray," or "bumpy." We can separate out these various impressions into different types. Further, for different types of impressions, we can use models of the relationship of an impression, depending on the type of impression, to the physical light we encounter at different levels of detail. In many cases, the statements we can reliably make about the relationship between physical light and the impression we form will be very crude. However, even simple approximate relationships provide us with significant insight into how we should model light interactions to produce the appearance of an object.

In computer graphics, we combine descriptions of physical light and human perception to form images. To form an image, we need to model each object's shape, material, and the light incident on the object. Given these ingredients, we can generate an image for a human observer at a specific location and view direction.

Light, perception, and image formation are each topics that could be the subjects of a book, or series of books, on their own. Here, we briefly discuss some basic ideas from these areas that are needed as background for the detailed material models we will present in the following chapters.

2.1 LIGHT

Light is basic to our existence, and we think of it in many different ways. Light is the product that comes from the sun or a lamp that allows us to see things. Light leaves a source, strikes objects, and eventually hits our eyes. We only see objects for which there is a direct, unobstructed path for light to follow from the object to our eyes. If there is an unobstructed path from a light source to the object, the object will appear bright to us. If the path from the light source to the object is blocked, the object will look dark, or shadowed, to us.

More formally, we are considering visible light, which is electromagnetic radiation in the wavelength band between roughly 380 nm and 780 nm. Light is variously modeled as quanta, waves, or geometric rays depending on the length scales involved, as diagrammed in Figure 2.2. At atomic length scales, quantum mechanical effects are important. At scales within an order magnitude of the wavelength of light (100 nm to 10 microns), wave phenomena are important. At the scale of most human activity (mm to km), geometric optics serve to accurately model the light interactions that leave an object and arrive at our eyes.

In geometric optics, we model the light as traveling along straight paths between surfaces, as illustrated by the sample ray paths shown in Figure 2.3. Ray paths begin at light

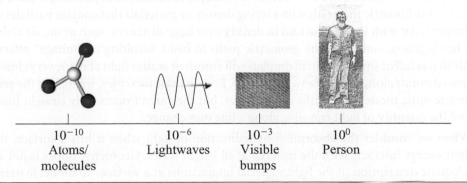

$$10^{-10} \qquad\qquad 10^{-6} \qquad\qquad 10^{-3} \qquad\qquad 10^{0}$$

Atoms/ molecules	Lightwaves	Visible bumps	Person

Figure 2.2: Light wavelength relative to atomic and human length scales (logarithmic in meters).

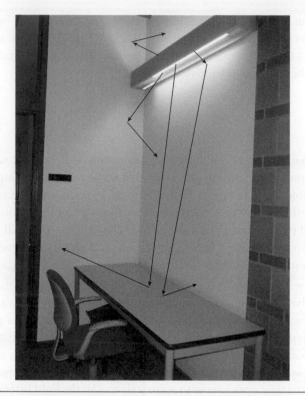

Figure 2.3: In geometric optics, light is modeled as traveling in straight lines.

sources, for example, a lamp or the sun. As rays hit other surfaces, they may be either absorbed or redirected in a new direction. A couple of variations in this simple description are volumetric materials with varying density or materials that contain particles or droplets. Air with large variations in density over large distances, such as the air above a hot highway, can cause the geometric paths to bend, resulting in "mirage" effects. Air that is full of smoke or small droplets will absorb or scatter light at many very closely spaced points along the ray between objects. Even in these two cases, we still use the geometric optic model. The paths are still lines, but they aren't necessarily straight lines, and the quantity of light traveling along a line may change.

When we consider the absorption or redirection of light when it hits a surface, the light energy interacts with the material at all length scales. Geometric optics is not an adequate description of the light/material interactions at a surface. To model material appearance, we encapsulate these interactions in the form of scattering distributions (such as the distribution illustrated in Figure 2.4) that describe what amount of light

Figure 2.4: The effect of a material on incident light is represented as a scattering distribution. In this image the distribution of laser light scattered by the surface is made visible using artificial fog manufactured for stage lighting effects.

leaves a surface in each direction as a function of the amount and direction of incident light. These distributions can be obtained by measuring the light leaving a surface. Alternatively, the small-scale interactions can be modeled by quantum, wave, or geometric techniques to form the scattering distribution. A fundamental observation is that these detailed interactions encapsulated in the scattering distribution only depend on the material, not on the overall scene. They can be measured or simulated once and then reused in many environments. These scattering distributions do not need to be recomputed in the course of computing an image, but simply evaluated for incident and exitant angles as required.

The encapsulated description is relatively simple, because of the independence of light transfers. The amount of light scattered by incident light from a particular source is the same regardless of whether there is also light coming from another light source. We can, for example, solve for the effect of light source A on a scene, and then solve for the effect of light source B on the same scene, and obtain the result for using both by taking the sum of the results, as shown in Figure 2.5. Light coming from source A will do nothing to enhance or diminish the light from source B scattered by surfaces. The light scattering distribution functions we use for materials can be used as we consider individual light paths in our solution, rather than having to consider all light paths simultaneously.

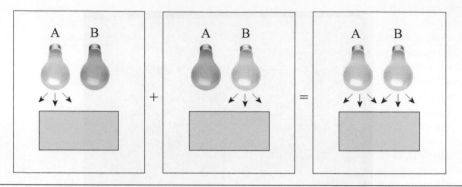

Figure 2.5: The effect of two lights is the sum of their independent effects.

The ability to encapsulate detailed, small-scale interactions into functions while computing the bulk of light transfer in a scene using geometric optics is a very powerful concept. It is what allows us to accurately simulate light transfer by following the paths of thousands or millions of rays using a desktop PC, rather than using months of supercomputer time computing electromagnetic wave solutions on computational grids that divide scenes into segments of less than a micron.

Models based on physics are used in many areas of graphics, particularly animation. Mathematical techniques are adapted from various fields of engineering and science. A consequence of using the geometric optic model for light transfer is that the mathematics used are different from many of the other fields that graphics draws on. When studying fluid flow, for example, the activity at a point in the material depends on the difference in some quantity like pressure or density between the point and its immediate neighbors. In modeling a continuous material, the neighborhood is shrunk to infinitesimal, and the differences between points are modeled as derivatives and the phenomena are modeled as differential equations.

In considering light transport, we have quite a different situation. Consider looking at points on a sidewalk on a sunny day (Figure 2.6). The light reflected from the points on the sidewalk does not come from the points on either side of it. We could paint all of the sidewalk around each point black, and the light coming from the points would remain substantially the same. The light coming from the points does depend on the very distant sky and sun that direct energy at the points along straight line paths. One of the points is darker because a less distant object (the photographer) is blocking the direct sun, but not all of the distant skylight. Instead of estimating the light by taking derivatives in the neighborhood of the point, we need to compute the light incident from all directions above the point. We need to sum up the incident light from the continuum of directions above the point. As a result, to solve the

Figure 2.6: The light on a point can depend on distant sources and can be independent of its immediate neighborhood.

light transfer problem, we use primarily integral, rather than differential, equations. In some cases, light transfer will also depend on local scattering within the material. In such cases the light transfer is described by integro-differential equations. The form of these equations influences the way the material models are formulated and encoded.

Although it challenges our everyday experience, it is critical in modeling appearance that light itself does not have color. Quoting Newton's *Optiks*: "For the Rays to speak properly [they] are not coloured. In them there is nothing else than a certain Power and Disposition to stir up a Sensation of this or that Colour" [246]. Light energy is distributed over various wavelengths. Different wavelength distributions produce the *perception* of different colors when they hit our eyes. As we follow light from source to object to eye, we need to model the changing wavelength distribution, not the color, of the light.

In typical natural environments there is a distribution of light energy through the whole visible spectrum. For example, Figure 2.7 shows the reflectance of a blue flower. With a few exceptions, such as lasers or light emitting diodes, we don't often encounter light at a single wavelength or narrow wavelength band. Except for a few cases, such as fluorescent lights that have spikes, at a few wavelengths the variation of light energy leaving objects in a scene as a function of wavelength is smooth. The overall smoothness of most wavelength distributions is one of the phenomena that make it possible to accurately simulate light transfers with relatively crude models of spectral variation.

The discussion of wavelength versus color leads us to the general consideration of human perception and judgments related to light and appearance.

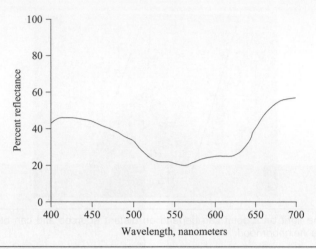

Figure 2.7: The wavelength distribution from natural objects is typically smooth.

2.2 HUMAN PERCEPTION AND JUDGMENTS

As just noted, the appropriate models of light to use are dictated by the scales that are relevant to humans, in particular, to human perception. Besides dictating the appropriate scales, our understanding of human perception and judgment informs us about what aspects of light we need to simulate, and how precisely we need to simulate these aspects to produce accurate appearance.

Brightness and color are two ways we judge materials. Another type of judgment we make is the directionality of a material's light interactions, that is, whether the object is shiny or dull, opaque or translucent. We also judge whether the material is uniform or textured (i.e., whether it appears to have scale variations of color and/or geometry). Considering our perception of brightness, color, directionality, and texture provide insights into what light interactions are important to model.

2.2.1 LUMINANCE AND BRIGHTNESS

Our eyes are sensitive to light in the 380 to 780 nm wavelength band. We only need to be concerned with light in this range leaving an object to generate an image reproducing the object's appearance. This is a major simplification of relating physical models to our perception. In special cases, such as fluorescent materials that emit visible light as the result of absorbing light in nonvisible bands, other wavelengths might have some impact on the light ultimately leaving an object. However, outside of studies, such as whether fluorescent materials added to a detergent will really make your "whites whiter," light outside the visible band rarely enters into modeling appearance.

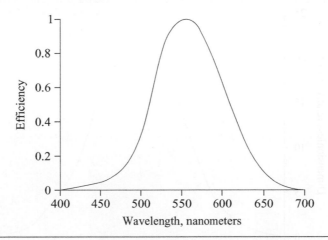

Figure 2.8: The luminous efficiency curve shows the sensitivity of eyes to light as a function of wavelength.

Our eyes are not equally sensitive to all wavelengths in the visible range. The sensitivity of human eyes over the visible range is given by the luminous efficiency function, which is a bell-shaped function peaking at 550 nm, as shown in Figure 2.8. The convolution of the luminous efficiency function with a light distribution is defined to be luminance. Luminance is the area under the curve formed by multiplying the luminous efficiency curve by the spectral distribution wavelength, as shown in Figure 2.9. Because luminance is a measure of light that is really useful in vision, lightbulbs are labeled with the luminance they produce as well as the electric power they consume. As a side note, because there are different ways to physically produce light with varying amounts of the electric power emitted as heat rather than visible light, it is possible that different bulbs produce the same luminance for different electrical power consumption.

Luminance is a measure of the light energy that is useful, but we are not linearly sensitive to luminance. Our sensation of the amount of light we are seeing is called brightness. A surface with twice the luminance does not look twice as bright. The variation of brightness as a function of luminance can be roughly modeled as a log or cube root function. This sublinear variation in sensitivity reduces the accuracy required in the estimation of light arriving from an object. Light variations that can be recorded by even an inexpensive light meter may not necessarily be detected visually. Not only is our ability to detect light variations not linear, it is relative as we adapt to the overall light level in a scene.

The perception of variations of light levels is also a function of the spatial frequency of the variation, as illustrated in Figure 2.10. For very low spatial frequencies (left

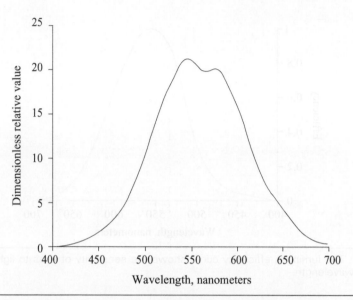

Figure 2.9: The luminance is the area under the curve formed by multiplying the spectral distribution wavelength by the luminous efficiency curve. This curve shows the result for the blue flower distribution.

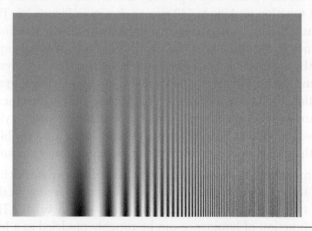

Figure 2.10: Our ability to detect variations in luminance depends on the spatial frequency of the variations.

side of figure), or very high-frequency variations (right side of figure), large changes in luminance are needed to be detected, again reducing the accuracy of the estimates required. The spatial level of detail at which we need to model objects is limited by the falloff of sensitivities at high spatial frequencies.

2.2.2 COLOR

When we are asked to describe an object, our response is likely to be naming its predominant color. For example, we might ask "Which sample?" when looking at Figure 2.11. A likely response is "the green one" rather than "the flat one with the dull finish." Reproducing the color of an object is key in modeling its appearance. A lot of work in studying appearance has focused on color alone. Color perception is consistent across populations and cultures, as evidenced by the basic color names for similar color groupings that are found in nearly all languages [20]. A significant proportion of the population (around 8 percent of the male population, 0.4 percent of the female population [91]) is color-blind. However, this means for most that they have difficulty discriminating between particular colors (usually red and green) rather than that they have no color perception at all.

Our eyes are not sensitive to all possible variations in spectral distribution. A very simplified description of our visual system is that at normal light levels incident light is processed by three sensors: one signal corresponding to the quantity of light at shorter wavelengths, one in the mid-range, and one at the longer wavelengths. These three types of sensors are the cones in our eyes. The signals are combined in various ways to produce our perception of color. The physiology of the receptors that produce color are relatively well understood, and their sensitivities as a function of wavelength have been measured.

At low light levels the cones are not sensitive to light, and our vision is the result of signals from the rods in our eyes. There is only one type of rod rather than three for different wavelength bands, and as a result, at low light levels we do not perceive color.

Figure 2.11: Color is a major visual attribute we use to refer to an object's appearance.

We don't use the sensitivity functions of the cones explicitly for image synthesis, but we do use the very powerful observation that the color we perceive is based on three independent signals. This means that all the colors we perceive can be represented by a vector of three values. Basis functions that can be used to unambiguously compute colors from spectra have been defined by the International Commission on Illumination (CIE), and are shown in Figure 2.12. These basis functions are referred to as X, Y, and Z and were determined by psychophysical experiments. These basis functions are not the sensitivities of the eyes' cones, but they are constructed so that any two spectra that map to the same values of X, Y, and Z will be perceived as the same color. This mapping, that is, the projection of the spectrum onto the X, Y, and Z basis functions, is the same as the calculation of luminance from the spectral distribution and the luminous efficiency curve. Formally, the XYZ coordinates are found by convolving the spectra with the functions. Roughly speaking, spectra that map to the same values of XYZ appear to be the same color, as illustrated in Figure 2.13. Different spectra that appear to be the same color are referred to as *metamers*. Overall viewing conditions also affect color perception, so that matching colors by matching XYZ values is a very simplified description of evaluating color.

Color displays work by emitting light from red, green, and blue elements. Each of these elements emit light across the spectrum, and the light from each element can be characterized by XYZ coordinates. The red elements have a higher value of X, green elements a higher value of Y, and blue elements a higher value of Z. To display an arbitrary color XYZ, the relative intensities of the red, blue, and green elements are adjusted

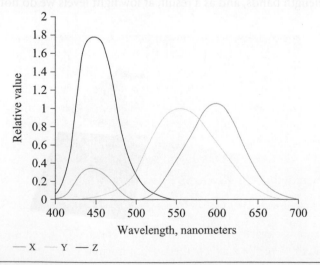

Figure 2.12: XYZ sensitivities for the standard observer.

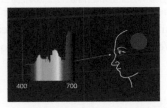

Figure 2.13: Different spectra can look the same.

so that their sum matches the color to be displayed. For example, the color yellow has high values of X and Y and a relatively low value of Z. The elements would be adjusted so that red and green have high values and the blue element has a low value.

The three signal characteristics of color perception do not guarantee that it is always adequate to simply sample three wavelengths to compute the color perceived from a particular spectral distribution. A detailed material model should be defined as a function of wavelength. How finely the spectral dependence should be sampled depends on the particular material and scene. In practice, the rather smooth variations in spectral distributions make it possible to use sparse sampling. Furthermore, the spectral samples often used in graphics are rarely obtained by sampling in a narrow wavelength band, but rather are recorded over broader bands, such as by the red, green, and blue values recorded by a digital camera.

The perceptions of color and brightness are effects with common terminology and well-defined scales. In many applications concerned with appearance, such as photography, print, and television, reproducing color and brightness are the only issues. These applications start with nature providing the light from a physical object arriving at a camera sensor or film plane, and the task is to produce a print or television display that provides the same stimulus to viewers as would observing the object directly. Appearance is reproduced by ensuring that brightness and color response stimulated by the display are the same as a direct view of the object. This in part accounts for why color has been the main aspect of appearance that has been studied. This is not to say that color reproduction is simple or a fully solved problem. Conversion to XYZ coordinates and the use of simple brightness/luminance functions are extraordinarily simplified descriptions of how color is faithfully reproduced. Many other perceptual factors in the viewing context need to be considered, and many alternatives to the XYZ color space have been developed.

Unlike photography or television, we aren't interested in just reproducing one image of an object. We aren't given a description of the light reaching the viewer for an existing object—we need to predict it. The spatial and directional distribution of the light, as well as the spectral distribution, affect our impression of object appearance. If we want to generate an image that looks like a red carpet, it is not enough to light up an array of red pixels. We need to account for directional and spatial variations on the object.

2.2.3 DIRECTIONAL EFFECTS

Directional effects are impressions of an object's appearance that result from the directionality of the scattering of light by the object. We can observe directional effects by noting whether we see changes in an object as we change our view of the object. The directional effects we classify here are due to structures at a length scale shorter than that visible to the eye. Directional effects can be observed on completely flat surfaces. Descriptions that we attach to these impressions include shiny, hazy, glossy, matte, dull, translucent, or transparent. Unlike color, we don't have a universally accepted name for this type of effect, or specific definitions for when something is "shiny" versus "glossy" or "translucent" versus "transparent." These attributes are attached to an object, even when the object is viewed under different illumination conditions [96].

Despite the absence of universal definitions, directional effects are clearly important. Terms and classifications can be found in a variety of contexts and fields of study. In home decorating, the term *surface finish* is often used. Paints of the same color are designated as matte or gloss finish, metal is weathered or polished, and ceramics are glazed or unglazed. When referring to the term *gloss*, various sorts of paints may be gloss, semigloss, eggshell, satin, or low-luster. Surfaces may be categorized by their sheen or how reflective they are.

In natural sciences, directional effects are used in classification. In geology, for instance, one way minerals are characterized is by their "luster"— their appearance beyond color, with specific definitions of terms such as adamantine, metallic, greasy/oily, earthy/dull, waxy, and vitreous. In grading gems such as diamonds that are adamantine, specific directional effects are referred to as brilliance, fire, and scintillation. In plant pathology, the health of a plant may be diagnosed by whether leaves are shiny or dull.

Directional effects are also used in classifications in other fields. For example, in archaeology, beads are an artifact that are used to date finds based on what is known about bead making [175]. Along with characteristics such as light and color, beads are judged on "diaphaneity," or their ability to transmit light. A bead is opaque if no light passes through it, translucent if light passes through but objects cannot be seen distinctly through the bead, and transparent if objects can be seen distinctly through the bead. As an example in a much different area, water clarity monitoring, the turbidity of water is sometimes characterized visually. A common test is at what depth a black-and-white disk is no longer visible.

The physical stimulus for these visual impressions is clearly related to a material's light scattering function, but the relationship is not as clear as that between wavelengths and color. Because of the commercial impact of consumer judgments of these effects, there has been some work in correlating directional light scattering measurements with human judgments. In the effort to established these correlations, Hunter and Harold [152] defined different types of gloss: specular ("brilliance of highlights"); sheen ("shininess at grazing angles"); luster ("contrast between specularly reflecting and other areas"); absence-of-bloom ("absence of haze, or milky appearance"); and distinctness of image ("sharpness of mirror images"). A wide variety of standardized tests for these types of gloss have been defined by different industries. They involve measuring light scattering at particular angles and establishing a scale based on judgments relative to a "perfect" material; for example, sheen might be rated relative to the appearance of light reflected from a black glass.

In the study of human vision, the nature of directional effects has been studied in a variety of ways, including the effect of directional scattering on the perception of overall three-dimensional object shapes. However, there has not been a focused effort on relating specific perceptions to the physical scattering function. Only preliminary work has been done in computer graphics modeling to examine these effects. Westlund and Meyer [334] explored how to convert industrial measurements into light scattering models. Pellacini et al. [263] performed psychophysical tests to establish perceptual gloss dimensions to a light scattering model. For the types of materials tested, they found that gloss perception had two perceptual dimensions. However, there is no general measure yet to predict when two scattering functions will produce the same impression of shininess or gloss. The directionality of physical light scatter can be viewed as a very high-dimensional space [219]. It is unknown how many perceptual dimensions there are for general material types. Modeling the quantity of light scattered in a preferred direction (mirror direction) versus the quantity scattered in all directions (diffusely) is important.

Similar to gloss measurements, there are industrial standard tests to characterize transparency. For example, haze in transparent plastic film is measured as the light scattered more than 4 degrees from the direction passing directly through the film [152]. Opacity is measured to determine how well paint covers by measuring how much light is reflected when paint is applied to a white backing rather than a black backing. In the human vision literature, the characteristics of images that produce judgments of transparency and translucency have been studied both for thin objects [228] and recently more generally [97]. Perception of translucency is more complex than simply assessing whether light passes through an object. Translucence can be perceived when light comes from in front of the object as a result of the apparent spreading of incident light within the object.

In the past, an impediment to relating judgments to physical quantities for directional effects was the difficulty of controlling the scattering function to conduct controlled experiments. For experiments in color, the intensity of lights of various spectra could be controlled and projected together to perform color-matching experiments. Experiments for thin transparency were made using an "epscopister," which was a disk with a wedge cut out that, when spun at different rates, would allow some fraction of light through, simulating various levels of transparency [228]. Arguably, this was not actually measuring the perception of transparent materials [177], which is why more recent work [97] has produced different results. For measuring perceptions of shininess or sheen, there is no physical way to gradually alter the scattering distribution of surfaces in a controlled fashion. The capability we have now to generate images from scattering functions is removing this impediment to studying human perception of directional effects. Computer graphics imagery is being used ever more commonly in psychophysical experiments. By using imagery generated from numerically controlled scattering functions, our understanding of these relationships will accelerate in the coming years.

2.2.4 TEXTURES AND PATTERNS

Another factor in judging appearance is texture or pattern. Descriptions of texture are even more varied than those used for directional variations. Even the word "texture" does not have a uniform meaning; for example, it is applied to microscopic phenomena in material science and tactile phenomena in foods. Even by the definition of visual variations, many different terms may be used in different areas. Painted surfaces may be described with terms such as crackled, stippled, or swirled. Different types of wood veneer are described by their "grain figures" or typical textures, such as cathedral, oval, flakes, burl, flame, or fiddleback. Carpet textures are sometimes referred to as plush, shag, or sculpted. More specific classifications include the textures of igneous rocks, described as phaneritic, aphanitic, porphyritic, glassy, vesicular, and fragmental [164].

Technically, texture spatial visual variation on an object's surface is on a much smaller scale than the size of the object, but a much larger scale than the wavelength of light. The perceived variations may be due to spatial variations in directional or spectral scattering characteristics, or to small-scale geometric structures such as bumps or pores. Regardless of the cause, people are able to judge surfaces as either uniform or not, that is, whether there is a texture or pattern.

Despite the wide variation in physical origin and the terms used to describe it, the perception of texture has been studied extensively in both human and computer vision literature. A great deal of work has been inspired by Bela Julesz, who in a seminal paper [165] used the then-new tool of computer-generated patterns to conduct experiments in which observers saw textures only without any other physical context. His results launched a search for perceptual channels for texture that are analogous to the role of cones in color. The problem posed was whether there were features of textures that would predict when a person would judge two textures to be different. While no such channels have been found, there is evidence that texture perception is related to the vision system's mechanism for tuning features of different orientations and spatial frequencies. This observation has been exploited in computer graphics to synthesize large areas of texture formed by spatial variations of spectral reflectance from small spatial samples [143]. The levels of contrast and randomness are important features in discerning different textures [329].

2.3 IMAGE SYNTHESIS

With some basic ideas about light and perception outlined, we move to the process of forming a synthetic image. Illustrating this process shows the role that modeling material appearance plays in producing a visually accurate image.

An environment consists of a set of objects, each defined by a shape and material description, and at least one light source. Any number of images could be created from such an environment, with each image corresponding to a particular viewpoint, view direction, and view frustum (i.e., field of view), as shown in Figure 2.14. The image is formed by projecting the objects in the environment that are seen through the frustum onto an image plane that spans the field of view and is perpendicular to the view direction. In a digital image, the image is discretized into pixels, and the display values for a specific pixel are set by determining the light that will arrive at the viewer from the object visible through that pixel.

For completeness, a couple of other image synthesis features should be noted. First, pixels cover an area, not just a point, and so an estimate of some average of the light arriving through the pixels needs to be found to avoid aliasing or jagginess in the final image. Second, the light values obtained will range through all the values possible in nature, which of course cannot be displayed. Color transformations and tone mapping, which exploit the effects described in the previous section, need to be applied to convert the image to a displayable range.

Before averaging light values or mapping them to displayable units, however, the light that would arrive through a pixel needs to be determined. The light that leaves an object depends on the *incident light* and the object's *shape* and *material*.

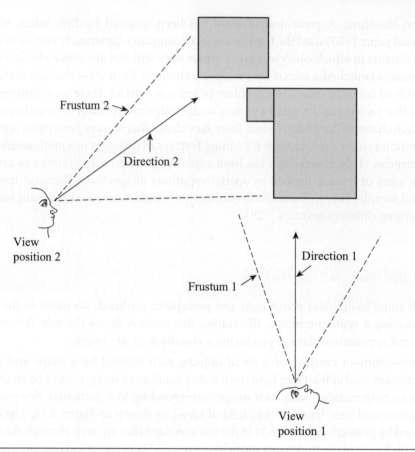

Figure 2.14: Specifying view position, direction, and frustum.

2.3.1 SHAPE

By shape, we mean the large-scale form or geometry of an object. The shape is needed to correctly place the image of an object with respect to other objects in a scene to determine what other objects are occluded and what areas are cast into shadow by the object. Fine-scale geometric variations exist as part of the object's material in the object we incorporate. Similar to the choice of model of light transfer to use, the definition of whether object geometry is part of its shape and/or material depends on the scale of the problem being considered. For a close view of a tree branch, a leaf is defined by a flat shape, with the number of lobes or points dependent on the type of tree. In an aerial photograph, a leaf is a small facet in a tree canopy material that covers the terrain. A rectangular rubber sponge is an example of an object that can be equally well modeled with different classification of what is shape. The sponge can be considered a simple rectangular shape, with a complicated map of its material characteristics of voids and sections of rubber. The sponge could also be modeled as a very complex shape, including all the holes and a very simple uniform rubber material.

Many methods can be used to represent shape. The area of computer-aided geometry is devoted to the study of shape representation, and extensive descriptions of representations, such as NURBs (nonuniform rational B-splines), polygon meshes, subdivision surfaces, and implicit surfaces, are documented at length in other references [31, 92, 330]. We will not discuss the various methods for defining shapes. Many considerations are involved in selecting a representation, including ease of design and compactness of representation. For rendering appearance, the essential feature of a shape representation is that given a ray in a particular direction, the position and orientation of the intersection of the ray and the shape's surface can be efficiently computed.

2.3.2 INCIDENT LIGHT

The light incident on an object comes directly from light sources and/or interreflections or scattering from other objects, as shown in Figure 2.3. The incident light will vary both in spectral composition and magnitude with direction from the object surface, as well as from position to position on the surface.

Many methods can be used to compute the interreflections of light between objects in an environment. These methods, referred to as "global illumination" methods, include ray tracing, radiosity, photon mapping, and hybrids of these various approaches. Thorough discussions of these methods can be found in Dutre et al. [84]. In these methods, paths of light are followed either explicitly or implicitly. Global illumination methods begin with the assumptions that shapes and the scattering functions that describe how each object material will redirect light have been defined. Some approaches, such as the original radiosity method, restrict the types of shapes or scattering functions that can be included in the solution. More recently, combinations of more sophisticated algorithms and faster processing speeds have resulted in Monte Carlo-based algorithms that can accommodate arbitrary input.

In real-time rendering methods, global illumination is often approximated and represented as a map. The approximation can come from offline calculations or may be captured from a physical environment.

For rendering appearance, the essential feature of a global illumination method, or a real-time approximation of global illumination in the form of a map, is that for a given ray direction, the quantity of light from that direction at a particular point can be efficiently computed.

Figure 2.15: Same shape, different materials.

2.3.3 MATERIAL

The object material determines how the incident light is redirected by the object at each point on the object's surface. The model of the material needs to account for the perceptual effects that were discussed in the previous section: the spectral variations that account for color, the scattering variations that account for directional effects, and the small-scale spatial variations of surface material and geometry that account for the perception of texture. The effect of material is illustrated in Figure 2.15. The shape and incident light are the same in each image, but the material in each case is different.

Material models have existed in computer graphics as long as there have been shaded images. It is impossible to form a shaded image of an object without assuming some material model that describes how light or dark the object is as a result of its orientation to a light source. However, advances in material modeling lagged on research in shape and global illumination for many years. Recent advances in inexpensive digital cameras that allow the capture of rich material variations, and increased processing power for computing complex effects, coupled with demands for increasing visual realism in computer-generated films and games, have pushed forward the area of material modeling.

2.4 SUMMARY AND FURTHER READING

The background we need for modeling materials is an understanding of the physics of light and human perception, and how they come together in the process of forming an image. The key ideas we will use are listed in the following.

Light
- For the human scales we normally model, geometric optics (light traveling along straight line paths) can be used to model light transfer.
- The interaction of light and material can be modeled independently of the environment containing the material.
- Complex light/material interactions that occur at small scales requiring more complicated models than geometric optics can be encapsulated into scattering distributions.
- Light is described by wavelength distribution, not by specifying a color.

We will show the use of physics results in constructing models for computer graphics; we won't derive them. For the quantitative background on the physics of light needed to do the derivations, the best starting point is a first-year college physics text. A particularly accessible treatment is given in chapters 34 through 39 of *Fundamentals of Physics*, volume 2, by Halliday et al. [134]. For a more qualitative background on the physics of light, a useful book is Feynman's *QED: The Strange Theory of Light and Matter* [94].

Human Perception
- We are sensitive to visible light, but are not accurate light meters.
- We characterize materials by color. However, color is a perceptual, not physical, quantity. In psychophysics, methods have been developed to convert quantities of light expressed as a function of wavelength into three-dimensional colors.
- We characterize materials by the directionality of how they scatter light, using terms such as glossy, matte, turbid, and so on.
- We characterize materials by texture—spatial variations in geometry and spectral characteristics that occur on a much smaller scale than that of objects.

We build on these observations by building material models that are functions of wavelength, direction, and spatial location. We rely on physics and measurement to quantify our models, since we can't accurately estimate light values with our vision system.

As in the case of physical light, for a more detailed understanding of perception, a good starting point is a comprehensive text such as Palmer's *Vision Science: Photons to Phenomenology* [257]. A qualitative discussion of vision and how characteristics of human vision are exploited in art is given in *Vision and Art: The Biology of Seeing* by Livingstone [206].

A brief description of the relationship of wavelength to color is given here in terms of simple colorimetry. The more general area of color appearance, which takes into account the whole visual context of a sample being observed, is examined in Fairchild's *Color Appearance Models* [91]. A practical guide to digital color in a variety of fields, including computer graphics, is given in Stone's *A Field Guide to Digital Color* [303]. A summary of standards for directional effects is given in Hunter and Harold's *The Measurement of Appearance*. For industrial appearance applications, these are referred to as "geometric" effects. Finally, texture perception is treated in Palmer's book [257]. A more qualitative discussion can be found in Julesz's *Dialogues on Perception* [166].

Image Formation

- An image is formed by computing the light that would be incident on the eyes through each pixel for a particular view.
- The light arriving through each pixel depends on the shape, incident light, and material of the object visible through the pixel.

We assume a basic knowledge of forming a computer graphics image. Texts such as Shirley et al.'s *Fundamentals of Computer Graphics* [288] describe projecting three-dimensional objects on a two-dimensional image plane and processes such as anti-aliasing. A detailed discussion of the appropriate color transforms and tone mapping that need to be applied to the light calculated through each pixel is given in Reinhard et al.'s *High Dynamic Range Imaging* [272].

For the next few chapters, we will focus on the modeling of materials. In the final chapters, we will consider how these models are encoded to be related to shapes and evaluated in global illumination systems to form images. We start in Chapter 3 with the first step in the modeling process, observing and classifying real-world materials.

3 OBSERVATION AND CLASSIFICATION

Modeling materials begins with observation. We need to look at what makes each material in the real world look different from other materials. The observation skills we need are similar to those developed by artists. However, we don't want to just observe the appearance of a particular object in a particular setting. Object appearance depends on shape, illumination, and our perception, as well as on the material itself. We need to develop a critical eye to discount these other factors.

As discussed in Chapter 2, for any material there are spectral, directional, and spatial variations. There are many types of variations in each of these categories, and for many materials just one or two types of variations determine appearance. By classifying materials by the types of variations that are important, we can greatly simplify the mathematical and numerical models we need to reproduce material appearance.

Our approach is shown at a high level in Figure 3.1. Material modeling does not start in front of a computer or by working from our often faulty visual memories. We start by looking carefully at the material we want to simulate, and possibly make some measurements. After this step we can turn to selecting the appropriate models and determining parameters to drive a numerical simulation.

The art-inspired observational approach has previously been applied by Wolfe [338] in analyzing synthetic imagery to understand three-dimensional rendering techniques. Here, we apply the visual analysis process Wolfe describes for achieving visual literacy when observing physical materials in order to understand how to model them.

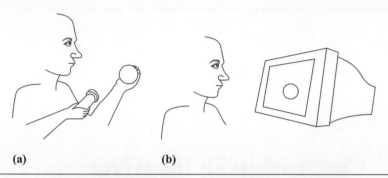

(a)   (b)

Figure 3.1: Modeling a material is a two-part process: (a) The real-world material has to be observed carefully to understand the factors that determine its appearance, and (b) then an appropriate mathematical model can be selected and adjusted to simulate the materials appearance numerically.

3.1 A TOUR OF MATERIALS

In this section, we consider examples of materials as they are classified for modeling in computer graphics. We define the terms that describe materials using images of real objects, and diagram their interaction with light. Light interactions can be viewed in two ways. First, we consider how individual light rays incident on an object are scattered or redirected. Then, we consider the rays that we need to follow to form an image. We follow the scattered rays backwards from a viewpoint to see how the simple single ray interactions lead to the formation of an image. In the following chapters we will define the interactions mathematically.

The most familiar and basic light scattering is regular or mirror reflection, as shown in Figure 3.2a. Each light ray reflects into one single direction, as shown in Figure 3.2b. Because each ray reflects in a single direction, rather than splitting and scattering upon reflection, the reflected rays stay organized. Figure 3.2c shows rays followed backwards from the viewer to objects in the environment. Because the rays stay in the same order as they were when they left the previous objects, a sharp image is formed just as though you were looking directly at the objects. We will refer to this regular, or mirror, reflection as a *pure specular* reflection. An indication that an object is a pure specular reflector, or has a component of pure specular reflection, is that you can see sharp images of other objects reflected in the material.

In Figure 3.2, objects are as sharp *and* proportioned as they are when viewed directly, because the mirror is flat. Figure 3.3a shows another object, a pitcher, with pure specular reflection. The shapes of other objects reflected in this object are distorted, not because of a different material property, but because the shape of the specular object is not a plane. The individual light material interaction is the same as in Figure 3.2b.

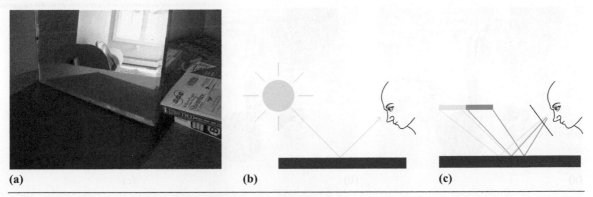

Figure 3.2: Mirror or pure specular reflection: (a) A typical mirror, (b) an individual ray reflects from a mirror in a single direction, and (c) tracing backwards from the viewpoint, the rays stay organized on reflection and form a sharp image.

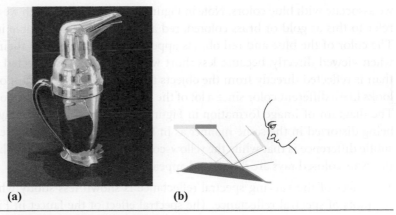

Figure 3.3: The nonplanar shape of the pure specular object shown in (a) results in the distortion of objects reflected on it. The direction of the rays is altered by the shape (b), but they do not overlap or split upon reflection, so the reflect images of objects appear sharp.

However, the organization of the rays forming an image is different, because of the difference in object shape, as diagrammed in Figure 3.3b. This is an example of needing to discount the effect of the overall shape in assessing the class of material.

Pure specular reflection may be spectrally selective. We generally think of a mirror as colorless, or possibly silver. This is just a way of describing a material that reflects all wavelengths the same way. Figure 3.4a shows a pure specular object that is specularly selective—it reflects a higher fraction of the incident light of the range of mid and longer wavelengths that we associate with a yellow color rather than shorter wavelengths that

  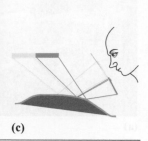

(a)   (b)   (c)

Figure 3.4: Spectrally selective reflection: (a) A metal faucet that does not reflect all wavelengths of light equally, (b) the color of objects is reflected when they are reflected in the faucet, and (c) spectral selection, not directionality, differentiates this material from that shown in Figures 3.2 and 3.3.

we associate with blue colors. Note in Figure 3.4b that even though we would generally refer to this as gold or brass colored, red and blue colors are visible in the reflection. The color of the blue and red objects appear slightly different in their reflection than when viewed directly, because less short wavelength light is reflected from the faucet than is reflected directly from the objects themselves. The reflection of the white sink looks like a different color since a lot of the light leaving the sink has not been reflected. The diagram of image formation in Figure 3.4c shows rays following directions and being distorted in the same manner as in Figure 3.3b. The images are still sharp. The subtle difference is that while the yellow-colored rays are reflected with the same color, the cyan-colored rays are darker and appear greener.

The effect of the varying spectral reflectance is shown less subtly when we consider the plots of spectral reflectance. The spectral effect of the faucet in Figure 3.4 on the light coming from the white sink and the red plastic cap is diagrammed in Figure 3.5. The upper right diagram shows the selectivity of the reflectance. A small percentage of energy is reflected for incident light with a relatively short wavelength (i.e., the wavelengths we associate with blue are absorbed). Incident light in the rest of the spectrum—the middle section that we associate with green and yellow, and the longer wavelengths that we associate with orange and red—is almost all reflected rather than absorbed.

The magnitude of the effect of this selectivity on the reflected images of objects depends on the spectrum of light leaving a particular object. For the red object in the image, there is a relatively small amount of light energy in the wavelength band absorbed by the faucet, as shown in the left diagram in the second row of Figure 3.5. The spectrum of the reflection of the red object, shown in the right diagram in the second row, is nearly

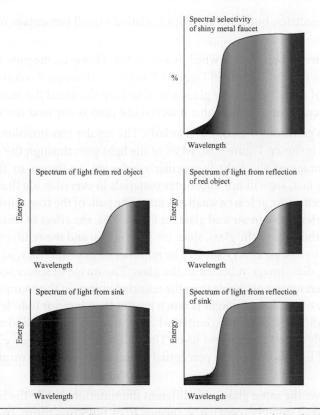

Figure 3.5: In the upper right diagram, the spectral dependence of the faucet is shown as percent reflectance as a function of wavelength. The effect of this selectivity on the red object and white sink are shown in the second and third row of diagrams, respectively.

the same as the spectrum initially leaving the object. The spectrum of light leaving the white sink is shown in the left diagram in the third row. An object that is white is reflecting light more or less evenly across the spectrum. On reflection from the faucet, the light in the shorter wavelengths is absorbed, as shown in the right diagram in the third row. This partial light absorption on reflection results in the sink color appearing to be yellow rather than white.

Pure specular reflection occurs at smooth surfaces. For a surface to have a high percentage of incident light reflected, very little light enters the surface to be scattered or absorbed. A basic classification of materials is whether they are metallic or dielectric. Metals are materials that easily conduct electricity, and dielectric are those that do not. An implication of easily conducting electricity is that light, which is electromagnetic energy, does not scatter through a metal. Pure specular surfaces that reflect a high percentage of incident light are metals. Pure specular reflection can also occur from dielectrics, but generally with a relatively small percentage of incident light reflected.

We think of mirrors being glass, which is a dielectric. However, the pure specular reflection we see in a mirror, such as in Figure 3.2, is from a thin metal coating on either the front or back of a clear glass. The glass is used to keep the metal flat and dimensionally stable. The interaction of light with a material like glass is our next consideration.

Light may also go through an object regularly. The regular transmission we are used to seeing in glass is shown Figure 3.6a. Most of the light goes through the glass, although a small percentage of the light is specularly reflected, as shown in the top path in Figure 3.6b. In fact, we will not encounter materials in everyday life that only transmit light without reflecting at least a small amount. The path of the transmitted light is bent at the boundaries between air and glass. In Figure 3.6a, the effect of this bending is difficult to see at the edge of the glass, since the glass is thin and the redirection of the light ray compared to free air is very small. The reflection is pure specular, so we see a sharp, but somewhat dim, image reflected in the glass. The image of leaves seen through the window is much more noticeable than the reflected objects in the room. This is because the magnitude of outdoor daylight is much greater than interior light levels. The order of magnitude differences are discounted when we directly look around a room and our eyes continually adjust to the light level. The difference between perceived and actual magnitudes of light is one of the perceptual effects we need to discount as we observe materials.

Figure 3.7 shows the same glass with different illumination. While the light reflected is still the same very small percentage, it appears to be reflecting more. In Figure 3.7, less

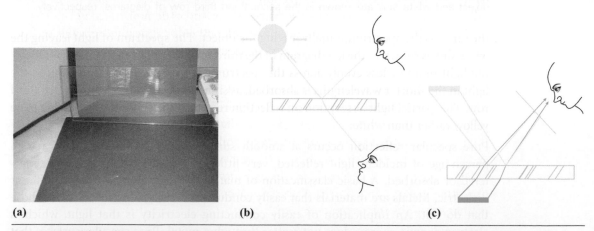

(a)   (b)   (c)

Figure 3.6: (a) A piece of glass reflecting and transmitting light. (b) An individual light ray will split, with a small fraction reflected, and the rest being bent as it passes through the glass. (c) The resulting image from the glass shows both objects seen through the glass and reflected from the glass, appearing sharp.

Figure 3.7: The same material from Figure 3.6a is shown with different illumination.

light has been directed at the black cards, so there is very little light coming through the glass. As a result, the reflection of the outdoor light (with the quantity of light from the window being equal in both Figure 3.6a and Figure 3.7) is much more noticeable. In this case, to make the correct judgment about the interaction of the material with light, we must discount the particular illumination as well as our perceptual distortion of light magnitudes.

For metals, the fraction of light reflected by pure specular reflection is nearly the same for all angles of incidence. For dielectrics like glass, though, the fraction of light reflected is higher at grazing angles, an effect referred to as Fresnel reflection. A glass viewed at near normal (i.e., looking perpendicular at the glass) and grazing angles are shown in Figures 3.8a and 3.8b, respectively. The change in the balance between the fraction of light transmitted and the fraction of light reflected at these angles is diagrammed in Figures 3.8c and 3.8d. Unlike Figures 3.6 and 3.7, the light from behind the glass, the white document, is not changing. In this case, the relative visibility of the document behind the glass changes because a higher percentage of the light from the vase and can are reflected at the near grazing viewing angle than at the near normal viewing angle.

In all of the images of glass we observe that the colors of the reflected objects are the same as the colors as we see them directly. A general property of dielectrics is that the light that is reflected by pure specular reflection will not be specularly selective.

The appearance of objects reflected and transmitted through a thin piece of flat glass is a result of following relatively simple ray paths that generally preserve the objects'

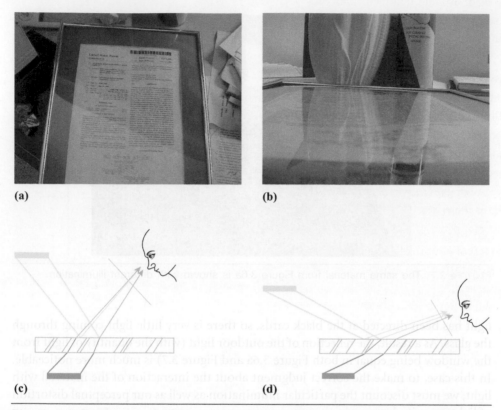

Figure 3.8: The fraction of reflected light changes with angle for a dielectric material. The upper row shows a piece of glass shown from a near normal viewing direction (a) and a grazing viewing angle (b). The bottom row illustrates that the fraction of light reflected at the grazing angle (d) is much greater than at the normal angle (c).

appearance. As in Figure 3.3, the different ray paths formed by the changing surface orientation for smoothly shaped or faceted glass objects form distorted images of the surroundings, as illustrated in Figures 3.9a and 3.9b and diagrammed in Figure 3.9c. There is no significant difference in the material in Figures 3.9a and 3.9b, but the shape of the object makes a difference in the visual impact between the disjointed images in the faceted object, and the distorted but continuous images in the smooth object. While there are simple light interactions at each surface, either a pure specular reflection or regular transmission, the combination of multiple reflections and redirections of each ray as it passes through the object and reaches the eyes results in a complex appearance. Note that at each boundary between materials there may be a reflection as well as a transmission.

Figure 3.9: Refraction and reflection from more complicated glass shapes such as a (a) smooth object and a (b) faceted object. The rays passing through the object may reflect and transmit at each boundary (c).

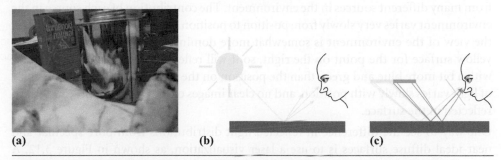

Figure 3.10: (a) Somewhat blurred reflections are seen in a can that is not purely specular. (b) An individual ray is reflected into a set of rays centered in a direction near the mirror direction. (c) Each ray direction traced back in forming an image is a mix of reflections of different areas on the reflected objects.

Many materials are shiny or glossy, but not purely specular. An example of a shiny but not pure specular object is shown in Figure 3.10a. In these materials, incident beams of light are distributed into a cone or lobe of directions centered near the direction of mirror reflection (Figure 3.10b). The result of this is that when you are looking at such materials, the light reflected from each point of the surface includes light from a range of surfaces in the environment, instead of just reflecting one point. Therefore, instead of seeing sharp edges reflected, everything looks blurred. In Figure 3.10c, the light coming from the center ray being traced is partly from the yellow and partly from the cyan surfaces. The result is that a mix of the two colors will be seen at that point, rather than a sharp edge between cyan and yellow. By observing the reflections in the paint can in the image, you can see that how blurred things look depends on how close the objects being reflected are to the glossy surface. If objects being reflected are relatively close to the glossy object, the cross section of the cone from which a point is reflecting light is relatively small, and lines like those between the yellow and blue surfaces above are only blurred a bit. As the objects get further away, the cross section of the cone becomes large. Distant objects do not appear with any detail at all when reflected in such a shiny surface.

Objects that appear to have the same shading of light and dark regardless of how you view them (as long as you don't block a significant source of light from the environment as you move your head) are diffuse. Diffuse reflection can be seen in the two images of the unglazed ceramic dog in Figure 3.11a. Choosing a single position, like the end of the dog's nose, the images can be compared to see that their shade is the same in both views. An ideal diffuse object reflects an incident ray of light as light rays of much lower magnitude in all directions, as shown in Figure 3.11b. The light coming from any position on a diffuse object when viewed from any direction is the result of light coming from many different sources in the environment. The contribution of each source in the environment varies very slowly from position to position on the surface. In Figure 3.11c, the view of the environment is somewhat more dominated by the cyan surface than yellow surface for the point on the right, so it will reflect a somewhat different color with a bit more blue and green than the position on the left. The magnitude and color of light varies slowly with position, and no clear images of the environment can be seen reflected in the surface.

One way to see the difference in reflected light distributions from pure specular and near-ideal diffuse surfaces is to use a laser visualization, as shown in Figure 3.12. A fine cloud of particles is sprayed into a box, so that the particles scatter the laser light as it travels through space. In Figure 3.12a, the laser light is directed from the upper left to a flat sheet of glass. The reflection of the beam can be seen in the glass. The glass is a pure specular reflector, but only reflects a small fraction of the light from the top surface, so the reflected beam is noticeably dimmer. The reflected beam continues to the right side of the box, where it illuminates a single spot. In Figure 3.12b, the laser is directed at a white paper napkin. No single beam is reflected. Instead, the light reflected in all directions appears as a cloud of light around the illuminated spot on the napkin. The light scattered in all directions is clearly dimmer than the incident beam. Rather than producing a small spot of light on the right wall of the box, the entire right side of the box receives light from the illuminated portion of the napkin.

So far, we have considered spectral and directional variations but not spatial variations. For example, the material on the dog in Figure 3.11 is spatially uniform. All of the spatial variations in shading are due to the different environmental views from different positions on the surface. For most objects, the material on a surface varies with position

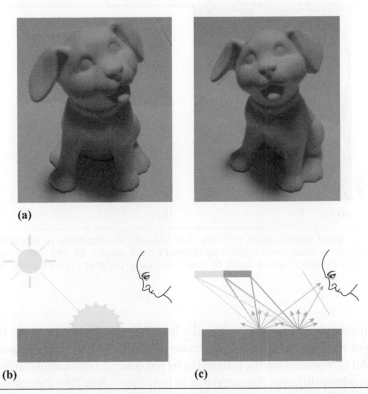

Figure 3.11: (a) This dog figurine here has a diffuse surface, so the shading at any point stays the same from any view. (b) An ideal diffuse material reflects an incident light ray as rays are distributed evenly into all directions. (c) Tracing rays backwards from a diffuse reflector, all rays have a mixture of light from the yellow and cyan surfaces.

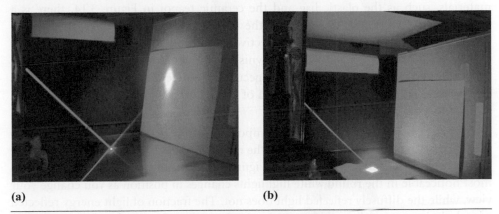

Figure 3.12: Laser light directed at a surface through mist is used to visualize the directionality of surface reflection from (a) a smooth piece of glass and (b) a paper napkin.

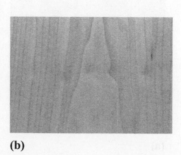

(a)   (b)

Figure 3.13: Most objects have surfaces with spatially varying material properties. (a) These variations have been applied as different color glazes. (b) The variations in the amount of light reflection are a result of how the tree grew that produced this wood.

as in the materials in Figure 3.13. On the left, the spatial variation is in the spectral selectivity of the reflectance. For many materials, modeling the spatial variation is the most critical component for the material to be recognized. For example, different pieces of wood may have different characteristics in how they reflect light directionally, but we recognize them as wood by characteristic spatial variations of higher and lower levels of reflectances, as seen in Figure 3.13b.

Materials may show a combination of specular and diffuse reflection. In dielectric materials, such as the plastic bag and the ceramic teapot in Figure 3.14, there is a difference in the spectral selectivity of the different components of reflection. The diffuse reflectance may be spectrally selective, such as the pink color of the diffusely reflected light in Figure 3.14a, or the brownish-red, green, white, and dark brown diffusely reflected light in Figure 3.14b. The specular component of reflectance, however, is white; that is, the wavelength distribution of the light that is reflected specularly is the same as the incident light.

The separation of diffuse and specular components can be observed by moving around the object without changing or blocking the main light sources. Two views of an object with combined reflectance are shown in Figure 3.15. The specularly reflected light here most noticeable in the round white highlights changes in position as you change your view, while the diffusely reflected light does not. The fraction of light energy reflected specularly is very small in this example, on the order of a couple of percent. Only the white highlights corresponding to the reflection of the light source are obvious,

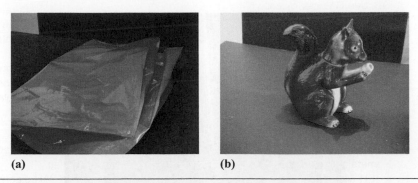

Figure 3.14: Objects, such as the plastic bag (a) and the glazed ceramic (b), may have a combination of diffuse and specular reflectance.

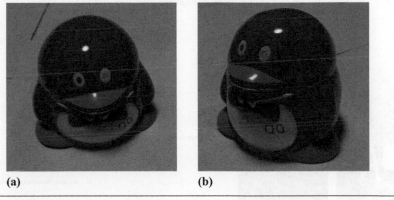

Figure 3.15: The separation of diffuse and specular components reflected from an object can be observed by changing your view of an object.

although the entire room is reflected specularly. Looking closely, a dim distorted reflection of the environment can be seen in these images. This effect is similar to the glass example in Figure 3.6.

Diffuse reflection never has an orientation, but blurred specular reflection may. Surfaces such as brushed steel (Figure 3.16) have elongated rather than round highlights even when the light source being reflected is round. Surfaces with elongated highlights in one direction are referred to as being anisotropic reflectors.

Analogous to diffuse reflection, thin surfaces may diffusely transmit light. As an example, in Figure 3.17, the cylinder is made of an opaque material, while the letter A is made from a thin diffusely transmitting (or translucent) material. When lit from the

Figure 3.16: Anisotropic materials have elongated specular highlights rather than round.

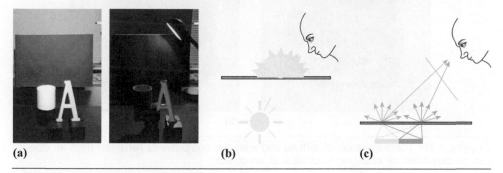

(a)   **(b)**   **(c)**

Figure 3.17: (a) An opaque cylinder and a transmitting letter A are lit from the front on the left and from the back on the right. (b) When a light ray hits the back of a thin diffusely transmitting surface, it is scattered in all directions on the other side. (c) Similar to diffuse reflectance, the light transmitted diffusely through a sample transmitting surface is a combination of the light coming from the yellow and cyan surfaces.

front, as shown on the left, the surfaces look similar. When lit from the back, however, as shown on the right, the material in the letter A transmits the light so it appears brighter. Because the transmission is diffuse, however, it is not possible to see objects clearly through the letter A.

Diffuse light transmission as shown in Figure 3.17 is due to light being scattered multiple times within a material. This is referred to as subsurface scattering and can occur

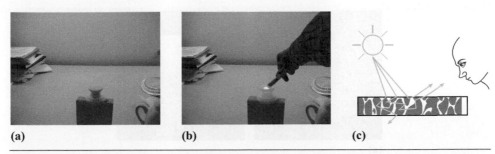

(a)   (b)   (c)

Figure 3.18: (a) An object composed of a material that scatters light internally. The effect of subsurface scattering is often subtle (a) until dramatic illumination, such as the laser light (b), is used. (c) Some of the light is scattered back to the viewer from points that are distant from the point of incidence.

in dielectrics, not metals. It is not confined to thin surfaces. In Figure 3.18, an object with subsurface scattering is shown. Figure 3.18b though shows an extreme example of illumination. A green laser is directed at the top of a small piece of stone. Besides being reflected from the top, the light is scattered in the material and is visible emerging from the sides of the stone. The multiple scattering paths are diagrammed in Figure 3.18c.

The light scattering properties within a material may vary spatially in three dimensions. Figure 3.19 shows two examples. In Figure 3.19a, the alabaster vase scatters light, as is particularly evident when it is lit from above (a, *right*). The vase is composed of veins of material, some which scatter light and some which do not. Figure 3.19b shows the Beinecke Library at Yale. Since it contains rare books and manuscripts, little light is allowed inside. Slabs of stone are used as windows. From the outside (b, *left*) the stones appear as diffuse reflectors of sunlight. On the inside (b, *right*), the artificial illumination is very low, and the sunlight scattered through the veined stone is visible.

The different ways that materials interact with light scatters shown so far depend primarily on their microstructure and chemical composition. The appearance of material also depends on small-scale, yet visible, geometric structures. Just as some materials are characterized primarily by the spatial variations in reflectance, other materials are characterized primarily by their small-scale geometric structure. Small is defined as orders of magnitude smaller than the overall object. Figure 3.20a shows a piece of plastic with a pattern pressed into it that changes the surface from smooth to bumpy. The bumps cause a variation in shading due to the change in surface orientation, as shown in Figure 3.20b. The small-scale geometric structure shown here is characteristic of leather material, and this structure is used in the production of plastic physical materials that look like leather.

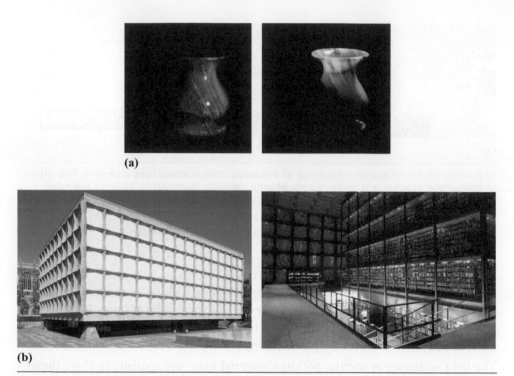

Figure 3.19: Examples of objects with volumetrically varying material properties. (a) An alabaster vase exhibits subsurface scattering effects, particularly when lit from above (*right*). The highlights on the front of the vase indicate that the vase also reflects light specularly from the top surface. (b) The Beinecke library that has thick stone as "windows" that let only small amounts of the bright daylight in. *Source*: From photographs of Beinecke Library by Michael Marsland © 2007 Yale University.

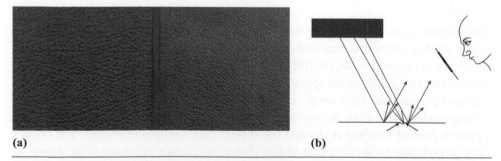

Figure 3.20: (a) A piece of plastic has spatial variations in its appearance due to small geometric variations pressed into it. (b) The variations of light and dark seen on the plastic are not due to variations in the fraction of light reflected, but variations in the orientation of the surface.

Some materials require accounting for the combined effects of different types of reflection and transmission as well as small-scale geometry effects. In Figure 3.21a when we view a leaf lit from above, we see the spatially varying diffuse reflectance and small-scale indentations. In Figure 3.21b when we change the view and lighting, we also see specular reflectance and diffuse transmission.

On some materials we see vibrant hues, which change as we change views. The examples shown in Figure 3.22 are typical, where we see all the colors of the rainbow. These types of colors are explained by considering the wave nature of light, and require special models to predict this behavior. Although the color effects are similar, different

(a)   (b)

Figure 3.21: Plant leaf material exhibits spatially varying diffuse transmission as well as diffuse and specular reflection. Leaves also have a small-scale geometric structure, showing indentations where the veins go through the leaf.

(a)   (b)   (c)

Figure 3.22: Vibrant colors spanning the rainbow are visible in some materials. These colors are modeled by the wave nature of light.

phenomena are responsible for the colors in these two examples. In Figure 3.22a, on the CDs, the colors appear as the result of small grooves the same size of the wavelength of light causing diffraction. In Figure 3.22b, on the wrapping paper, the colors appear as the result of the transmission and reflection of light through very thin layers of material that cause interference. Figure 3.22c illustrates that incident white light is reflected as different hues depending on view direction.

The example material types we have considered here are not an exhaustive set. They are a good starting point though for classifying the materials we observe in everyday objects. Models for all of these material types have been developed for computer graphics applications.

3.2 EXAMPLES OF MODELING CLASSES OF MATERIALS

We can't formulate numerical models simply using the classifications just discussed. We can, however, select and specify reasonable parameters for models of materials that are used by many basic computer graphics rendering systems. Most systems allow reflectances to be specified for surfaces, not volumes, so examples like Figures 3.18 and 3.19 can't be approximated. Most systems also allow specifications only in terms of red, green, and blue (or another three-dimensional color space), rather than in terms of wavelengths, so effects such as those shown in Figure 3.22 can't be specified. For other types of materials though, we can specify spectral dependence by assigning percentages of red, green, and blue to each of the components of reflectance or transmittance. We can specify the directionality of a material's interaction with light by the relative values of red, green, and blue that we assign to each of these components.

For a test object, we use a model of the head of a jackal defined as a triangle mesh. To best recognize materials, we need to see them in some plausible context. This allows us to better interpret the incident light the material is scattering, and therefore better infer what the material is. In this case, we place the model in a cubical room with beige (ideal diffusely reflecting walls) and a spherical overhead light source.

Figures 3.23a through 3.23c shows the results of modeling the object as a specularly reflecting metal. In Figure 3.23a, the red, green, and blue values of pure specular reflectance are set to be equal and to a relatively high value. In Figure 3.23b, the red and green values are set higher than the blue value to give the effect of brass, similar to Figure 3.4. Notice the darker brass color at the base of the ears where the object is reflected in itself. This is the result of light undergoing two reductions in magnitude as it is reflected twice by the spectrally selective reflectance. In Figure 3.23c, the material is modeled as glossy, rather than as pure specular. The reflections of the light source, which appear as sharp-edged white spots in Figure 3.23a, are blurred.

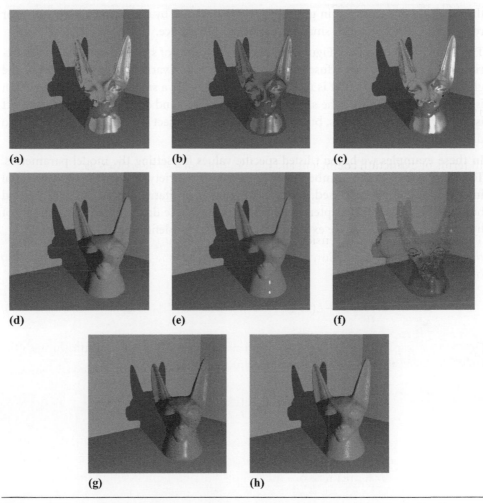

Figure 3.23: A model rendered as composed of various materials: (a) a pure specular reflector, (b) a spectrally selective pure specular reflector, (c) a glossy specular reflector, (d) an ideal diffuse reflector, (e) a combination of ideal diffuse and pure specular reflectors, (f) a thin regularly transmitting glass shell, (g) a material with spatially varying reflectance, and (h) a material with spatially varying small-scale geometry.

Figure 3.23 also shows the results of rendering the object as though it were made of three different dielectric materials. In Figure 3.23d, it is modeled as an ideal diffuse reflector, making it look similar to the glazed ceramic material shown in Figure 3.11. In Figure 3.23e, the material is a diffuse reflector with a small component of pure specular reflection, producing a material similar to the plastic penguin in Figure 3.15. Finally, the model is shown as a thin glass shell in Figure 3.23f, by specifying a high value for regular transmission and a small pure specular reflectance.

The final row of images in Figure 3.23 shows the results of spatial variations in a material. In Figure 3.23g, the diffuse component of reflection varies with position, while the glossy specular component is uniform. In Figure 3.23h, a small-scale spatial variation is applied to the surface. The spatial frequency of light and dark shading on the object is similar in the two images, but the effect is that the object appears to be made of two different types of material.

In these examples we haven't listed specific values for setting the model parameters. To give meaning to the numbers, and to express the variety of ways the light material interactions can be expressed, we need to make quantitative definitions of light and how it is scattered. In Chapter 4, we will focus on these definitions and examples of how material properties are expressed in terms of these definitions.

4 MATHEMATICAL TERMS

In Chapter 3, we observed and classified materials we encounter in day-to-day life. We observe the appearance of materials resulting from the combined effects of light, shape, and the properties of the materials themselves, filtered through the properties of our human visual system. Observation provides guidance in how to model materials, but it doesn't give us precision needed for digital modeling. The interaction of light and materials occur physically, not in perceptual terms, so we need to consider characterizing materials in quantitative physical terms, rather than qualitative perceptual terms. We could devise completely perceptually-inspired models for individual materials and define parameters to adjust them. However, that would not guarantee that objects looked correct when viewed in combination or as conditions change. Perceptual observations let us categorize materials as dielectric versus metallic, dull versus shiny. Within these categories, though, we need physically-based models with parameters with physical meaning so that we can measure materials, adjust them, and reuse them in scenes to produce effects consistent with what we observe in the real world.

To make physically-based numerical definitions, we need to define various expressions for how incident light energy is distributed by a material with respect to position, direction, and wavelength. In Chapter 3, we saw how material interactions depend on the material characteristics at a particular position or in a particular direction. We also saw an instance in which the light reflected in a particular direction depended on the light from *all* incident directions. We need a mathematical mechanism that allows us to specify particular direction, position, or wavelength values, and then lets us add up all the particular values for all directions, positions, or wavelengths. The mechanism that lets us do this is the calculus. For our purposes, a complete calculus course is not required. We only rely on the basic concept from calculus that we can divide the quantities we are interested in into infinitesimally small pieces, which approach zero in size but still have meaning. We can take ratios of them to specify values at particular points. We can add up the small pieces at all points to find the quantity for the object as a whole.

Expressing directional variation introduces complications in addition to the concept of using infinitesimals. However, directional variations are essential to modeling appearance. The key quantity in defining light transfer in a particular direction is radiance. The key quantity for expressing the directional effect of materials on the incident radiance is the bidirectional reflectance distribution function (BRDF). There are many materials that require an extended definition of scattering beyond the BRDF, but they are readily understood once radiance and BRDF are defined. We will introduce some foundations for the definitions of these quantities. Throughout, when units are used, the SI (Systeme Internationale d'Units) system will be used.

4.1 ENERGY AS A FUNCTION OF TIME, POSITION, AND DIRECTION

We denote energy as Q. The SI unit for energy is Joules. Since we are interested in light *transfer* and not in its storage, we will only be dealing with the rate that it moves through an environment per unit time. The rate of energy transfer per unit time is power, expressed in the SI system as watts. Wattage ratings are familiar on lightbulbs. Lightbulbs aren't rated to produce or absorb a particular quantity of energy, rather to consume electrical energy at some rate. The power radiated is referred to as the *radiant flux*. To express the average flux Φ over a period of time, we would measure the energy ΔQ transferred through some time period Δt and find:

$$\Phi = \Delta Q / \Delta t \qquad (4.1)$$

To find the flux $\Phi(t)$ at a particular instant, we consider differential period of time dt, which is the quantity Δt as it approaches zero. The differential amount of energy dQ transferred in dt is:

$$\Phi(t) = dQ/dt \qquad (4.2)$$

Light travels at nearly 300 million meters per second. We are not going to consider generating images at that time frame, so we are not going to carry the dependence of flux on time any further in our definitions.

4.1.1 POSITION

Next, we need to consider how the flux of light Φ varies with position. We examine how to do this in detail to illustrate how taking the ratio of quantities that are approaching zero in magnitude allows us to express the energy transfer for a particular point. First, let's consider the radiant energy Φ leaving a surface A, as shown on the left in Figure 4.1.

The average flux leaving per unit area, or radiant exitance M, is the total flux leaving divided by surface area A, or

$$M = \Phi/A \qquad\qquad (4.3)$$

To express the radiant exitance from a particular point (x, y), first consider breaking the surface A into small pieces ΔA, as shown in the center image in Figure 4.1. Each of the small pieces ΔA_i will have a flux $\Delta \Phi_i$ associated with it. The sum of the fluxes $\Delta \Phi_i$ will be the total flux Φ. For example, suppose we had a flux of 10 watts (w) leaving from an area of 1 meter squared (m^2), for an average exitance M of 10 w/m^2. We could divide that area into four areas, ΔA_1, ΔA_2, ΔA_3, and ΔA_4, each of 0.25 m^2. We might find that a $\Delta \Phi_1$ of 2 w leaves from area ΔA_1, and 3 w, 4 w, and 1 w from ΔA_2, ΔA_3, and ΔA_4, respectively. Obviously, the flux from each area is lower than from the whole. However, if we compute the radiant exitance for each of the four areas, we have that M_1 is (2 $w/0.25$ m^2) or 8 w/m^2, and M_2, M_3, and M_4 are 12, 16, and 4 w/m^2, respectively. These radiant exitances are not all smaller than the original, and generally are the same order of magnitude. We have started to characterize the dependence of how the radiant exitance varies with position, as M is different for each of the four smaller areas.

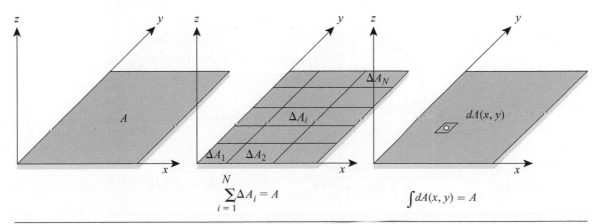

Figure 4.1: A finite area A on the *left* can be considered as a set of small surfaces ΔA, as shown in the *center*, or as an infinite number of differential surfaces dA, as shown on the *right*.

We can continue to divide up the areas into smaller pieces, as illustrated in the center image in Figure 4.1 for N smaller areas. The flux from each piece will continue to get smaller. However, the ratio of flux per unit area will stay the same magnitude. We will have a better estimate of the spatial variation of radiant exitance from the surface. The limit of this process is to divide up the area into infinitesimally small areas dA, and consider the flux $d\Phi$ from each of these areas. The infinitesimally small area dA is located at a single point (x, y), rather than covering some range of values of x and y on the surface. By considering this infinitesimally small area dA, we can define the radiant exitance $M(x, y)$ at a particular position:

$$M(x, y) = d\Phi(x, y)/dA \qquad (4.4)$$

The radiant energy per unit time and area arriving at a surface is called the *irradiance E*. It is defined in the same manner as M, with the only difference being whether the radiant energy is approaching or leaving the surface.

4.1.2 DIRECTION

When we consider very small objects with light leaving them, such as a small light source, we are interested in the flux in a particular direction. Similar to considering a full surface for defining radiant exitance, lets begin with considering a set of all directions. In the case of a small object, we can think of all directions around the object as a unit sphere around the object, as shown on the left in Figure 4.2. Any direction from the object is specified by a point on the unit sphere. Any set of directions from the small light-emitting object can be indicated as a surface on the unit sphere. A set of directions is referred to as a *solid angle*. The area of a unit sphere is 4π, and the set of all directions

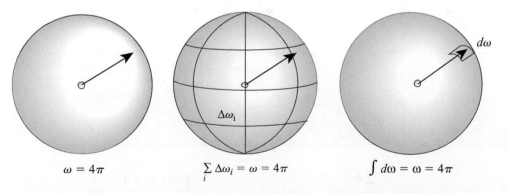

$$\omega = 4\pi \qquad \sum_i \Delta\omega_i = \omega = 4\pi \qquad \int d\omega = \omega = 4\pi$$

Figure 4.2: The set of all directions around a small object is described by a sphere of radius one surrounding it (*left*). This sphere of all directions ω subtends 4π steradians. The sphere of all directions can be broken up into a set of smaller sets of directions $\Delta\omega$ (*center*). Finally, a particular direction is associated with a differential set of direction $d\omega$ (*right*).

from a point in the center of the sphere is defined to be 4π steradians. Steradians are the three-dimensional analog of radians as a measure of an angle on the plane. On the plane, the set of all directions around a point is 2π radians.

The radiant flux per unit solid angle is called the *radiant intensity*. For a small object with total radiant flux Φ, the average radiant intensity I over the solid angle of all directions, that is, over ω of 4π steradians, is:

$$I = \Phi/4\pi \qquad (4.5)$$

Similar to the consideration of radiant exitance, we can localize the radiant intensity to sets of directions by considering the flux that is leaving through each of the set of directions defined by dividing up the sphere of all directions into small areas on the sphere, as shown in the center in Figure 4.2. Finally, we can express the intensity for a particular direction by considering the infinitesimally small flux $d\Phi$ through an infinitesimally small set of directions $d\omega$ represented as a differential area on the unit sphere.

Besides defining the meaning of a differential set of directions, we need coordinates to specify a particular direction. We specified a particular position using the (x, y) coordinates on surface A. We can specify a direction from the small object by setting up a spherical coordinate system around the small object, as shown in Figure 4.3. We denote the angle a direction makes with "straight up" as θ, which is referred to as the polar angle. We choose an arbitrary direction perpendicular from "straight up," in this case to the right as a second reference. A plane is defined by the center of the object, and by being perpendicular to the up direction. The projection of a direction onto this plane makes an angle ϕ with the second reference direction, and ϕ is referred to as the

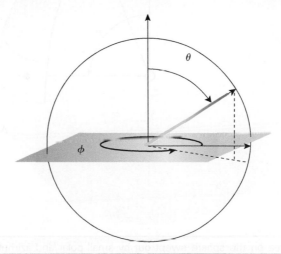

Figure 4.3: To specify directions, we define a spherical coordinate system using a polar angle θ and azimuthal angle ϕ.

azimuthal direction. Together, θ and and ϕ specify a direction. We will use Θ to compactly denote the direction $(\theta, \phi.)$ To specify the intensity I in a particular direction, rather than an average intensity, we define:

$$I(\Theta) = d\Phi(\Theta)/d\omega \qquad (4.6)$$

We can express the differential solid angle $d\omega$ in terms of differential angles $d\theta$ and $d\phi$ by considering the area swept out on the unit sphere by these angles. As shown in Figure 4.4, the height of the small patch swept out is $\Delta\theta$ (or the differential $d\theta$ in the limit as $\Delta\theta$ becomes infinitesimal). The width of the patch depends on the value of θ, with the patch being very thin near θ equaling zero and wide at θ equaling $\pi/2$. In fact, the width of the patch is given by $sin\theta d\phi$. The intensity I (watts w/steradian sr) then can also be expressed as:

$$I(\Theta) = d^2\Phi/sin\theta \, d\theta \, d\phi \qquad (4.7)$$

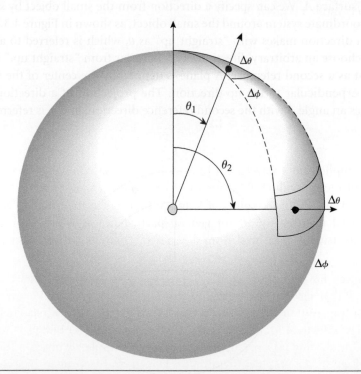

Figure 4.4: The area on the sphere swept out by small polar and azimuthal angles increases as the center of that area varies from the polar angle.

In describing light transfer, we are concerned with the simultaneous flux per unit area and solid angle. Similar to other quantities, we will form this by taking a ratio involving differentials Φ, A, and ω. A differential flux $d\Phi$ leaves in a solid angle $d\omega$. An infinitesimally small portion $d^2\Phi$ of that $d\Phi$ leaves from the differential surface dA. A problem, though, is what area should be considered to define dA? In understanding light transfer between objects, and from an object to the eye, we want to define a quantity of light transfer that is independent of a particular object, but has meaning anywhere in space. A surface dA that is uniquely defined for a particular direction is a differential area perpendicular to the direction of travel Θ.

The impact of defining light transfer per unit time, solid angle, and area in the direction of travel is to somewhat complicate the definition of light leaving a particular surface. This is because, unlike the small object radiating in all directions that we considered in defining intensity, a surface radiating energy has a particular orientation. In Figure 4.2, the direction of "straight up" is arbitrary. For a surface, however, the surface normal defines a unique direction. We will consider the surface normal as the axis from which the polar angle θ is measured. If another object is in a direction for which θ is less than $\pi/2$, it will receive radiant energy from the surface. However, if the direction of an object has a value of θ greater than $\pi/2$ it cannot receive radiant energy—it is behind the surface. A surface looks largest, that is, has the largest "projected area," when viewed along the surface normal. The surface varies in apparent size with the cosine of the view direction θ, as shown in Figure 4.5.

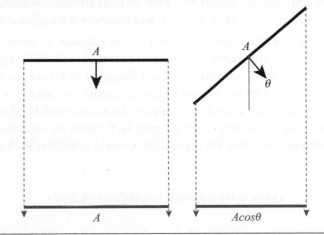

Figure 4.5: The apparent size of surface A is larger on the left when it is projected in the direction of its surface normal, than on the right when it is projected in a direction at an angle θ to the normal.

4.2 RADIANCE

To account for this effect of the apparent area decreasing with view direction, the key quantity radiance in a particular direction Θ is defined as the radiant flux per unit solid angle and unit area projected in the direction θ. The radiance L is defined as:

$$L(\Theta) = d^2\Phi(\Theta)/cos\theta\, dA\, d\omega \tag{4.8}$$

Understanding the *cosθ* in the denominator of the definition of radiance is one of two difficult concepts in the mathematical description of how light interacts with materials. One way to think of its convenience, is to think of a small patch of diffuse material, such as the right ear of the dog shown in Figure 3.11a. Looking straight at the ear in the right image, the ear appears to have a certain brightness, and a certain amount of light energy from it reaches our eye. Looking at the ear at a more glancing angle in the left image, the patch is just as bright, but overall less light from it reaches our eye, because the area the light is coming from is smaller from our new point of view. The quantity that affects our perception of brightness is the radiance. The radiance of the patch for a diffuse material is the same for all directions even though the energy per unit time depends on the orientation of the view relative to the surface.

As discussed in Chapter 2, we form an image by computing the light that arrives at a visible object through each pixel. We can make the statement "computing the light" more specific now, and say that we want to compute the radiance that would arrive from the visible object. The radiance has been defined so that if we compute the radiance at an object point in a particular direction, in clear air the radiance along a ray in that direction will be constant. We qualify this with "in clear air" since volumes of smoke or dust might absorb some light along the way, and therefore the radiance would change.

The other variable that we want to account for in addition to time, position, and direction, is wavelength. Implicitly, since we are concerned with visible light in the span of 380 to 780 nm, all of the quantities we have discussed so far are for energy in that band. To express flux, irradiance, radiant exitance, intensity, or radiance as a function of wavelength, we consider the quantity at a value of λ within a small band of wavelengths between λ and $\lambda + d\lambda$. By associating a $d\lambda$ with each value, we can integrate spectral values over the whole spectrum. We express the spectral quantities such as the spectral radiance as:

$$L(\lambda, x, y, \Theta) = d^3\Phi(\lambda, x, y, \Theta)/cos\theta\, dA\, d\omega\, d\lambda \tag{4.9}$$

To simplify this notation, we denote the two-dimensional spatial coordinate x, y with the boldface **x**. In many cases, we will want to indicate whether light is incident on or leaving the surface. Following Philip Dutre's online Global Illumination Compendium at *http://www.cs.kuleuven.ac.be/phil/GI/*, we will use the convention that $L(\lambda, \mathbf{x} \leftarrow \Theta)$ is incident at $\mathbf{x}$ from direction Θ, and that $L(\lambda, \mathbf{x} \rightarrow \Theta)$ is leaving the surface in direction Θ.

The terms we have discussed so far in this chapter—flux, exitance, irradiance, radiant intensity, and radiance—are *radiometric* quantities. Radiometric quantities are used for all electromagnetic radiation, whether or not the radiation is in the band of visible wavelengths. In the design of illumination, *photometric* quantities are used. For each spectral radiometric quantity, an analogous photometric quantity can be defined by integrating the quantity over all wavelengths with the luminous efficiency curve (discussed in Chapter 2) as a weighting function. The photometric analogs of the radiometric quantites are indicated with a subscript v. For example, denoting the luminous efficiency curve as $V(\lambda)$, the luminance L_V leaving a surface, which is the photometric analog of radiance, is computed from radiance expressed in standard SI units using:

$$L_V(\mathbf{x} \rightarrow \Theta) = K_m \int_\lambda L(\lambda, \mathbf{x} \rightarrow \Theta) V(\lambda) d\lambda \qquad (4.10)$$

where K_m is equal to 680 lumens per watt.

4.3 REFLECTANCE AND BRDF

We can describe how materials affect the path of light now by expressing how the radiance leaving a surface is related to the radiance incident on a surface. For a pure specularly reflecting material, there is only one possible direction that light leaves the surface for a given incident direction. In terms of the spherical coordinate system we are using, light that is incident within a differential solid angle $d\omega_i$ from direction (θ_i, ϕ_i) is reflected in a differential solid angle ω_r in direction $(\theta_i, \phi_i + \pi)$. For these types of materials all we need to do then is specify how much, if at all, the radiance is reduced after it is reflected. We can express this as a simple fraction that we will call reflectance ρ_s. For a pure specular material, such as the mirror in Figure 3.2a, we can express this as:

$$\rho_s = L_r/L_i \qquad (4.11)$$

As demonstrated in the image of the faucet in Figure 3.4a, this may vary with wavelength, and as demonstrated with the reflection from the glass, this may also vary with the angle of incidence (see Figure 3.8). Therefore, we define the specular reflectance more generally as:

$$\rho_s(\lambda, \theta_i, \phi_i) = L_r(\lambda, \theta_i, \phi_i + \pi)/L_i(\lambda, \theta_i, \phi_i) \qquad (4.12)$$

For pure specular reflection, the solid angle that light is reflected into is the same as the solid angle of the incident light, and the projected area of the surface in the direction of incidence is the same as the area projected in the direction of reflection. This means that for specular reflection the ratio of the exitant flux to the irradiance is the same as the ratio of the reflected radiance to incident radiance. This is a unique situation for pure specular reflectance. In general, we use the term *reflectance* to express the ratio of the reflected energy flux per unit area to the irradiance. This ratio must always be between 0 and 1. In general, this ratio only expresses the fraction of energy that is not absorbed or transmitted by a material, it doesn't express how light is redirected by reflection.

To describe how a surface redirects light, we consider light incident on the surface with radiance $L(\lambda, \mathbf{x} \leftarrow \Theta_i)$ within a differential solid angle $d\omega_i$. The irradiance dE_i on the surface that will be either absorbed or redirected is:

$$dE_i(\lambda, \mathbf{x} \leftarrow \Theta_i) = L(\lambda, \mathbf{x} \leftarrow \Theta_i)cos\theta_i d\omega_i \tag{4.13}$$

The $cos\theta_i$ term appears because the radiance L measures energy per unit area dA in the direction of travel Θ_i, and that direction projected into the orientation of the surface we are considering is $cos\theta_i dA$. The $d\omega_i$ term enters in because we want to know the effect of energy coming from a single direction representing a differential section of all the possible directions above the surface. The light reflected by the surface in each direction can be described by the radiance in each direction. The effect of a material redirecting light is then given by a function that is the ratio of the radiance reflected in a particular direction Θ_r as a result of the total incident flux per unit area from another direction Θ_i as shown in Figure 4.6. This ratio is referred to as the bidirectional reflectance distribution function (BRDF), f_r:

$$f_r(\lambda, \mathbf{x}, \Theta_i \rightarrow \Theta_r) = dL_r(\lambda, \mathbf{x} \rightarrow \Theta_r)/L_i(\lambda, \mathbf{x} \leftarrow \Theta_i)cos\theta_i d\omega_i \tag{4.14}$$

4.3.1 DISTRIBUTION FUNCTIONS

The BRDF is a distribution function, not a reflectance. It describes how the radiance is distributed in different directions, rather than expressing the fraction of energy reflected. For a general surface, some finite amount of incident energy from direction Θ_i is redirected into the hemisphere of all directions about the surface. If we look at any one reflected direction we are considering only an infinitesimally small solid angle $d\omega_r$. If we consider the redistribution of energy to be roughly even over all directions, the magnitude of the reflected radiance must be infinitesimally small relative to the magnitude of the incident radiance.

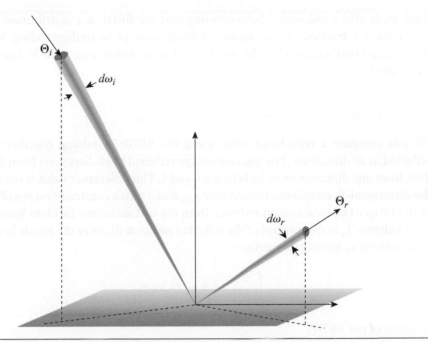

Figure 4.6: BRDF relates the radiance reflected to the radiance incident on a surface.

To better understand why a distribution function rather than a fraction is used, consider a specific numerical example. Suppose an incident radiance of 100 $w/m^2 - sr$ is normal to the surface in a solid angle subtending 1 percent of the hemisphere of 2π sr above the surface. The irradiance is $100 \times cos\,0 \times 0.01 \times 2\pi$ or about 6.3 w/m^2. If all of this incident light is reflected evenly in all directions, the reflected radiance in the direction of the surface normal would be $6.3/\pi$ or about 2 $w/m^2 - sr$. If we consider a smaller incident solid angle, one-tenth this size (as we approach estimating the effect of light incident from a single direction), the reflected radiance by the same analysis would be 0.2 $w/m^2 - sr$ for the same incident radiance of 100 $w/m^2 - sr$. As we let the solid angle approach zero, the reflected radiance would approach zero. However, if we characterize the distribution of light as the ratio of the reflected radiance and a differential solid angle that we reflect into, and let both incident and reflected solid angles go to zero at the same rate, we get a quantity that does not go to zero. For both incident solid angles of 0.01 and 0.001 steradians considered above, we would calculate the ratio of reflected radiance to the solid angle ($\Delta L_r/\Delta\omega_r$) as about 32 $w/m^2 - sr^2$. This is why rather than expressing the light distribution as a ratio of radiances, we express the distribution as a ratio of differential radiance per differential solid angle and a radiance. Understanding that the BRDF is a distribution function rather than a fraction, is the second difficult concept to understanding how light is described mathematically (the first being the projected area term in the radiance definition).

4.3.2 ENERGY CONSERVATION AND BRDF

We can compute a reflectance value using the BRDF by adding together the light reflected in all directions. The fraction energy reflected to all directions from light incident from one direction must be between 0 and 1. This reflectance value is referred to as the directional-hemispherical reflectance ρ_{dh}, and it puts a constraint on possible values of the BRDF. The total exitant radiance from the surface for the incident beam of light with radiance L_i is the integral of the reflected radiance dL_r over the whole hemisphere of directions ω_r leaving the surface:

$$\int_{\omega_r} dL_r(\lambda, \mathbf{x} \rightarrow \Theta_r) cos\theta_r d\omega_r$$

In terms of the BRDF:

$$\int_{\omega_r} f_r(\lambda, \mathbf{x}, \Theta_i \rightarrow \Theta_r) L_i(\lambda, \mathbf{x} \leftarrow \Theta_i) cos\theta_i d\omega_i cos\theta_r d\omega_r$$

Since the incident radiance and direction do not depend on reflected direction, these terms can be treated as a constant outside of the integral:

$$L_i(\lambda, \mathbf{x} \leftarrow \Theta_i) cos\theta_i d\omega_i \int_{\omega_r} f_r(\lambda, \mathbf{x}, \Theta_i \rightarrow \Theta_r) cos\theta_r d\omega_r$$

The directional hemispherical reflectance then is this quantity divided by the incident flux per unit area, $L_i(\lambda, \mathbf{x} \leftarrow \Theta_i) cos\theta_i d\omega_i$, giving:

$$\rho_{dh}(\lambda, \mathbf{x} \leftarrow \Theta_i) = \int_{\omega_r} f_r(\lambda, \mathbf{x}, \Theta_i \rightarrow \Theta_r) cos\theta_r d\omega_r \qquad (4.15)$$

The restriction that ρ_{dh} be between 0 and 1 is a constraint on the possible values that $f_r(\lambda, \mathbf{x}, \Theta_i \rightarrow \Theta_r)$ can take on. For a diffuse surface that has the same reflected radiance in every direction, the value of f_r is the same in each direction. With f_r a constant, we can find a relationship between the BRDF of a diffuse surface and its directional hemispherical reflectance, which is that f_r is equal to ρ_{dh}/π. For a specular surface, the directional hemispherical reflectance is just equal to the specular reflectance ρ_s. In the integral on the right of Eq. 4.15, since there is nonzero reflected radiance only in one direction for a single direction, the value of f_r is nonzero for a single direction. Since the solid angle for a single angle is a differential approaching zero, to make the product in the integral on the right equal to a finite value, the value of f_r for a specular surface approaches infinity.

4.3.3 RECIPROCITY AND BRDF

An additional restriction on the BRDF is known as *reciprocity*. The principle of reciprocity for light transfer says that light paths are reversible. That is, as shown in Figure 4.7, if it is possible for light to travel from P to Q, then it is also possible for light to travel from Q to P. An everyday example of this is that a person P who can see person Q's eyes in a mirror can also be seen by Q. The mirror can't allow reflections in one direction but suppress them in the other. Reversibility implies that the BRDF must remain the same when the direction of incidence and reflectance are reversed:

$$f_r(\lambda, \mathbf{x}, \Theta_i \to \Theta_r) = f_r(\lambda, \mathbf{x}, \Theta_r \to \Theta_i) \tag{4.16}$$

Energy conservation is a basic thermodynamic requirement. However, there has been considerable discussion over the years whether the reciprocity of the BRDF is a basic consequence of thermodynamic or quantum-mechanical principles. The results of some experiments have appeared to show a failure of the reciprocity relationship, although such failures have subsequently been found to be due to measurement errors. Theoretical analysis and careful experiments on everyday materials have confirmed the validity of the reciprocity of the BRDF [124, 295, 296].

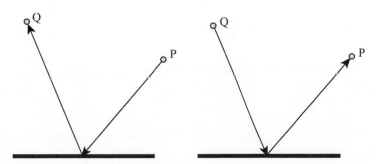

Figure 4.7: The reciprocity of BRDFs is a consequence of the reversibility of light paths. If light can follow the path shown from P to Q on the left, it can also follow the path shown from Q to P on the right.

The definition of BRDF provides a framework to describe how different materials interact with light. In general, surfaces are not pure specular, ideal diffuse, or a combination of the two. In Chapter 5, we will consider general models that have been developed to describe the BRDF of surfaces. We will also consider extensions of the basic idea of the BRDF to account for scattering within volumes of material.

5 GENERAL MATERIAL MODELS

In the previous chapters we have seen how the appearance of materials depends on how they interact with light. We need to model how a material scatters light, whether it is reflected, transmitted, or undergoes multiple scattering events within the material. We have developed notation and terms that allow us to express quantitatively how the light leaving a material is related to the light incident. We now will look at how models are developed for different materials using these terms. In this chapter, we consider models that apply to a wide range of materials. In Chapter 6, we will focus on combinations of models for light scattering and small-scale geometric structures that have been developed for specific materials.

One approach for representation material models would be to store values of the reflectance for densely sampled values of position, wavelength, and direction (i.e., for $x, y, \lambda, \theta_i, \phi_i, \theta_r, \phi_r$). A table of such densely sampled models would require an enormous amount of storage for even simple objects. In addition to computational inefficiency, this is not a useful representation for a user to specify materials. Using just a table, how could a user specify that he or she would like something shinier, grayer, or bumpier? Models are needed that give users some handles to adjust the appearance when creating a material.

Instead, we want to find functions or simpler numerical tables that represent materials. A number of different criteria can be used to guide the construction of a good representation. Criteria include capturing the visible effects discussed in Chapter 3, obeying the physical constraints of conservation of energy, and reciprocity, compactness, complying with the electromagnetic wave theory of light, ease of evaluation, and meaningful parameters for user input. Different approaches choose to emphasize some subset of these criteria and ignore others.

The most basic material models are bidirectional reflectance distribution functions (BRDFs) that describe the spectral and directional characteristics of a material at a spatial location. Although BRDFs often have complicated derivations and form, they generally reduce to evaluating an expression. In this chapter, we first examine different general models for BRDFs, and then consider more general scattering functions.

The derivation of many BRDFs is complicated, because they include the derivation from physical principles borrowed from optics, and then add to that derivation modifications for computational efficiency. We do not consider the derivation of the models in detail, but only to the extent needed to understand the limitations of the models and how to specify the parameters.

Most models are named after the authors of the papers that originally introduced them. In general, when these models are implemented in rendering systems they are not exactly in the form that they were originally presented. There are no compliance standards for implementing any particular model. In many cases, features in original models that were lost for efficiency sake are later rediscovered as useful enhancements or insights. For a deep understanding of models, rereading the original papers remains worthwhile.

We begin with the reflection and transmission at a smooth surface between two homogeneous materials. This solution provides some basic relations used in many other models. We then consider three approaches to constructing light reflection models for more complex materials and surface structures: empirical, analytical first principles, and simulation from first principles. We discuss some issues regarding complex spectral interactions. Finally, we consider expanding the modeling of scattering from surfaces to volumes of material.

5.1 REFLECTION AND REFRACTION FROM A SMOOTH SURFACE

Nearly all BRDF models make use at base the reflection and transmission characteristics of a smooth surface. Understanding how light interacts with a smooth surface provides some basic bounds on forms of the BRDF. The smooth surface results also provide a complete model for shiny opaque surfaces like stainless steel and clear transmitting surfaces like glass.

By a smooth surface, we mean a surface that looks flat and infinite when viewed at the scale of the wavelength of light (on the order of a micron). Formally, the requirement that a smooth surface has variations much smaller than the wavelength of light is known as the *Rayleigh criterion*. Smaller variations, such as on the scale of an atomic radius, or larger variations, such as geometric features visible to the eye, aren't considered. For a smooth surface, the equations for the electromagnetic waves impinging on a surface, known as Maxwell's equations, can be solved explicitly. The solution gives the directional and spectral variations of reflection and transmission. The details of the solution can be found in textbooks on optics or radiation [289].

Since light is electromagnetic energy, its interaction is governed by the properties that quantify the material's interaction with electric and magnetic fields. In the solution to Maxwell's equations, these properties are expressed as the index of refraction n and a coefficient that captures the tendency to absorb electromagnetic waves κ. The value of n is the ratio of the speed of light in a vacuum to the speed of light in a material. The value of κ is zero for dielectrics, which do not conduct electricity, and greater than zero for metals, which do conduct electricity. Values of κ and n are found by measurement and can be looked up in handbooks or online resources [256]. Generally, understanding and applying the results of the smooth surface solution for computer graphics requires only knowing some rough estimates of typical values of these constants for common materials.

The solutions of Maxwell's equations give simple relationships for the directionality of reflection and transmission, which are shown in Figure 5.1. The light incident from a direction θ_i is reflected in a direction θ_r that makes the same angle with the

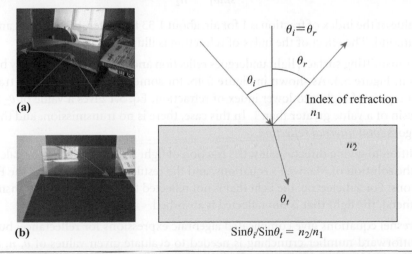

Figure 5.1: The direction of reflection from a smooth surface is in the "mirror" direction (a), and the direction of transmission is given by Snell's Law (b).

Figure 5.2: Mirror reflection and conservation of energy specify a model that allows the rendering of smooth surfaces. Here, only the spectral dependence of the specular reflection is different in the left and right images.

surface normal, and which is in the same plane as the incident light direction and the surface normal. Using just this simple information for directionality and imposing energy conservation (i.e., we cannot let the specular reflectance exceed 1), we have a model for mirrorlike surfaces such as those shown in Figure 5.2.

The directionality of transmission is a bit more complicated. Most metals have a high tendency to absorb electromagnetic energy, so transmission of visible light is not observed. For dielectrics, a change in the speed of light in the material causes a change in the direction. This change in direction is called *refraction*, and is expressed by Snell's Law:

$$\frac{sin\theta_2}{sin\theta_1} = \frac{n_1}{n_2} \tag{5.1}$$

The value of the index of fraction is 1 for air, about 1.33 for water, 1.5 for glass, and 2.42 for diamond. The effect of the index of refraction is illustrated in Figure 5.3.

For a transmitting surface, light undergoes reflection and transmission at every boundary, as in Figure 5.4. As shown in Figure 5.4b, for some angles when light is traveling from a region of higher to lower index of refraction, Eq. 5.1 gives a value of θ_2 that is the arcsin of a value greater than 1. In this case, there is no transmission, and the light undergoes *total internal reflection*.

In addition to giving directionality, the fraction of light reflected can also be calculated from the solution of Maxwell's equations, and the results are referred to as the Fresnel equations. For a dielectric, the light that is not reflected from the surface is transmitted. For a metal, the light that is not reflected is absorbed.

The Fresnel equations give complicated algebraic expressions for reflectance, but only straightforward number crunching is needed to evaluate given values of θ, n, and κ. We will refer to this particular function for the specular reflectance $\rho_s(\theta)$ as $F(\theta)$. The explicit dependence on $(\theta_i, \theta_r, \phi_i, \phi_r)$ is omitted, and the function is zero unless $(\theta_i = \theta_r)$

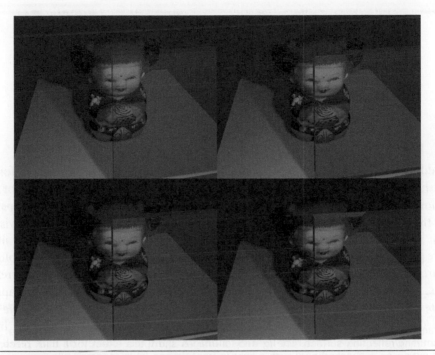

Figure 5.3: The effect of the index of refraction is visible in how much the image of an object is offset when viewed through the material versus when the object is viewed directly.

and $(\phi_i = \phi_r + \pi)$. The definitions of a and b are just to gather up expressions that are repeated in $F(\theta)$ and make the final equation simpler to write.

$$2a^2 = \sqrt{(n^2 - \kappa^2 - sin^2\theta)^2 + 4n^2\kappa^2} + n^2 - \kappa^2 - sin^2\theta$$

$$2b^2 = \sqrt{(n^2 - \kappa^2 - sin^2\theta)^2 + 4n^2\kappa^2} - (n^2 - \kappa^2 - sin^2\theta)$$

$$\rho_s(\theta) = F(\theta) = 0.5 \left(1 + \frac{a^2 + b^2 - 2asin\theta tan\theta + sin^2\theta tan^2\theta}{a^2 + b^2 + 2asin\theta tan\theta + sin^2\theta tan^2\theta} \right)$$

$$\left(\frac{a^2 + b^2 - 2acos\theta + cos^2\theta}{a^2 + b^2 + 2acos\theta + cos^2\theta} \right)$$

(5.2)

The value of these equations is that they provide general insight into reflective behavior. The interpretation of these reflectances is much easier to understand when evaluated for a series of incident angles θ for a particular material. Figure 5.5 shows the result for glass—n equal to 1.5, κ equal to 0—as well as for water and diamond. For these

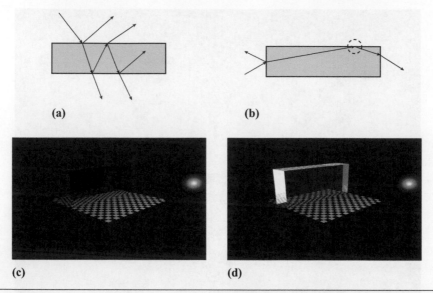

(a)   **(b)**

(c)   **(d)**

Figure 5.4: For a dielectric material, light is transmitted and reflected at every boundary. When traveling from a dense (higher value of n) to a less dense material, there may be no transmitted ray (b). Multiple bounces are required to get the accurate image of the transmitting/reflecting surface. The (c) and (d) images show this effect for a thick piece of glass sitting on a checkerboard with a light in front. Image (c) is rendered allowing only 2 reflections, whereas image (d) has 15.

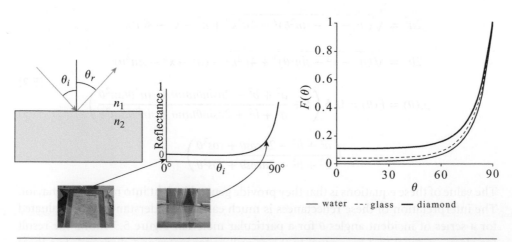

Figure 5.5: For a dielectric material, the reflectance increases with the angle of incidence.

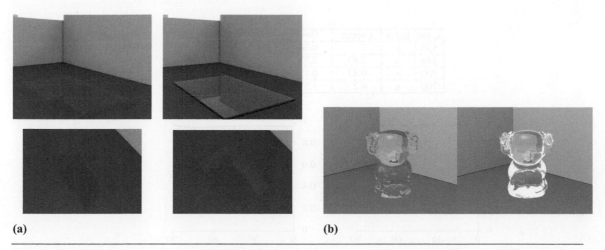

(a)   **(b)**

Figure 5.6: Without and with Fresnel effect (a): grazing view and top-down view. Effect of Fresnel on complex shape (b).

dielectrics, the fraction of light reflected strongly depends on the angle of incidence. The reflectance is very low until the incident angle is greater than 60 degrees. Although the high reflectance values are for a relatively small portion of the possible directions of incidence, the visual impact of this Fresnel effect is very noticeable when rendering glass and crystal. Synthetic results comparing the effect of just using a single low value of reflectance and accounting for the increase of reflectance with increasing incidence angle are shown in Figure 5.6.

For metals, there is not a dramatic change as the angle of incidence nears grazing, since the reflectance is high at all angles, as shown in Figure 5.7. The values of n and κ vary with wavelength. Silver has a high value for all visible wavelengths, while gold and copper have higher values near the red end of the spectrum (700 nm), resulting in the different color appearance of these metals. All of the metals have high reflectance at all wavelengths at near grazing angles. The implication of high reflectance at all wavelengths is that all of the metals tend to look gray or white when viewed at grazing angles.

Eq. 5.2 is an example of a result of derivations developed in another discipline. Another series of modifications of Eq. 5.2 has been not to change the effect, but to make Fresnel reflectance more efficient to compute in graphics applications. Since Fresnel reflectance variations are most important for dielectrics, a simplified version with κ set to zero is often used, and the equation simplifies to:

$$F(\theta) = \frac{(g-c)^2}{2(g+c)^2} \left\{ 1 + \frac{[c(g+c)-1]^2}{[c(g-c)+1]^2} \right\}$$
$$c = cos\theta$$
$$g^2 = n^2 + c^2 - 1$$

(5.3)

λ, nm	Index	Copper	Gold	Silver
550	n	1	0.34	0.12
550	κ	2.93	2.37	3.34
700	n	0.41	0.17	0.14
700	κ	4.2	3.97	4.52

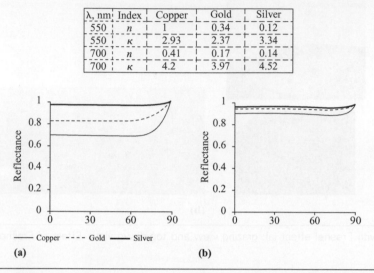

(a)   (b)

Figure 5.7: Reflectance as a function of angle for three metals—gold, copper, and silver—for two different wavelengths: (a) $\lambda = 550$ nm, (b) $\lambda = 700$ nm.

Since you need to know a technical standard name of a material to look it up, requiring the value of n to model a material for computer graphics is impractical. Cook and Torrance [56] note that if you know or can estimate the reflectance at normal incidence (θ equals zero), you can evaluate Eq. 5.3 with everything known except for the index of refraction. This results in estimate of n as:

$$n = \frac{1 + \sqrt{F(0)}}{1 - \sqrt{F(0)}} \tag{5.4}$$

With this insight relating normal reflectance and the index of refraction, an even simpler approximation of Eq. 5.3 was developed for quick evaluation in computer graphics by Schlick [285]:

$$F(\theta) = F(0) + (1 - cos\theta)^5(1 - F(0)) \tag{5.5}$$

From a practical point of view, for metals it is easier to measure the value of reflectance as a function of wavelength than it is to measure the values of n and κ. A simple approximation for the spectral change at grazing angles is just to linearly interpolate between the spectral values found for near-normal incidence angles and white at grazing angles [56]. If the Schlick approximation is used, this is simply a matter of evaluating Eq. 5.5 at each wavelength sample.

Using $(1 - F(\theta))$ as the transmittance of a material like glass only takes into account what happens at the smooth surface. As light moves from the surface through the glass, some light may be absorbed. Clear, transmitting glass may absorb different percentages of light at different wavelengths, resulting in a colored appearance. Impurities in the glass results in different colors. Iron oxide occurring in common glass results in a greenish tint that becomes more pronounced when multiple interreflections are viewed in common household mirrors [190]. The attenuation of radiance $L(s)$ compared to its initial radiance $L(0)$ as it travels through a uniform absorbing material with a thickness s is given by the Beer–Lambert–Bouguer Law:

$$L(s) = L(0)e^{-\sigma_a(\lambda)s} \tag{5.6}$$

The quantity $\sigma_a(\lambda)$ is the absorption coefficient of the material. This is an instance of a volumetric effect in a material. Volumetric effects will be discussed in greater detail in Section 5.7.

5.2 EMPIRICAL MODELS

Empirical, or phenomenological, models use combinations of functions that capture the major features of reflection we commonly observe, such as the diffuse reflectance in all directions, and the concentration of light scattering in a direction near the specular for glossy materials.

Empirical models do not attempt to simulate reflection or scattering in detail from the basic laws of physics. They define a set of mathematical functions that can be controlled by a small number of parameters. The functions are chosen to best fit reflectance behavior. The goal of empirical models is to have a small number of parameters that are easy to relate to the observation of a material.

5.2.1 LAMBERTIAN REFLECTANCE

Lambertian, or "ideal diffuse," reflectance, as described in Chapter 4, is in a sense the opposite of specular reflection. Instead of all light being reflected in a single direction, it is reflected in all directions with the same radiance. Unlike specular reflection, this is not the result of solving Maxwell's equations for some particular surface configuration. It is an approximation of the observed behavior of many materials. While real materials usually deviate from Lambertian for angles of view or incidence greater than 60 degrees, the Lambertian model is used for its computational simplicity. For measurement purposes, some materials have been designed that are very close to being to Lambertian, such as Spectralon from Labsphere Inc.

Figure 5.8: Diffuse looks the same from different views.

Figure 5.8 shows the puppy shape from Figure 5.2 rendered with Lambertian reflection. Because Lambertian reflection does not have to be recomputed as the view changes, it is commonly used in interactive applications.

Lambertian and specular reflection can be combined to approximate a material. Figure 5.9 shows a progression of approximating a material. In the upper left, the penguin shape is white diffuse. In the upper right, spatial variation is added to the spectral reflectance values. In the lower left, just the light source is reflected with a specular component. For efficiency, many interactive applications only consider the light source when applying the specular reflectance. Finally, in the lower right, all objects in the environment are considered when computing the specular reflection.

5.2.2 PHONG REFLECTANCE

A popular model that moves beyond simple specular plus ideal diffuse was developed by Phong and presented in a classic paper [264]. Many subsequent models can be viewed as variations and improvements on this basic model.

The Phong model was originally expressed as a reflectance function for setting shades in an image, rather than as a BRDF formulated for computing radiance. The goal of the model was not to accurately simulate light transfer, but to give the impression of a three-dimensional shaded surface illuminated by a directional light source. The development paid attention to computing within the 0 to 255 range imposed by using 8 bits per channel to store an image. The model is not grounded in the physics of light, but was inspired by physical observation. In Phong's paper [264], the effectiveness of the model is demonstrated comparing a rendering of a sphere and a photograph of a real sphere.

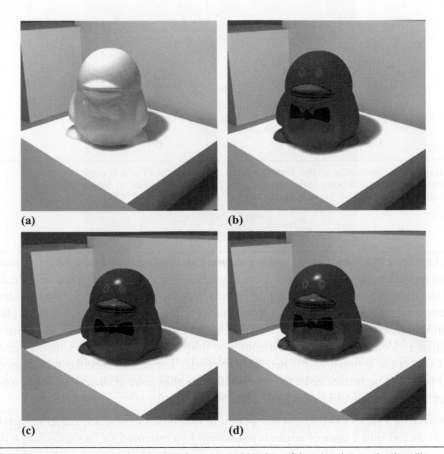

(a)   (b)

(c)   (d)

Figure 5.9: Materials can be modeled as a combination of Lambertian and mirrorlike reflectance. The material can also have spectral values that vary with position. Here, a scanned object is shown as white Lambertian (a), spectrally varying with position (b), with mirrorlike reflection of the light source (c), and with mirrorlike reflection (d) of the entire environment.

The model is given in terms of the angle θ_s between the view angle (θ_r, ϕ_r) and the angle of mirror reflection $(\theta_i, \phi_i + \pi)$ (Figure 5.10). As presented in the original paper [264], the function is given in the following terms:

$$d = \text{environmental diffuse coefficient}$$

$$W(\theta) = \text{specular coefficient}$$

$$C(\lambda) = \text{reflection coefficient}$$

$$\rho(\theta) = C(\lambda)[cos\,\theta_i(1-d) + d] + W(\theta_i)cos^p\theta_s$$

(5.7)

where p is a parameter controlling the shininess of the material.

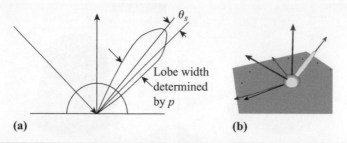

Figure 5.10: Geometry of the Phong model: (a) empirical Phong model, (b) three-dimensional view of Phong reflectance. *Source*: 3D view of Phong reflectance from US National Institute of Standards.

The key element in this equation, that is now commonly referred to as *Phong reflectance*, is the term that raises the cosine of the angle between the angle of specular reflection and the view direction to a power p. The term $W(\theta_i)$ that varies with angle of incidence is generally not used. The factor d is an artifact of incorporating an estimate of global illumination effects into a reflectance model. The effect of $cos^p\theta_s$ is to spread out the specular reflection into a cone of angles. For simple viewing software with viewer and light sources at infinity, this is necessary to render any sort of specular reflection of a light source. The mirror reflection of an infinitely thin cone of directional light would never be visible or would illuminate a single pixel.

Considering a surface and a light source pair in isolation, defining a specular reflectance that is spread into a cone of angles is equivalent to a mirrored surface reflecting a light incident from a cone of angles, as shown in Figure 5.11. In systems where it is too expensive to compute the effects of area light sources, applying Phong reflectance to the reflection of the light source is a substitute to produce an area effect from a directional or point light.

A physical interpretation of this spread of light into a cone of angles is that it is the effect of a slightly rough surface distributing the light in directions near the mirror angle. For simple viewing programs, the Phong model is typically expressed as:

$$\rho_{Phong}(\Theta_i \rightarrow \Theta_r) = k_d cos\theta_i + k_s cos^p\theta_s \qquad (5.8)$$

where k_d and k_s can take on different values for red, green, and blue.

The separate ideal diffuse and specular components are shown in Figure 5.12. The larger the value of p, the smaller the specular highlights formed by the reflection of the light source. Using the Phong model, different colors can be assigned to the specular portion of reflection (Figure 5.13).

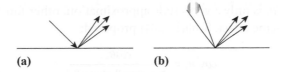

(a)   **(b)**

Figure 5.11: When viewed in isolation, the blurred reflectance of a point or directional source (a) looks the same as the mirror reflection of an area source with blurry edges (b).

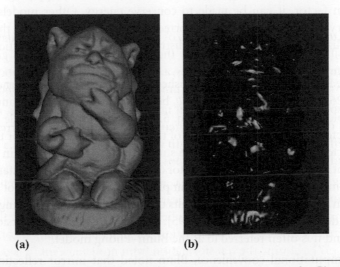

(a)   **(b)**

Figure 5.12: The (a) diffuse and (b) specular ($p = 0.5$) components of a Phong reflectance viewed separately.

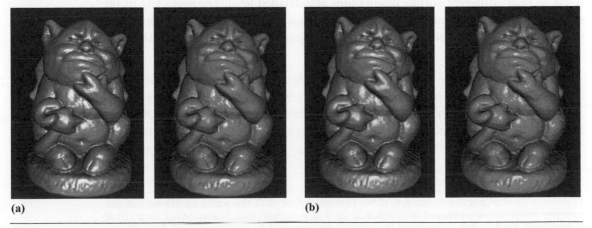

(a)   **(b)**

Figure 5.13: Phong reflectances with different shininess parameters p and different colors assigned to the specular reflection: (a) increasing p (white specular) and (b) increasing p (colored specular).

Since the term $cos^p\theta_s$ is only a very crude approximation, other functions can be used to accomplish the same effect. Schlick [284] proposed:

$$cos^p\theta_s = \frac{cos\theta_s}{p - pcos\theta_s + cos\theta_s} \qquad (5.9)$$

The classic Phong model has been frequently criticized as unphysical, since it does not obey conservation of energy. Lewis [200] showed that by applying an appropriate correction factor, it can be made to conserve energy. Other models correct for energy conservation by introducing the correction factor, or by replacing the $cos^p\theta_s$ with other normalized functions that create distributions around the direction of mirror reflection.

Soon after the Phong model was first published, Blinn introduced an alternative form to compute it [26]. He noted that the angle θ_s between the view direction and the mirror direction could be replaced with θ_h in Eq. 5.8. The angle θ_h is the angle between the "halfway" vector H, which is the bisector of the angle between the vector to the source L and the vector to the viewer V, and the surface normal N, as shown in Figure 5.14. Taking the dot product of the halfway vector and normal is more computationally convenient to compute than $cos\theta_s$. Using θ_h in place of θ_s, however, does not produce the same function. The difference in the results of using the two different angles has been examined in depth by Fisher and Woo [95]. Many systems use this version of Phong reflectance, and it is often referred to as the Blinn–Phong model.

Besides a computational convenience, Blinn noted that mirror reflections are only observed when the surface normal is aligned with the halfway vector. While the main surface has a normal N, at a microscopic level the surface has height variations that result in many different surface orientations at a detailed level. The spreading of the specular lobe can be thought of as the result of microsurfaces oriented in the direction of the halfway vector H with a likelihood related to $cos\theta_h$. Figure 5.14 shows in

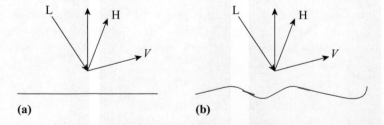

(a)   (b)

Figure 5.14: For a smooth surface, if the halfway vector isn't the same as the normal, no specular reflection is observed in direction V (a). For a surface that is somewhat rough at a microscopic level, some portions of the surface are oriented in the direction of the halfway vector even when the halfway vector isn't the same as the main surface normal (b).

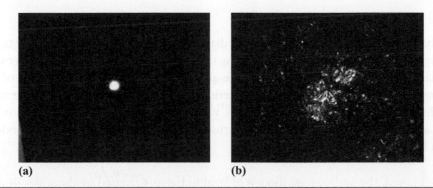

(a)   **(b)**

Figure 5.15: A macroscopic example of the spreading effect of a rough surface. For a surface that is somewhat rough at a microscopic level, some portions of the surface are oriented in the direction of the halfway vector even when the halfway vector isn't the same as the main surface normal. (a) A photograph of a small light source reflected in a mirror; and (b) a photograph of a small light source reflected in crumpled foil.

one dimension the effect of a slightly rough surface resulting in some portion of the surface oriented in the direction of the halfway angle. Figure 5.15 shows photographs of the effect with a surface with macroscopic roughness. A small light source on the left is reflected in a smooth mirror. On the right, the mirror is replaced with crumpled foil. Surfaces on the foil that are oriented correctly for specular reflection are distributed over a larger area, resulting in a larger bright area. Blinn cited examples in the optics literature of other functions used to model the likelihood of the surface microstructure being oriented with the halfway vector, and the use of these functions in formulating true BRDF models. This insight influenced the development of many computer graphics reflectance models.

As a side note on the Phong model, a frequent source of confusion is that the paper that introduced the Phong reflectance model also introduced Phong interpolation. Phong interpolation is a technique to make objects approximated as flat facets appear smooth. One way to do this is with Gouraud shading, which computes a shade at each vertex and then interpolates these shades across the facets. Phong interpolation takes this a step further and computes normals at each vertex and interpolates the normals across each flat facet. This is relevant to computing specular highlights on flat facets. For example, the appearance of a bright spot in the middle of a triangle with more dimly shaded vertices would not be possible if the shades were simply interpolated from the triangle vertices. Phong interpolation and Phong reflectance, however, are separate concepts and do not have to be used together. Phong reflectance can be applied to any geometric object including, for example, an implicit surface for which a normal can be computed explicitly at any point rather than approximated by interpolation.

5.2.3 WARD REFLECTANCE

The basic Ward reflectance model [326], diagrammed in Figure 5.16, is similar to the Phong model, except that rather than using the cosine term to a power, it uses an exponential function. The exponential term is parameterized by an average slope of the microscopic surface roughness. This function for describing the spread of the specular lobe in terms of microscopic surface variation was one of the forms that originally appeared in the optics literature discussed by Blinn. The original Ward model is given by:

$$f_r(\Theta_i \to \Theta_r) = \rho_d / \pi + \rho_s \frac{1}{\sqrt{cos\theta_i cos\theta_r}} \frac{e^{-tan^2\theta_h / \alpha^2}}{4\pi\alpha^2} \tag{5.10}$$

The value of α represents the standard deviation of the surface slope, where a uniform slope of zero would be a smooth surface. Small values of α (i.e., less that 0.1) model a very nearly smooth surface. Normally, α is adjusted by the user to get a particular appearance, or by fitting measured BRDF data, rather than somehow trying to measure the shape of the microscopic surface.

The normalization of the Ward function has recently been corrected by Duer [79], resulting in the form:

$$f_r(\Theta_i \to \Theta_r) = \rho_d / \pi + \rho_s \frac{1}{cos\theta_i cos\theta_r} \frac{e^{-tan^2\theta_h / \alpha^2}}{4\pi\alpha^2} \tag{5.11}$$

Ward's reflectance model obeys reciprocity. The factor $\frac{1}{4\pi\alpha^2}$ approximately normalizes the specular term so that energy is conserved. The approximation becomes poor

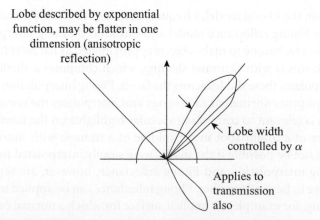

Figure 5.16: Geometry of Ward's reflectance model.

for α, greater than 0.2, but at that point the term is very broad and an ideal diffuse approximation would suffice. The effect of the normalization is to reduce the peak of the specular reflectance as the spread of the specular lobe gets wider. Another view of the normalization is to note that in Figure 5.14, as the fraction of the rough surface that is not oriented in the same direction as N increases, the fraction that is oriented toward N must decrease.

In an extended form of the Ward model, the specular lobe can be anisotropic by expressing different slopes for different directions on a surface (e.g., for a set of grooves, the slope is zero along the grooves and potentially steep perpendicular to the grooves). This results in the width of the lobe being different in the direction out of the page than it is in the page:

$$f_r(\Theta_i \to \Theta_r) = \rho_d/\pi + \rho_s \frac{1}{cos\theta_i cos\theta_r} \frac{e^{-tan^2\theta_h(cos^2\phi_h/\alpha_x^2 + sin^2\phi_h/\alpha_y^2)}}{4\pi\alpha_x\alpha_y} \tag{5.12}$$

The basic model can just be assigned to a surface, and the only geometric information needed at any point is the normal that can be viewed as the z axis of a local coordinate system. For the basic model, how the y and x axes are locally assigned has no effect on the reflectance values calculated. However, with an anisotropic reflectance, the orientation of the different slopes needs to be specified on the surface. In the examples shown here, the direction of the x and y axes are taken to be aligned with the global coordinate system.

Since the Ward model is developed in physical terms of incident and reflected radiance, it works (by design) in a system that simulates physically accurate global illumination. Physically accurate material models can only be expected to predict realistic appearance when used in the context of a physically accurate global illumination system. Even the most carefully derived reflectance functions will produce artificial-looking materials if they are not placed in a natural setting with accurately computed lighting input. The variations of models shown in Figures 5.17 and 5.18 were rendered using the Radiance [187] software system.

The darker orange in the ridges of the model in Figure 5.18 is not specified by the material definition, but is due to the fact that this is a global illumination solution. Rays are reflected from the object to itself, altering the reflected spectrum and intensifying the color on each reflection.

Anisotropic reflection has a significant impact on appearance, but for a complicated object its effect is only clear when the effect of isotropic or anisotropic reflection with a different orientation is displayed.

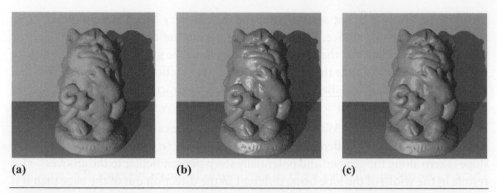

(a)   (b)   (c)

Figure 5.17: Ward reflectance used with a Lambertian component: (a) ideal diffuse, (b) diffuse plus white glossy specular, and (c) diffuse plus white anisotropic glossy specular.

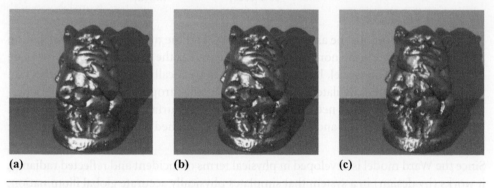

(a)   (b)   (c)

Figure 5.18: Ward reflectance without a Lambertian component and with a high specular component, giving the appearance of metal: (a) metal, isotropic glossy; (b) metal, anisotropic (horizontal) glossy; and (c) metal, anisotropic (vertical) glossy.

The Ward model for the specular lobe can readily be applied to the transmitted ray as well, as shown in Figure 5.19. These transmitting models are rendered with the same surface spectrum as the others. They appear darker and a different color though, because the light is not primarily from the bright-white light source reflected from the front surface of the object, but is being transmitted through the object from the dimmer grayish-green wall and floor. Observing the shadow of the object on the right also demonstrates the effect of a material on its surroundings when a global illumination solution is computed.

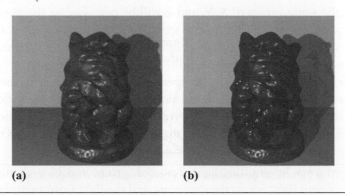

(a)   **(b)**

Figure 5.19: The Ward model applied to the transmitted component: (a) ideal diffuse transmission, glossy specular reflection; and (b) combined diffuse, regular transmission, glossy specular reflection.

5.2.4 LAFORTUNE REFLECTANCE

The cosine lobe model described in Lafortune et al. [185] is a different generalization of the Phong model. Like the Ward model, it is formulated in physical terms. Instead of just describing peaks of reflection around the specular direction, it allows the definition of lobes (possibly anisotropic) around any axis defined with respect to the surface as shown in Figure 5.20. By appropriate normalization, a lobe in any direction can be defined as an element of a BRDF that both conserves energy and obeys reciprocity. Important other axes for defining lobes are just off the specular direction, the normal direction, and the direction of the source (for backscatter).

The general form of the reflectance can be expressed as:

$$f_r(\Theta_i \to \Theta_r) = f_r(u \to v) = \rho_s[C_x u_x v_x + C_y u_y v_y + C_z u_z v_z]^p \qquad (5.13)$$

where u and v are vectors in the incident Θ_i and reflected Θ_r directions expressed in a coordinate system were the z axis is the surface normal (see Figure 5.21), C_x, C_y, and C_z are coefficients determining the direction and proportions of the lobe, and p defines how narrow it is. Sets of functions of this form can be summed to form the BRDF for a single material.

The Lafortune model includes previous models. If p is set to zero in Eq. 5.13, the result is Lambertian reflectance. An energy-conserving version of the original Phong reflectance (not Blinn–Phong) is obtained by choosing:

$$-C_x = -C_y = C_z = \sqrt[p]{\frac{p+2}{2\pi}} \qquad (5.14)$$

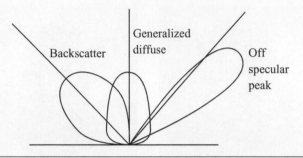

Figure 5.20: The Lafortune generalizes the Phong model to multiple lobes.

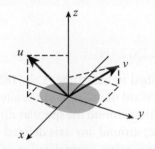

Figure 5.21: The Lafortune model is expressed in terms of vectors expressed in a local coordinate system on the surface. *Source*: Redrawn from Lafortune et al. [185]. © 1997 ACM 1997. Included here by permission.

An example of a BRDF that the Lafortune model can represent that previous models could not is generalized diffuse reflectance (Figure 5.22). In general, even surfaces that appear matte or diffuse don't reflect radiance evenly in all directions. The reflection may peak in the direction of the surface normal and fall off at near-grazing viewing angles. The effects shown here are found using $C_x = C_y = 0, C_z = 1$, and p is equal to 0, 0.5, and 2, respectively.

The Lafortune model, unlike Phong or Ward, also provides a mechanism for defining backscatter, which is the tendency of some materials to scatter light preferentially back into the incident direction. The $cos^p\theta$ distribution can be interpreted as the likelihood that a surface microfacet is oriented normal to the incident direction. In Figure 5.23, the sum of a Lambertian term and a backscatter lobe is illustrated.

While backscatter can be important, most notably in the rendering of the moon, as ambient interreflections increase the visual effect of backscattering on the appearance

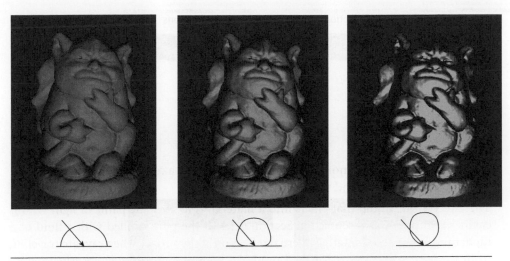

Figure 5.22: Diffuse fall-off modeled as a Lafortune lobe.

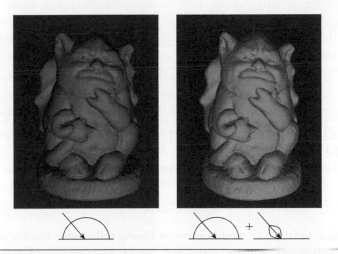

Figure 5.23: Backscattering modeled with a lobe in the Lafortune model.

of natural materials is reduced (Figure 5.24). Some man-made materials, such as those used in road signs, are designed to be sharply reflective back into the incident direction. These *retroreflective* materials require an explicit definition of a backscatter lobe to be adequately modeled.

No interreflections   Interreflections

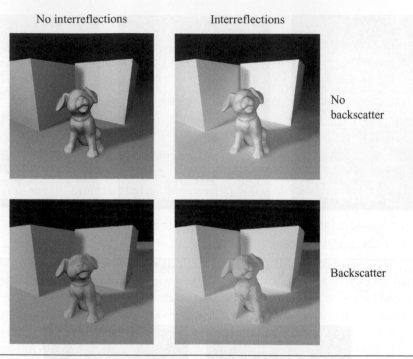

No
backscatter

Backscatter

Figure 5.24: The effect of backscattering compared to Lambertian reflection diminishes when light interreflections are taken into account.

With summing functions, there become a large number of parameters C_x, C_y, C_z, and p to be defined for specifying reflectance. This makes the model inconvenient for user interfaces. The Lafortune model has been used for fitting masses of measured BRDF data into a compact representation (e.g., [196]).

5.2.5 ASHIKHMIN–SHIRLEY ANISOTROPIC PHONG REFLECTANCE

The Ashikhmin–Shirley [8] modification of Phong reflectance has the feature that it includes an explicit term for the Fresnel reflectance. The specular reflectance increases as the angle of incidence increases. The diffuse component is appropriately reduced at these angles to maintain energy conservation. The formulation also maintains reciprocity and allows for anisotropy. The model parameters for anisotropic reflection are Phong-type exponents p_u and p_v that control the shape of the highlight in the directions of two tangent vectors on the surface that are perpendicular to the surface normal. Parameters R_s and R_d respectively specify the fractions of incident energy reflected specularly and diffusely. The Fresnel component is computed with Schlick's approximation.

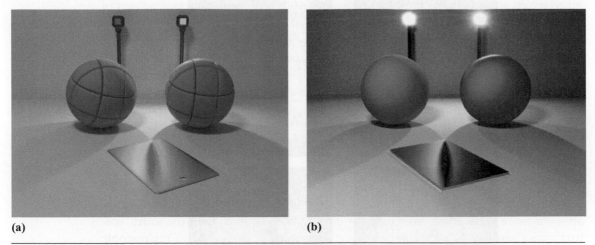

(a)   (b)

Figure 5.25: Lafortune (a) and Ashikhmin–Shirley (b) models simulating increased Fresnel reflectance at grazing incident/viewing angle. *Source* (a) From Lafortune et al. [185] © 1997 ACM; (b) from Ashikmin and Shirley [8] © 2000 AK Peters. Included here by permission.

The model is given by:

$$f_r(\Theta_i \rightarrow \Theta_r) = \rho_s(\Theta_i \rightarrow \Theta_r) + \rho_d(\Theta_i \rightarrow \Theta_r)$$

$$\rho_s(\Theta_i \rightarrow \Theta_r) = \frac{\sqrt{(p_u + 1) + (p_v + 1)}}{8\pi} \frac{cos\theta_h^{p_u cos^2\phi_h + p_v sin^2\phi_h}}{cos\theta_h max(cos\theta_i, cos\theta_r)} F(cos\theta_h) \quad (5.15)$$

$$\rho_d(\Theta_i \rightarrow \Theta_r) = \frac{28R_d}{23\pi}(1 - R_s)\left(1 - \left(\frac{1 - cos\theta_i}{2}\right)^5\right)\left(1 - \left(\frac{1 - cos\theta_r}{2}\right)^5\right)$$

$$F(cos\theta_h) = R_s + (1 - R_s)(1 - cos\theta_h)^5$$

A similar effect can be accomplished in the Lafortune model by summing an imperfect diffuse lobe and a specular lobe that increases by the amount the diffuse lobe falls off. Comparable images from the original papers on the two models are shown in Figure 5.25. The difference in contrast in rendering with this model versus the Ward model that renders with a Lambertian term for the diffuse component is shown in Figure 5.26 for a couple of different forms of the specular lobe.

5.3 ANALYTICAL FIRST PRINCIPLES MODELS

Another class of methods derives functions for light scattering that start at a more detailed level of modeling of the surface, rather than trying to capture the behavior of the surface as a black box. These are referred to as "first principles" models because

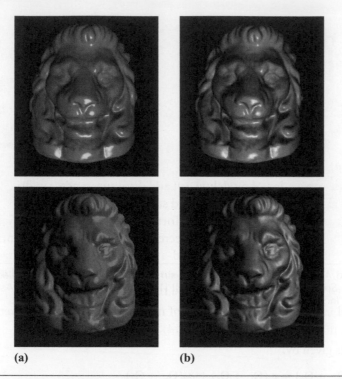

(a)   (b)

Figure 5.26: Fall-off in diffuse component results in greater contrast in the Ashikhmin–Shirley model (b) relative to Ward model (a), as is apparent both from rendering an isotropic highlight with light from front (*top* row) and softer anisotropic highlight with light from right (*bottom* row).

they apply basic principles of physics to a surface's microscopic structure, and build up the bulk behavior of how the surface redirects light. They make use of the material properties n and κ and then use either geometric or wave optics to describe how light interacts with a nonsmooth surface.

5.3.1 MICROFACET DISTRIBUTIONS

Analytical models begin with modeling the surface geometry at the microscopic level (Figure 5.27). Rather than explicitly model the small geometric features, general reflectance functions use statistical models. Statistical models are used because the variation in surface height is assumed to be irregular and random. Different methods for generating a random surface can be hypothesized, resulting in different distributions. Beckmann and Spizzichino [19] demonstrate building a random surface in one dimension by coin flipping. As shown in Figure 5.28, as steps are taken to the right, based on

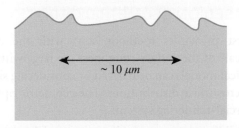

Figure 5.27: First principles techniques start with a model of the surface at the microlevel; this shows model interaction of light with material.

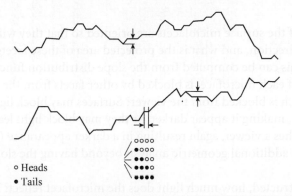

○ Heads
● Tails

Figure 5.28: A method for constructing a random surface. *Source*: Redrawn from Beckmann and Spizzichino [19], © 1987 Artech House Publishers.

the results of flipping a coin four times, the surface moves up or down one or two units, or stays at the same level.

A statistical model for surfaces in reflectance models generally takes the form of giving the distribution of facets that have a particular slope. One possibility is the Gaussian distribution of surface slopes used in the Ward model. Another is to assume the variation in height of the surface is Gaussian, and then derive the slope distribution. This assumption results in the Beckmann distribution function in terms of the slope parameter α:

$$D_{Beckmann}(\theta_h) = \frac{1}{\alpha^2 cos^4 \theta_h} exp - (tan\theta_h/\alpha)^2 \qquad (5.16)$$

The assumption of a microfacet distribution function is a starting point for first principles methods for both geometric optics and wave optics approaches.

5.3.2 MODELS BASED ON GEOMETRIC OPTICS

Geometric optics first principles methods start with the assumption that the microfacets and the scale of the surface roughness are large with respect to the wavelength of light. Analytical models can be derived by considering simple ray interactions at the facets of the microsurface distributions. The geometric optics models are found commonly in commercial-rendering systems.

A methodology for building up a geometric optics model for reflectance from a surface distribution was originally developed in optics and radiation transfer, and was described in the context of computer graphics in Blinn [26]. A model can be composed from the following factors:

- How many of the surface microfacets are oriented so that they will reflect light in the view direction, and what is the projected area of these facets in the view direction? This can be computed from the slope distribution function.
- How much of each microfacet is blocked by other facets from the incident light and how much is blocked from the viewer? Surfaces may block light incident on another facet, making it appear darker, or they may block light leaving the facet before it reaches a viewer, again resulting in a darker appearance (Figure 5.29). This requires additional geometric analysis beyond having the slope distribution function.
- When unobstructed, how much light does the microfacet reflect? This is given by a simple reflectance function, generally either pure specular or Lambertian.

Many different reflectance functions can be formed by varying the approach to each of these three issues. Examples of different forms of distribution functions have already been noted. One method for analyzing the effects of masking and shadowing is to assume that the facets form V-shaped grooves, as illustrated in Figure 5.29. This analysis was first introduced as graphics by Blinn [26] based on Torrance and Sparrow's [313] work in radiation heat transfer. While this shadowing model is commonly used, Ashikhmin et al. [9] challenged this approach, since long V-shaped grooves aren't consistent with the assumption of a random surface. They explored alternative shadowing functions to form custom reflectance functions for materials such as silk and velvet.

Finally, a differentiator between first principles methods using geometric optics is whether specular or Lambertian reflectance is assumed at each facet (Figure 5.30).

Popular first principles models are Blinn [26], Cook–Torrance [56], and Oren–Nayar [254] (Figure 5.31). In Blinn and Cook–Torrance, the microfacet reflectance is assumed to be specular, and in Oren–Nayar it is assumed to be Lambertian.

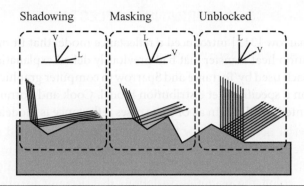

Figure 5.29: Facets may be shadowed, masked, or unblocked.

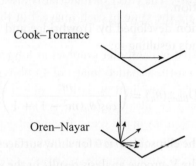

Figure 5.30: Blinn and Cook–Torrance assume specular reflectance at each facet, and Oren–Nayar assumes Lambertian facet reflectance.

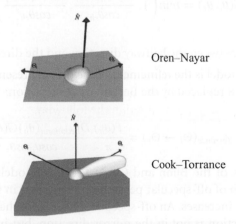

Figure 5.31: Basic shapes of Cook–Torrance (predicts off-specular peaks) and Oren–Nayar (predicts backscatter) reflectance functions. *Source*: Diagrams produced at the US National Institute of Standards and Technology.

5.3.3 BLINN AND COOK–TORRANCE REFLECTANCE

Torrance and Sparrow [313] introduced a reflectance model that fit measured data in optics and radiation heat transfer that had previously defied explanation. Blinn introduced the approach used by Torrance and Sparrow to computer graphics, and proposed a model based on a specific facet distribution model. Cook and Torrance then revised the model presented by Blinn. In all of these cases reflectance is modeled as:

$$f_r(\Theta_i \rightarrow \Theta_r) = \frac{F(\theta_h)D(\theta_h)G(\theta_i, \theta_r)}{\pi cos\theta_i cos\theta_r} \qquad (5.17)$$

where F is the Fresnel function, D is the facet distribution model, and G is the shadowing/masking function.

Blinn selected a distribution developed by Trowbridge and Reitz [314] motivated by modeling facets as ellipsoids resulting in:

$$D_{Blinn}(\theta_h) = \left(\frac{m^2}{cos^2\theta_h(m^2 - 1) + 1} \right)^2 \qquad (5.18)$$

where the eccentricity of the ellipsoids m is 0 for shiny surfaces and 1 for rough surfaces.

Blinn demonstrates that the V-groove analysis results in the shadowing/masking term:

$$G(\theta_i, \theta_r) = min\left(1, \frac{2cos\theta_h cos\theta_r}{cos\theta_{rh}}, \frac{2cos\theta_h cos\theta_i}{cos\theta_{rh}} \right) \qquad (5.19)$$

where θ_{rh} is the angle between the halfway direction and the direction of the viewer.

The Cook–Torrance model is the refinement of the model presented by Blinn, with the distribution in Eq. 5.18 replaced by the Beckmann distribution:

$$f_{r,Cook-Torrance}(\Theta_i \rightarrow \Theta_r) = \frac{F(\theta_h)}{\pi} \frac{D_{Beckmann}(\theta_h)G(\theta_i, \theta_r)}{cos\theta_i cos\theta_r} \qquad (5.20)$$

The principle features of the Blinn and Cook–Torrance models as far as directional effects is the prediction of off-specular peaks and the increase in specular reflectance as the angle of incidence increases. An off-specular peak means that the maximum value of the reflectance function is not in the mirror direction, but in a direction closer to a grazing angle. The off-specular peaks are the consequence of shadowing and masking causing asymmetries. The increase in reflectance with angle of incidence makes

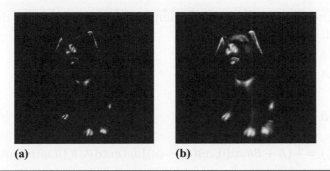

(a)   **(b)**

Figure 5.32: A comparison of Phong (a) and Blinn (b) specular highlights for the same lobe width (i.e., the angle at which the specular lobe is the value of one-half peak for both).

a noticeable difference over the Phong model with nominally the same lobe width. In Figure 5.32, the highlights look nearly the same at near-normal incidents to the surface, but are quite different at other angles.

While off-specular peaks are noticeable in some renderings, they aren't a first-order effect; it's difficult for people to tell from a picture if the position of the peak reflectance is correct. The major impact of the Cook–Torrance paper was in its treatment of the spectrum of the reflected light in the form of the Fresnel function, which depends on n and κ. The result of this treatment was that the plastic and ceramic materials they simulated had white (or the color of the light source) highlights, while metals had highlights the color of the base metal, even with a white light source. This was the first time this critical insight into reproducing the appearance of real materials appeared in computer graphics. Appropriately assigning the color of the specular component is a mechanism that can be used in any of the reflectance models to obtain metallic versus nonmetallic appearance.

5.3.4 OREN–NAYAR REFLECTANCE

The motivation for the Oren–Nayar model was that the edges of front-lit matte ceramic objects looked too dark if they were simulated as Lambertian. Rather than use an empirical function, they sought an analytical solution. The solution was found by using facets similar to Cook–Torrance, but assuming Lambertian, rather than mirror, reflection at the facet level. The V groove analysis for shadowing and masking effects was complicated by also needing to account for the effects of multiple Lambertian interreflections in the groove. A Gaussian slope distribution, similar to Ward, is used with the standard deviation of the slope equal to α. The full solution for Lambertian facets with reflectance ρ proved to be far more complicated than would ever be used in practice. Oren and Nayar found a simplified approximation to the solution is generally used:

$$A = 1.0 - 0.5\frac{\alpha^2}{\alpha^2 + 0.33}$$

$$B = 0.45\frac{\alpha^2}{\alpha^2 + 0.09} \tag{5.21}$$

$$f_r(\Theta_i \to \Theta_r) = \frac{\rho}{\pi}(A + Bmax[0, cos(\phi_r - \phi_i)])sin(max[\theta_r, \theta_i])tan(min[\theta_r, \theta_i])$$

The principle feature of the Oren–Nayar model is the prediction of backscattering, which is a consequence of facets oriented toward the light source diffusely reflect some light back to the source. When compared to a Lambertian surface, the Oren–Nayar model renders the object with less contrast (Figure 5.33). The higher the roughness specified in the Oren–Nayar method, the less contrast (Figure 5.34).

The result in each case are BRDF functions with lobes that have more complicated structures than those used in empirical models. The BRDF for the models in Figure 5.31 is specified by giving parameters for the microscopic surface geometry. However, since the microstructure is rarely known, the facet distribution parameters are normally treated as parameters similar to p in the Phong and Lafortune models for controlling the shape of these complicated distributions.

When specular and diffuse components are combined on an object in isolation, the differences in the model are discernible, but only with careful viewing (Figure 5.35).

Neither Blinn nor the Cook–Torrance models give backscattering, and Oren–Nayar doesn't give specular peaks. The models are often used together to produce a full BRDF.

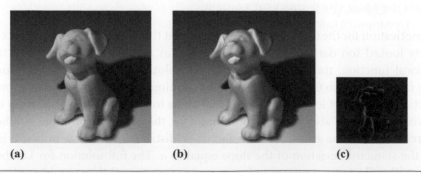

(a) **(b)** **(c)**

Figure 5.33: Comparison of Oren–Nayar (a) and Lambertian (b) with interreflections for the same diffuse coefficient; blue, Lambertian greater; yellow, Oren–Nayar greater (c).

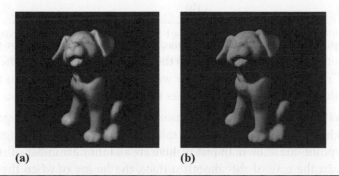

Figure 5.34: The effect of changing the standard deviation of the slope α, and so the roughness—(a) low, (b) high—in Oren–Nayar.

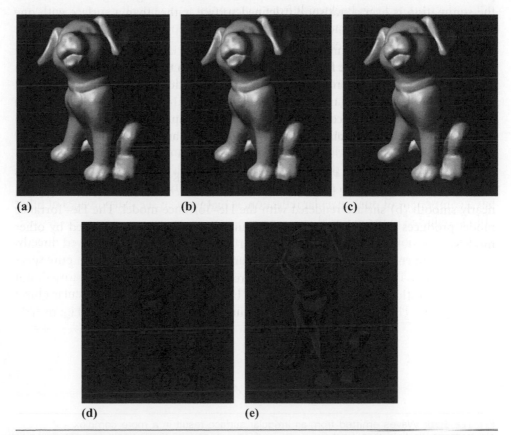

Figure 5.35: Comparison of Phong (a), Blinn (b), and Oren–Nayar (c) with comparable settings for diffuse and specular components. For many combinations of parameters and lighting conditions, the results are difficult to differentiate: (d) where Phong is less than Blinn and (e) where Oren–Nayar is less than Phong.

5.3.5 MODELS BASED ON WAVE OPTICS

Geometric optics provide models for perfectly smooth surfaces, and for surfaces with roughness that is significantly greater than the wavelength of light. The effects of surface variations of a size are on the scale of the wavelength of light needed to use solutions that include the wave nature of light, rather than simple ray interactions.

The problem is illustrated in Figure 5.36 using Huygen's principle. Huygen's principle states that each point acts as an individual spherical source of waves. In Figure 5.36, only a few sample points are shown. In reality there are an infinite number of emitters along each surface. In the case of the smooth surface, the timing of when the waves occur results in their sum forming exactly another plane wave. In the case of an irregular surface, on the right, the sum of the infinite number of spherical waves emitted from points on the surface is much more complicated. Complicating things further is that the summation is over a statistically defined surface, rather than a surface with one particular shape.

By making appropriate assumptions, such that the material is a perfect conductor and the curvature of the surface facets is large with respect to the wavelength of light, analytical solutions are possible. Kayija [167] derived a solution in the form of an integral that needed to be evaluated numerically. Later, He et al. [142] derived a solution in the form of a series that slowly converged. Subsequently, an approximation to this solution was presented as a set of spline functions controlled by an 80×80 matrix of control points.

The model by He et al. [142] is useful when predicting the appearance of a nearly smooth surface. Figure 5.37 illustrates the subtle differences between a smooth (a) and nearly smooth (b) surface rendered with the He–Torrance model. The He–Torrance model produces variations in sharp and blurred reflections not predicted by other models.

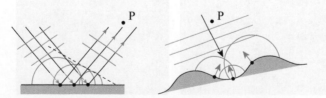

Figure 5.36: Waves emitted from an irregular surface result in a more complex electromagnetic field than from a smooth surface.

Figure 5.37: Effect of He–Torrance reflectance: a smooth surface (*left*) and a nearly smooth surface (*right*). *Source*: © 2004 Stephen H. Westin, Hong Song Li, and Kenneth Torrance, Cornell University.

5.4 SIMULATION FROM FIRST PRINCIPLES

Some models are developed by constructing a surface microstructure and then running a numerical simulation of the light scattering and storing the results in tabular form or as a set of coefficients of basis functions. An early example of this was presented by Cabral et al. [37] who computed a table of BRDF values by evaluating the visibility results of incident and reflected direction pairs on a small bumpy surface. The idea was further explored in Westin et al. [333] and Gondek et al. [118].

Westin et al. [333] define a hierarchy of modeling. At the finest level, they define BRDFs. At the next level, they define microgeometric structures, such as the fibers shown in Figure 5.38a. Rays are intersected from various directions at the microstructure, and the radiance reflected in different directions is stored in the form of spherical harmonic functions. The BRDF can then be evaluated from the spherical harmonic functions, and used to render the material on a macroscale, as shown in Figure 5.38b.

Gondek et al. [118] modeled both subsurface structure and surface microgeometry (top of Figure 5.39.) The subsurface structure is at a scale so small it is assumed that whatever rays enter the structure leave at essentially the same point on the surface. Rather than storing the results as spherical harmonics, they used a geodesic data structure (bottom of Figure 5.39.) An insightful result from this work is shown in Figure 5.40. In Figure 5.40a, surface roughness is increased. Since the reflection from the top surface of the material is white, increasing the roughness increases the fraction of white light reflected to the viewer everywhere except for the window reflections, which were white to start. The result is an object with apparently desaturated color. In Figure 5.40b,

(a)   **(b)**

Figure 5.38: (a) A microstructure for a first principles simulation; and (b) an object rendered with the resulting BRDF. *Source*: From Westin et al. [333], © 1992 ACM. Included here by permission.

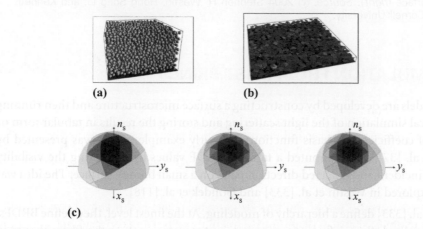

(a)   **(b)**

(c)

Figure 5.39: Simulation from first principles: (a), (b) microstructure models and (c) data structure for storing results. *Source*: From Gondek et al. [118], © 1994 ACM. Included here by permission.

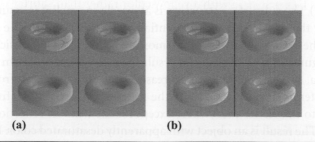

(a)   **(b)**

Figure 5.40: Gondek simulations of increasing surface roughness and decreasing pigment particle size. *Source*: From Gondek et al. [118], © 1994 ACM. Included here by permission.

transmitting pigment particles just below the surface are shown decreasing in size. The green color is due to the transmission of light through the particles during which the red and blue lights are absorbed. For smaller particles, there is a shorter path through each particle and less light is absorbed, and the material again appears to become desaturated.

First principles simulations don't provide interactive parameters that allow users to create materials with specific properties, as they can with functional models. The simulations could be used to build libraries of materials. However, with advances in physical capture techniques driven by the availability of inexpensive digital cameras, very little work has been done developing libraries with simulation.

5.5 SPECTRAL EFFECTS

The models discussed so far have focused on directional effects. Spectral effects have been accounted for implicitly in the Fresnel equations through the wavelength dependence of the material index of refraction. Specular and diffuse reflectance and transmittance may have different spectral distributions, and as demonstrated in Figure 5.40, the balance between these effects results in different color appearance. In this section, we more carefully consider some specific spectral variations that have complicated directional dependence.

The classic work on the spectral variations of materials is Nassau's *The Physics and Chemistry of Color: The Fifteen Causes of Color* [241]. Most of the causes he describes occur at the molecular or atomic level, scales that are not modeled in graphics applications. Furthermore, these spectral effects generally have directional characteristics that can be measured and used in the models we have already discussed in these chapters. However, there are three types of effects—*dispersion*, *interference*, and *diffraction*—that result in complicated spectral/directional dependence and that may require setting parameters at the microstructure level.

5.5.1 DISPERSION

As noted in the discussion of the Fresnel function for metals, the index of refraction is a function of wavelength. The index of refraction for glass is about 1.54 on the blue end of the spectrum and 1.5 on the red end. This spectral variation of the index of refraction is what causes different wavelengths of light to bend a different amount when they pass through glass, and causes white light to split into a rainbow of colors in a prism. This type of optical effect in prisms and lenses is discussed in optical texts such as Jenkins and White [159]. Dispersion is rendered by following separate ray paths for different wavelengths, rather than following one geometric path for R, G, and B. An example of dispersion produced by such spectral ray tracing is shown in Figure 5.41.

Figure 5.41: A lit object exhibiting color variations due to dispersion. *Source*: From Sun et al. [306], © 2001 Springer-Verlag.

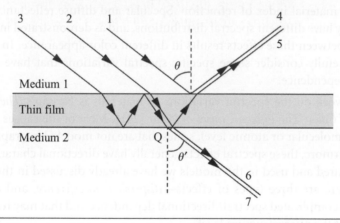

Figure 5.42: Geometry of interference. *Source*: From Sun et al. [306], © 1999 IEEE.

5.5.2 THIN FILM INTERFERENCE

Intense color can appear when light passes through a thin film, such as an oil slick on water on the street after it rains. In this instance, "thin" is defined as a length on the order of the wavelength of light. The geometry of the effect is shown in Figure 5.42 from Sun et al. [306], and it occurs when the thickness of the film is on the order of a wavelength of light. The phase of a wave, that is, where it has peaks and valleys, switches when light reflects off a boundary from lower to greater index of refraction, but does not change when reflecting from greater to lower index of refraction.

Suppose the materials are air, oil, and water (indices of 1, 1.5, and 1.3, respectively). Consider the paths from 1 to 4 and from 2 to 5 in Figure 5.42. When light reflects from 1 to 4 it undergoes a phase change. When it reflects on the way from 2 to 5 the phase does not change. However, if its path through the film is just one-half the wavelength, it will meet up with the first ray in the phase and they will add together, giving a much higher intensity for the light at this wavelength.

Many researchers have considered efficient rendering of interference effects, [148], [154], [155], [294]. Sun et al. [306] give pseudocode for ray tracing interference effects based on the following equations for the specular reflection or transmittance for a particular angle θ, wavelength λ, indices of refraction n_f, n_1, and n_2 (for film and the two surrounding media), and film thickness d:

$$\rho_s(\lambda, \theta) \ (or) \ \tau_s(\lambda, \theta) = cos^2 \frac{\delta(\lambda, \theta)}{2}$$

$$\delta(\lambda, \theta) = \frac{4\pi d}{\lambda}\sqrt{n_f^2 - n_1^2 sin\theta^2} + \delta' \tag{5.22}$$

for reflection $\delta' = 0$ for n_f between n_1 and n_2, else π

for transmission $\delta' = \pi$ for n_f between n_1 and n_2, else 0

5.5.3 DIFFRACTION FROM REGULAR STRUCTURES

Consider a surface with a regular structure, such as a sinusoid, instead of the irregular surface shown on the right in Figure 5.36. If the structure is on the order of the wavelength of light, the waves from the points on the surface will constructively and destructively interfere with each other, producing reflectances for a particular wavelength such as that shown in Figure 5.43. As you move the angle of view of the object, the light at each wavelength will change from being very intense to disappearing. Stam [297] and Sun et al. [307] have investigated solutions for the wave equation for this case, and they have produced approximations for rendering objects such as compact discs.

5.6 OTHER EFFECTS

Other effects at surfaces are polarization, phosphorescence, and fluorescence. While these influence many surfaces, they have noticeable visual effects only in specialized cases. Most rendering systems do not implement explicit models for these effects. Accounting for, and in the case of polarization taking advantage of, these effects are important in measuring material properties (see Chapter 7).

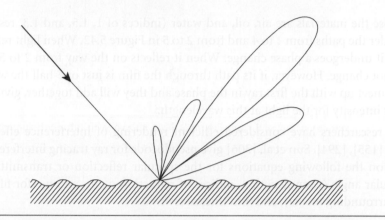

Figure 5.43: Reflection from sinusoidal microsurface. *Source*: Redrawn from Beckmann and Spizzichino [19], © 1987 Artech House Publishers.

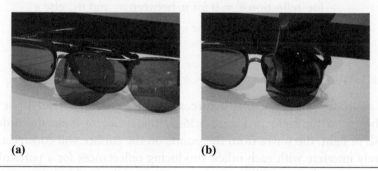

(a)   **(b)**

Figure 5.44: Photographs of sunglasses that are polarization filters. The relative orientation of two polarizations adjusts the amount of light transmitted through the filters.

5.6.1 POLARIZATION

Polarization, in addition to wavelength, is another attribute of light. It describes the orientation of the electromagnetic field in a plane normal to the direction of travel of light. Normally we see unpolarized light, which are light waves without any preferential orientation. If a polarization filter (such as the lens of polarized sunglasses) is used over a source, though, all of the light components perpendicular to the orientation of the filter are cut out, effectively reducing the radiance of unpolarized light by a factor of two (see Figure 5.44a). If a second polarization filter is used with an orientation perpendicular to the first, the light is completely blocked (Figure 5.44b).

A more general solution to Maxwell's equations for a smooth surface is expressed in terms of the state of polarization as well as for wavelength:

$$2a^2 = \sqrt{(n^2 - \kappa^2 - \sin^2\theta)^2 + 4n^2\kappa^2} + n^2 - \kappa^2 - \sin^2\theta$$

$$2b^2 = \sqrt{(n^2 - \kappa^2 - \sin^2\theta)^2 + 4n^2\kappa^2} - (n^2 - \kappa^2 - \sin^2\theta)$$

(5.23)

$$\rho_{s\perp} = F_\perp(\theta) = \frac{a^2 + b^2 - 2a\cos\theta + \cos^2\theta}{a^2 + b^2 + 2a\cos\theta + \cos^2\theta}$$

(5.24)

$$\rho_{s\parallel} = F_\parallel(\theta) = F_\perp(\theta)\frac{a^2 + b^2 - 2a\sin\theta\tan\theta + \sin^2\theta\tan^2\theta}{a^2 + b^2 + 2a\sin\theta\tan\theta + \sin^2\theta\tan^2\theta}$$

The two basis directions for the orientation are referred to as perpendicular ($\perp$) and parallel ($\parallel$). Eq. 5.3 for the unpolarized reflectance is just the average of the perpendicular and parallel reflectances. Parallel and perpendicular can be defined with respect to the plane of specular reflection (i.e., the plane defined by the incident and reflected directions), as shown on the left in Figure 5.45. The difference in reflectance for perpendicular versus parallel polarization are shown in the graphs on the right in Figure 5.45. The difference in the two orientations is quite large for dielectrics. Light reflected from a smooth dielectric, such as the surface of a body of water, is almost entirely polarized in one orientation. This polarization is what makes polarized sunglasses capable of removing the glare off of water while not turning the rest of the view black.

Wolff and Kurlander [339] developed a method to incorporate polarization effects into the Cook–Torrance reflectance model. The state of polarization can be expressed as a two-by-two matrix, called the coherence matrix (CM). The trace (sum of diagonal

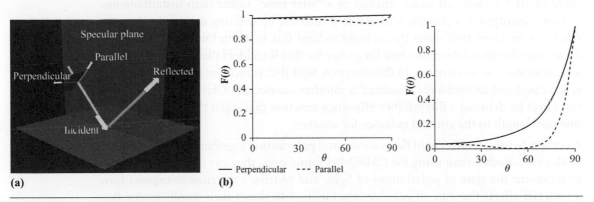

(a)   **(b)**

Figure 5.45: (a) Definition of the parallel and perpendicular directions as used to express the state of polarization of a ray of light. (b) Fresnel reflection of parallel and perpendicular polarized light for a typical metal (*left*) and a dielectric (*right*).

elements) of the matrix scales the radiance. The identity matrix scaled by one-half is the CM for unpolarized light. The effect of reflection on a polarization state can be expressed as a two-by-two coherence modification matrix (CMM). A reflected radiance with a polarization state is computed by geometrically transforming a ray's CM to the orientation of the specular plane of reflection of a material and then applying the CMM. Wolff and Kurlander [339] derived the CMM for the Cook–Torrance model in terms of the polarized Fresnel reflectances of a material. The modified model doesn't make substantial differences in object appearance when viewed directly. However, accounting for polarization does affect the appearance of both metals and dielectrics when they are reflected in a mirror or viewed through a polarizing filter.

Tannenbaum et al. [312] demonstrated the use of CMMs for rendering birefringent material. A birefringent material has different indices of refraction in different directions. The result of the difference in index of refraction is that two refracted rays are produced rather than one when light is transmitted through a birefringent material. The rays are refracted at different angles and have polarization states that are different. The rays following different paths may also be absorbed at different rates (i.e., may be affected by different values of $\sigma_a(\lambda)$ in Eq. 5.6) through the material. The difference in absorption results in spectral variations in the material referred to as *pleochorism*. Birefringence and polarization are important for specialized cases such as identifying minerals or simulating gems [312] (see Section 6.3.3).

5.6.2 PHOSPHORESCENCE AND FLUORESCENCE

Phosphorescence and fluorescence are discussed and modeled by Glassner [111]. In phosphorescence, light is absorbed and then diffusely reemitted at a later time. A time delay of 10^{-8} seconds or more qualifies as a "later time" rather than instantaneous. Glassner incorporates phosphorescence in a material by defining a phosphorescence efficiency function that scales the incident radiant flux to an emitted radiance, and a decay function that determines how long after the flux is incident that the emitted radiance continues to be nonzero. In fluorescence, light that is incident at one wavelength is absorbed and immediately reemitted at another wavelength. Glassner [111] models this effect by defining a fluorescence efficiency function that scales the incident flux at one wavelength to the emitted radiance for another.

A comprehensive treatment of fluorescence and polarization together is given by Wilkie et al. [337]. Rather than using the CM/CMM framework, they use Stokes' parameters to represent the state of polarization of light, and Mueller's matrices to express how a material affects the state of polarization. Figure 5.46 shows their results under two different lighting conditions.

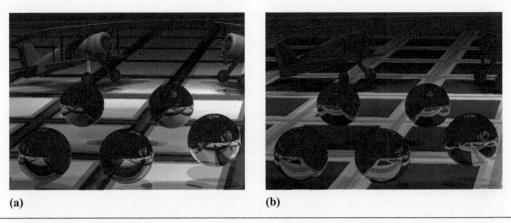

(a)   (b)

Figure 5.46: Renderings including polarization and fluorescent effects. (a) The image is illuminated with a standard D6500 light; and (b) the image is illuminated with a black light. The floor is fluorescent, the model biplane is a nonfluorescent dielectric, and the spheres are metal. *Source*: From Wilkie et al. [337], © 2001 Springer-Verlag.

5.7 SCATTERING IN VOLUMES

Light can scatter within volumes of material as well as from solid surfaces. Volumes of material include suspended particles in space, as well as tightly packed particles in volumes of light solid materials. In liquids and solids, this effect is referred to as subsurface scattering. Examples of volumetric materials that are suspended particles in air are clouds and atmosphere, shown in Figure 5.47. Clouds are volumes of water droplets or ice crystals that scatter and absorb light. Clear sky is actually volumes of molecules, with the scattering effect of the molecules in air only becoming evident when viewing volume thickness on the order of kilometers.

Figure 5.48 shows an example of particles tightly packed in a solid volume. The figure illustrates the appearance of a solid that scatters on a macroscopic length relative to an opaque solid with Lambertian reflectance. When lit from the front, the object with subsurface scattering appears brighter because some of the light that enters the surface is scattered back to the viewer. When lit from the back, the contrast is more dramatic, since light is transmitted and scattered from the back to the front of the object. With volumetric effects, the size of the object, as well as the material parameters, have an impact on the material appearance. The brightness of the same material is quite different for a thin and thick sample of it (Figure 5.49). For the same object and lighting conditions, the appearance will depend on the density of the particles in the solid, and on their properties (Figure 5.50).

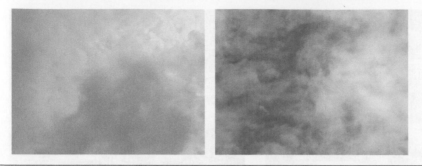

Figure 5.47: Clouds have different appearances based on the concentration of water droplets and ice crystals that scatter and absorb light.

(a)   (b)

Figure 5.48: Tightly packed volumes of particles in a solid produce subsurface scattering. The impact of the scattering depends on the illumination conditions. Here, a Lambertian material (a) is compared to a subsurface scattering material (b).

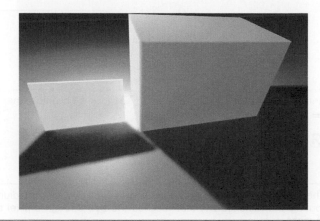

Figure 5.49: In computing the effect of subsurface scattering, the scale of an object matters. Two blocks of the same scattering material appear to have different brightness because of their differing thickness.

Figure 5.50: The magnitude of subsurface scattering is a function of the material properties. Here, the absorption coefficient is changed from image to image.

To understand volumes and subsurface scattering, we need to expand some of the mathematical definitions from Chapter 4. We show the full equation to be solved for volumes to identify the basic quantities needed to define a volume material, and to illustrate how the line between modeling a material and solving the global illumination problem becomes blurred. We briefly sketch the methods currently used to simulate subsurface scattering.

5.7.1 RADIANCE

The geometry of rendering a scene containing a volume of particles that affect visible light is shown in Figure 5.51. As in rendering a surface, the image is computed by finding the radiance (energy per unit time, solid angle, and projected area) $L(s)$ that would pass through an image pixel to the eye. Unlike the surface problem, in which it is adequate

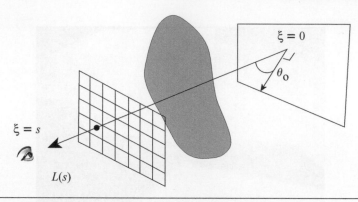

Figure 5.51: The geometry of rendering a scene with a participating medium. An image is formed by computing the radiance $L(s)$ that reaches the eye through a pixel by integrating along the line of sight.

to find the radiance of the closest visible surface, how the volume effects the light along the line of sight must be evaluated. Along the line of sight, four processes may occur: absorption, out-scattering, in-scattering, and emission.

Just as we think of surfaces that are composed of tiny microfacets as single infinitesimal surfaces dA, we model a volume of tiny particles as an infinitesimal volume dV. We model the interactions of light with a volume by considering how the radiance $L(s)$ of a beam of light changes as it travels through the volume dV. The value of $L(s)$ will change by some differential amount dL as it travels the distance ds through the volume. All of the interactions can be stated as the change in radiance per unit distance, that is, as dL/ds.

Absorption

Figure 5.52 shows absorption—some fraction of the beam of light is absorbed by the medium. The ability of the medium to absorb light is expressed as the absorption coefficient σ_a, the fraction by which the beam of light is reduced by absorption *per unit length* traveled along the line of sight:

$$\frac{dL(s)}{ds_{abs}} = -\sigma_a L(s) \tag{5.25}$$

Out-Scattering

Figure 5.53 shows out-scattering—some fraction of the beam of light is scattered by the medium. This light is absorbed by the medium and immediately reradiated, but in directions that are different from the original path. The ability of the medium to

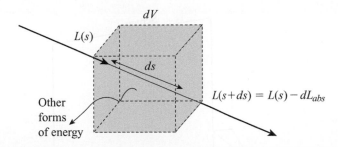

Figure 5.52: Absorption in a participating medium. Some of the incident light energy leaves the path in another form.

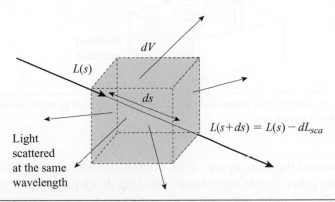

Figure 5.53: Scattering out of a participating medium. Some of the incident light energy leaves the path as light traveling in a different direction.

scatter light out of the path is expressed as the scattering coefficient σ_s, the fraction by which the beam light is reduced by scattering *per unit length* traveled along the line of sight:

$$\frac{dL(s)}{ds_{sca}} = -\sigma_s L(s) \tag{5.26}$$

Bohren [32] gives an example of a simple experiment that illustrates the difference between attenuation due to absorption and attenuation due to scattering. Referring to Figure 5.54, place two glass dishes of water on an overhead projector. Add ink to one dish and milk to the other. Its possible to add ink and milk at rates such that the projection through the two dishes is the same on the screen—they have each attenuated the beam from the projector by the same fraction. However, the dish of ink will look much darker than the dish of milk. The ink has attenuated the beam by absorption, the

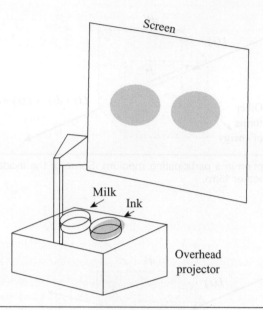

Figure 5.54: An experiment described by Bohren [32], illustrating attenuation by absorption and out-scattering.

milk has attenuated the beam by scattering. Bohren's book *Clouds in a Glass of Beer* [32] describes many other simple experiments that help develop a physical understanding of the interaction of visible light with participating media.

Because they both attenuate the radiance of a beam of light, the absorption and scattering coefficients are frequently combined into the extinction coefficient, σ_{ext}:

$$\sigma_{ext} = \sigma_a + \sigma_s \tag{5.27}$$

$$\frac{dL(s)}{ds} = -\sigma_{ext}L(s) \tag{5.28}$$

The effect of scattering relative to the effect of out-scattering is expressed as the single scatter albedo Ω of a medium:

$$\Omega = \frac{\sigma_s}{\sigma_a + \sigma_s} \tag{5.29}$$

Referring back to Bohren's milk and ink experiment, the two media have similar extinction coefficients. The milk has a high albedo relative to the ink.

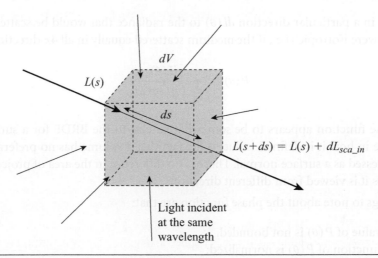

Figure 5.55: Scattering into the participating medium. Some incident light is scattered into the path.

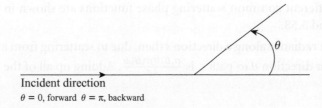

Figure 5.56: Definition of the angle in the scattering phase function.

In-Scattering

Scattering can also result in an increase in an radiance of the beam of light, as diagrammed in Figure 5.55. In-scattering from beams of light from other directions can increase the radiance along a line of sight. When discussing out-scattering, the direc-tionality of scattering was unimportant—all that mattered was that light left the path. For in-scattering, the directionality of scattering is important to understand to what extent light from other directions is scattered into the path.

The directionality of scattering is expressed by the scattering phase function $P(\theta)$, where θ is the angle between the direction of scattering and the original path, as shown in Figure 5.56. That is, forward scattering is in the direction for which θ is nearly zero. The phase function is a dimensionless quantity that is equal to the ratio of the radiance scattered in a particular direction $dL(\theta)$ to the radiance that would be scattered if the medium were isotropic (i.e., if the medium scattered equally in all 4π directions $d\omega$):

$$P(\theta) = \frac{dL(\theta)}{\frac{1}{4\pi}\int dL(\theta^*)d\omega} \qquad (5.30)$$

The phase function appears to be somewhat similar to the BRDF for a surface. The difference in how it is defined is due to the fact that a volume has no preferred direction expressed as a surface normal. There is no difference in the area of projection of a volume as it is viewed from different directions.

Two things to note about the phase function are that:

- The value of $P(\theta)$ is not bounded.
- The function of $P(\theta)$ is normalized:

$$\frac{1}{4\pi}\int P(\theta)d\omega = 1 \qquad (5.31)$$

A couple of different common scattering phase functions are shown in polar plots in Figures 5.57 and 5.58.

The increase in radiance along a direction s then, due to scattering from a beam of radiance $L'(\theta)$ from direction θ to path s, is $\frac{\sigma_s L'(\theta)P(\theta)ds}{4\pi}$. Adding up all of the contributions

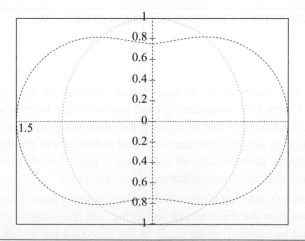

Figure 5.57: Rayleigh scattering phase function (isotropic shown with very light dotted line). This is typical for very small particles, such as the molecules in the atmosphere.

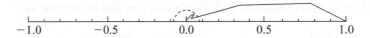

Figure 5.58: Scattering for a 525 nm radius sphere with index of refraction 1.5 (not normalized). This type of strong forward scattering is typical of water droplets in atmospheric clouds.

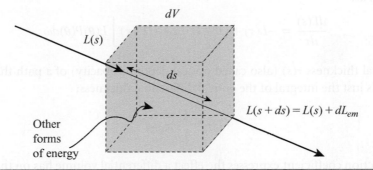

Figure 5.59: Emission in the participating medium. Energy in a form other than visible light enters the volume and causes the emission of visible light into the path.

from all directions gives the increase in direction s as:

$$\frac{dL}{ds_{in\_scat}} = \frac{\sigma_s}{4\pi} \int L(\theta) P(\theta) d\omega \qquad (5.32)$$

Emission

Finally, radiance may increase in a path due to emission within a volume, as shown in Figure 5.59. The increase can be modeled as a product of the absorption coefficient (which measures how dense the volume is) and the radiance L_e that would result from the emitter if it were infinitely thick:

$$\frac{dL}{ds_{em}} = \sigma_a L_e \qquad (5.33)$$

Putting together the four contributions to change in radiance along a path, the equation of transfer in a participating medium is:

$$\frac{dL(s)}{ds} = -\sigma_a L(s) - \sigma_s L(s) + \sigma_a L_e + \frac{\sigma_s}{4\pi} \int L(\theta) P(\theta) d\omega \qquad (5.34)$$

In terms of extinction coefficient and albedo, this can also be written as:

$$\frac{dL(s)}{ds} = -\sigma_{ext}L(s) + \sigma_{ext}(1 - \Omega)L_e + \frac{\sigma_{ext}\Omega}{4\pi} \int L(\theta)P(\theta)d\omega \tag{5.35}$$

The product $\sigma_{ext}ds$ is a dimensionless length in the medium called the *optical differential thickness*. Setting the function $d\tau$ equal to this dimensionless length, Eq. 5.35 can also be written as:

$$\frac{dL(s)}{d\tau} = -L(\tau) + (1 - \Omega)L_b + (\Omega/4\pi) \int L(\theta)P(\theta)d\omega \tag{5.36}$$

The optical thickness $\tau(s)$ (also called optical depth or opacity) of a path through the medium is just the integral of the optical differential thickness:

$$\tau(s) = \int_o^s \sigma_{ext}ds^* \tag{5.37}$$

The extinction coefficient expresses the effect a differential volume has on the incident light. The optical thickness of a medium expresses the effect of the entire extent of the medium. The optical thickness of a medium is a dimensionless length that can be used to compare the effects of volumes of medium. For example, a glass of milk of diameter 5 cm will attenuate a beam of light much more than the same glass filled with cigarette smoke at a density typically found in a restaurant. However, a volume of milk with optical thickness 1 will attenuate a beam of light exactly as much as a volume of cigarette smoke with optical thickness 1.

Looking at attenuation only, the radiance after traveling along a path s in a medium from a starting point at 0 is:

$$L(s) = L(0)e^{-\int_o^s \sigma_{ext}ds^*} \tag{5.38}$$

Solving Eq. 5.34 falls into the realm of computing global illumination. Computing the radiance at any point $L(s)$ depends on the radiance impinging on the volume $L(\theta)$. Determining the incident radiance $L(\theta)$ requires solving Eq. 5.34 along a ray in the direction of θ.

One simple approach to a fog volume material is to assume that the in-scattering term that makes the solution difficult can be replaced by a uniform emission term. This is usually chosen in an ad hoc fashion. The equation for the radiance becomes:

$$\frac{dL(s)}{ds} = -\sigma_{ext}L(s) + \sigma_{ext}L_e \tag{5.39}$$

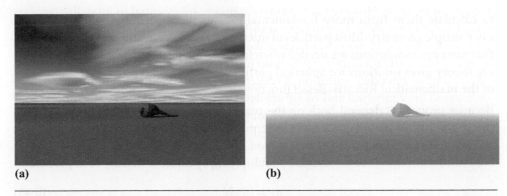

(a)   **(b)**

Figure 5.60: A scene without (a) and with (b) a simple uniform fog.

This can be solved to give:

$$L(s) = L_0 e^{-\sigma_{ext} s} + L_e(1 - e^{-\sigma_{ext} s})$$ (5.40)

where L_o is the radiance at the closest opaque surface along the path. The balances between the radiance of the opaque object and the volume are based on the distance through the fog. Figure 5.60 shows a simple scene with and without fog. To simplify the calculations and/or achieve different effects, the exponential term is sometimes replaced by a simple linear or quadratic function of distance.

Summary of the Input Needed

For a general volumetric medium, in addition to the input data required for a surface-only problem, the definition of a problem containing a participating medium requires the definitions of L_e, $P(\theta)$, σ_{ext}, and Ω as functions of position in the medium. Unlike the surface problem, in which geometry and reflectance properties are treated entirely separately, the definition of the geometry of a participating medium and its properties are closely coupled. If σ_{ext} is given directly as a function of location, the geometry of the medium is implied. The distribution of the medium may also be specified by giving partial pressure, volume fraction, or the density of the medium as a function of location. The values of σ_{ext} are computed by converting these quantities to densities, and using the mass coefficients of extinction (i.e., (fraction extinction/length)/(mass density)). The spatial distribution of scattering particles and gases may be constructed (e.g., by thoroughly mixing milk into water), but more often in environments of interest in graphics, they are determined by complex natural processes.

Similar to the study of surface reflectance, measured values of gas or particulate absorption and scattering properties may be used directly, or analytical models may be used to calculate them from more fundamental measurements of optical properties and microscopic geometry. Most particles of interest in visual applications are small enough that wave optics solutions are needed when forming analytical models. The Mie scattering theory gives solutions for spherical particles, which are expressed as combinations of the mathematical Riccatti–Bessel functions.

Because properties depend both on the particle details and the number of particles, the Mie solutions are generally given in terms of cross sections: C_{sca} for scattering cross section and C_{ext} for extinction cross section. The scattering and extinction coefficients are found from these cross sections by multiplying by number density N of particles:

$$\sigma_s = C_{sca}N \tag{5.41}$$

Code is available from many places to compute the Mie results, such as in the appendix to Bohren [32]. Figure 5.58 shows results computed with this code. Just having a code to compute Mie scattering doesn't solve the input problem. The complex index of refraction of the media being modeled is required, as is a size distribution of the particles in the medium.

Mie theory doesn't give good results for some particles of interest in rendering, such as those shown in Figure 5.61. Clouds composed of ice crystals are not well modeled with Mie theory [202]. Dobbins et al. [73] show that for irregularly shaped soot agglomerates, Mie scattering theory gives results for cross sections that can err by as much as a factor of two.

A special case of Mie scattering theory that is useful for rendering is scattering from very small particles, generally known as Rayleigh scattering. For this case the scattering cross section of particles is:

$$C_{sca} = \frac{8}{3}\frac{\pi D^2}{4}\left(\frac{\pi D}{\lambda}\right)^4\left|\frac{(n+i\kappa)^2 - 1}{(n+i\kappa)^2 + 2}\right|^2 \tag{5.42}$$

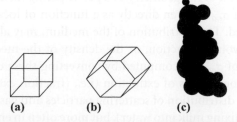

(a)   (b)   (c)

Figure 5.61: Common particle shapes that are not modeled well by the Mie theory: (a) cubic salt crystal, (b) hexagonal ice crystal, and (c) irregular soot agglomerate.

and the scattering phase function is:

$$P(\theta) = \frac{3}{4}(1 + cos^2\theta) \tag{5.43}$$

Cigarette smoke consists of particles with diameters less than 0.1 μm, and can be modeled as Rayleigh scatterers. The values of n and κ for smoke particles are on the order of 1.5 and 0.5, respectively. Number densities of particulates in a room with a couple of smoldering cigarettes is on the order of 50,000 cm^{-3} [201]. Since the scattering cross section is proportional to $\frac{1}{\lambda^4}$, much more light is scattered at short wavelengths (the blue end of the visible spectrum) than at longer wavelengths. As a result, scattered light from cigarette smoke generally looks bluish.

Molecular scattering has the same phase function. However, rather than modeling a molecule as a particle with diameter D, the scattering cross section is given by Liou [202], p. 166:

$$C_{sca} = 1.06\frac{8}{3}\pi^3\frac{{n^2 - 1}^2}{\lambda^4 N^2} \tag{5.44}$$

where index of refraction is approximated by:

$$(n - 1)10^8 = 6430 + \frac{2,950,000}{146 - \lambda^{-2}} + \frac{25,500}{41 - \lambda^{-2}} \tag{5.45}$$

where λ is in microns.

A typical value for the number density of molecules in the atmosphere N is 2.55×10^{19}cm^{-3}. The attenuation coefficient for molecular scattering becomes significant only over distances of kilometers. In the atmosphere, the $\frac{1}{\lambda^4}$ dependence in Eq. 5.44 is apparent in the blue color of the sky.

5.7.2 MEASURED PROPERTIES

Because measuring the shape, size distribution, and optical properties of particles of common participating media can be extremely difficult, it is often easier to rely on measured values for scattering and absorption coefficients. No tables are available for the diverse materials that are of interest in graphics, and values still need to be looked up from literature in geophysics, atmospherics, fire research, etc. For example, Gerber and Hindman [107] describe a workshop on measuring the interaction of light with aerosol particles. Measurements of absorption coefficients, mass of particles per unit volume of air, and albedo are given for various test cases using soot, methylene blue, salt, and Arizona road dust. For example, the samples of Arizona road dust had typical values of about 7×10^{-6}m^{-1} for absorption coefficient, and 0.7 for albedo.

To describe measured scattering distributions, fitting the Henyey–Greenstein function is generally used:

$$P_{HG}(\theta, g) = \frac{1 - g^2}{4\pi \left(1 + g^2 - 2g\cos\theta\right)^{\frac{3}{2}}}$$

(5.46)

For efficiency in graphics, Schlick proposed the approximation:

$$P_{Schlick}(\theta, g) = \frac{1 - g^2}{4\pi(1 - g\cos\theta)^2}$$

(5.47)

The parameter g indicates the asymmetry of the distribution. Liou [202] gives typical values of σ_{ext}, Ω, and g for cirrus clouds composed of ice crystals. For example, for cirrus uncinus, these values are 2.61 km^{-1}, 0.9999, and 0.84, respectively. Examples of diverse sources for particle properties include various references [27, 33, 73, 93, 201, 224, 236, 319].

Given the properties σ_{ext} and Ω for volumes of molecules in the gaseous state or particles suspended in air, the density distributions need to be defined by procedural methods or by fluid simulations. The radiance scattered from such distributions then needs to be computed using global illumination techniques such as Monte Carlo path tracing, radiosity, or photon tracing.

5.7.3 SOLID VOLUMETRIC MEDIA: SUBSURFACE SCATTERING

Many materials consist of dense sets of particles "trapped" in a volume bounded by a solid surface. The same principles apply within solids as for particles in air. However, the large number of scattering events that light undergoes in a solid medium allow approximations that facilitate more efficient calculations. For very dense packing, all of the scattering occurs in a microscopic layer near the surface, and the effect of the scattering is incorporated in the BRDF. One example of estimating BRDF by accounting for scattering effects in a microscopic volumetric layer has already been discussed in the context of first principle simulations in Section 5.4.

Kubelka–Munk Theory

Pigment particles in a binding medium that forms a paint or coating are an example of a case where the effect of a volume is to scatter light from the same surface point as the light was incident. A common method for computing the diffuse reflectance from pigment particles is the Kubelka–Munk theory [182–184], discussed by Haase and Meyer [132] as applied to modeling in graphics. The Kubelka–Munk theory considers thin layers of volumes of pigments. Unlike the problem of interference where "thin" is measured relative to the wavelength of light, in this case thin is measured relative to the diameter of the overall object. Each pigment i in a thin volume layer is characterized by the fraction of light K_i absorbed per unit length, unit weight fraction c_i, and the fraction of light S_i per unit length that is scattered back from the direction of travel. The reflectance of a paint layer that is thick enough that the substrate (the material painted) is completely hidden is given by:

$$R = 1 + \frac{K}{S} - \sqrt{\frac{K^2}{S} + 2\frac{K}{S}} \qquad (5.48)$$

$$K = \Sigma K_i c_i$$

$$S = \Sigma S_k c_i$$

Eq. 5.48 is applied on a wavelength-by-wavelength basis, allowing the spectral characteristics of the individual pigments to be combined into a spectral reflectance. As discussed by Callet [39], the values of K and S for layers in the Kubelka–Munk theory can be derived from σ_s and σ_a for general participating media. However, in practice, they are usually measured from a series of coatings with known density and thickness.

Many surfaces have multiple thin volumetric layers, and each has an associated reflectance R that accounts for reflections from the boundaries and backscatter in the layer, and a transmittance T that includes all the light that is not reflected back from the layer. The effects of multiple layers can be combined. The Kubelka–Munk theory results for "nonhiding" layers (coatings that do not completely obscure the substrate) were presented in the graphics literature in Dorsey and Hanrahan [75] for a layer of thickness d:

$$R = \frac{sinh(bSd)}{asinh(bSd) + bcosh(bSd)} \qquad (5.49)$$

$$T = \frac{b}{asinh(bSd) + bcosh(bSd)}$$

$$a = \frac{S + K}{S} \qquad (5.50)$$

$$b = \sqrt{a^2 - 1}$$

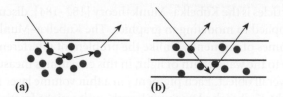

(a)   (b)

Figure 5.62: In the Kubelka-Munk theory, the effect of scattering through a mixture of pigment particle types (a) is modeled by finding weighted averages of the absorption and scattering values K and S. The effect of scattering in multiple layers containing different types of pigment particles (b) is modeled by computing composite values of reflectance and transmittance R and T.

The effects of a pair of layers with values R_1 and T_1 and R_2 and T_2 can be combined to produce a composite value of R and T:

$$R = R_1 + \frac{T_1^2 R_2}{1 - R_1 R_2} \tag{5.51}$$

$$T = \frac{T_1 T_2}{1 - R_1 R_2} \tag{5.52}$$

Figure 5.62 illustrates the two different structures for combinations of pigments. When there are multiple types of particles in one layer, as in Figure 5.62a, their effect is modeled by finding the weighted sums of K and S, as in Eq. 5.48. When there are multiple layers of material, each with a different mix of pigments, their effect is modeled by finding composite values of R and T, as in Eq. 5.51.

Combining Multiple Layers

Eq. 5.52 can be applied to combine the effects of scattering and absorption of layers independently of how R and T are determined. A more general notation of reflection and transmission from a layer, and the paths through two layers, are shown in Figure 5.63. The advantage of this generalization is that it allows for different values of R and T depending on the direction of incident light. This allows the inclusion of the Fresnel reflection and transmission at an infinitely thin layer between two media with different indices of refraction to be included in combining layers.

The reflectance from the top of the first of two layers 1 and 2 is given by:

$$R = R_1^+ + T_1^- R_2^+ T_1^+ + T_1^- R_2^+ R_1^- R_2^+ T_1^+ + \ldots \tag{5.53}$$

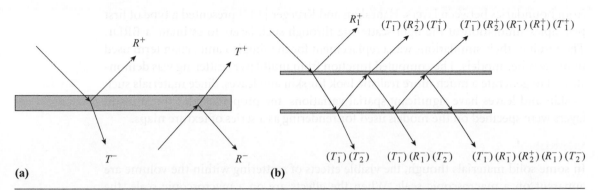

Figure 5.63: A more general model of thin layer reflectance and transmittance (a) allows for different values of R and T depending on which side of the layer light arrives. The combined effect of two layers (b) is an infinite sum of the paths through the layers where the attenuation along each path is the product of individual values of R and T for the original layers.

which is an infinite series that can be simplified to:

$$R = R_1^+ + T_1^- T_1^+ R_2^+ (1 + R_2^+ R_1^- + (R_2^+ R_1^-)^2 + \ldots) \tag{5.54}$$

$$R = R_1^+ + \frac{T_1^- T_1^+ R_2^+}{1 - R_2^+ R_1^-} \tag{5.55}$$

The sum of the infinite series is expressed explicitly, since the product $R_2^+ R_1^-$ is less than 1. For layers that are symmetric with respect to which side light is incident, Eq. 5.55 becomes Eq. 5.51. A similar general expression can be found for the transmission through two layers.

It may be straightforward to estimate R and T for a very thin layer with single scatter. The transmittance and reflectance can be computed for thicker layers by repeatedly applying Eq. 5.52 with identical values for the two layers. This process is referred to as *doubling*.

The values for R and T for arbitrary numbers of general layers of different materials can be obtained by starting at the bottom layer and alternately adding the effects of Fresnel reflection and transmission at infinitely thin layer boundaries and the effects of asorption and scattering in thin media layers. This process is referred to as *adding*.

The layers of material such as human skin or in leaves are composed of many reflecting and transmitting thin layers with complicated surface and volume scattering. The work in Hanrahan and Krueger [137] considers the effect of scattering with more complex directional effects within multiple thin layers, and reflecting and transmitting from boundaries between layers. Hanrahan and Krueger [137] presented a type of first principles simulation of the light scattering through such layers to estimate a BRDF. The result of their simulations was a replacement for the simple Lambertian term used in many other models. The computed function from multilayer scattering was demonstrated to generate a much more realistic look for skin and leaves. Since materials such as skin and leaves have significant spatial variations, the properties and thickness of layers were specified on the models used for rendering as a series of texture maps.

BSSRDF

In some solid materials though, the visible effects of scattering within the volume are apparent on a macroscopic scale. When the effects are on a macroscopic scale, the effect is referred to as subsurface scattering, and is described by what was defined by Nicodemus et al. in NBS 160 [251] as the bidirectional scattering-surface reflectance distribution function (BSSRDF). The geometry of BSSRDF is shown in Figure 5.64. Essentially it accounts for light incident on a surface at one location (x_i, y_i) entering the material and reemerging at (x_r, y_r).

To produce the effects of a true BSSRDF, rather than just altering the diffuse component of the BRDF by a simulation, the solid volume can be treated as a scattering volume and full global illumination methods used to follow light paths that enter the volume. This method was used to render the effects of subsurface scattering in stone by Dorsey et al. [76].

Treating solid or liquid subsurface scattering materials with general global illumination techniques is computationally inefficient. A key insight is that the concentration of particles in solid is very dense. In a general volume global illumination solution,

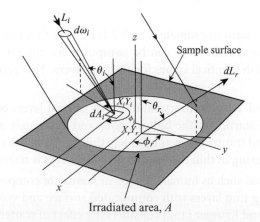

Figure 5.64: BSSRDF geometry. *Source*: From Nicodemus et al. [251]

scattering interactions are considered where there may be very long distances between scattering events. The mean distance light travels without being affected by the volume is $(1/\sigma_{ext})$. For the cirrus clouds example given above, this distance is 0.38 km, a distance that is on the scale of the size of the cloud. For a liquid subsurface scattering material like milk, $(1/\sigma_{ext})$ is about 0.2 mm, which is very small relative to the size of a glass of milk. When the light paths are very short, the general equation for light transport can be replaced by the diffusion equation. The equation is further simplified by the observation that after many scattering effects, the net result is isotropic scatter, regardless of the scattering phase function of individual particles. In the diffusion equation, the light at a point *within the medium* only depends directly on the radiance of light in the immediate neighborhood. The diffusion equation is a differential equation, rather than the integro-differential equation that represents the general light transport problem in volumes.

The diffusion approximation was originally applied to very dense clouds by Stam and Fiume [299] . Jensen et al. [163] adopted the diffusion approach and used the dipole diffusion solution originally developed to understand the subsurface scattering effects of blood when illuminated by a small source. This solution effectively gives a function for the radiance leaving a surface at a point x in direction Θ for incident irradiance E_i on a small area A_i at a point x_i. Summing the effects for multiple positions x_i sampling the entire surface gives the radiance leaving the object at $L(x \rightarrow \Theta)$. Specifically:

$$L_o(x \rightarrow \Theta) = \frac{F_t(x, \theta)}{F_{dr}(x)} M_o(x)/\pi$$

$$M_o(x) = F_{dt}(x) \left\{ C_1 \frac{e^{-\sigma_{tr} d_r}}{d_r^2} + C_2 \frac{e^{-\sigma_{tr} d_v}}{d_v^2} \right\} E_i A_i / 4\pi \tag{5.56}$$

where

$$C_1 = z_r \left(\sigma_{tr} + \frac{1}{d_r} \right), \ C_2 = z_v \left(\sigma_{tr} + \frac{1}{d_v} \right)$$

$$\sigma_{tr} = \sqrt{3\sigma_a \sigma_t'}, \ \sigma_t' = \sigma_a + (1-g)\sigma_s$$

$$d_r = \sqrt{r^2 + z_r^2}, \ d_v = \sqrt{r^2 + z_v^2}, \ r = ||x - x_i||, \ z_r = l_u, \ z_v = l_u(1 + 4/3A), \ l_u = \frac{1}{\sigma_t'}$$

$$A = \frac{1 + F_{dr}}{1 - F_{dr}}, \ F_{dr} = \frac{-1.44}{\eta^2} + \frac{.71}{\eta} + .668 + .0636\eta, \ \eta = \frac{n_2}{n_1}$$

Although this takes several lines to express, it can be evaluated in a straightforward way for one pair of points x and x_i given the material properties of the extinction coefficient, albedo, g in Henyey phase function, and the relative indices of fraction, with n_1 generally

1 for a material surrounded by air. The first line expresses the fact that the radiance leaving the surface $L_o(\mathbf{x} \rightarrow \Theta)$ is the radiant exitance $M(\mathbf{x})$ divided by π with corrections for Fresnel effects. The second line expresses that the radiant exitance $M(\mathbf{x})$ is the result of the energy $E_i A_i$ incident at another location $\mathbf{x_i}$ taking into account Fresnel effects and the multiple scattering effects (the term that includes the two coefficients C_1 and C_2). The term accounting for the multiple scattering includes the effects of the medium's extinction, scattering, and absorption coefficients and the distance r between the points $\mathbf{x}$ and $\mathbf{x_i}$.

The computationally complex aspect of this is summing over samples of the incident light for all points on the surface. Jensen and Buehler [160] form a hierarchy of surface incident light points, and the sum at each point to find the radiance leaving the surface uses clusters of points for areas that are distant on the surface. Lensch et al. [195] use an alternative hierarchy summing the incident light samples nearby a point on a texture map, and summing the results of more distant light samples at the vertices of the mesh representing an object. Many subsequent approaches have made rendering translucent objects with this approach possible at interactive rates. This approximation holds strictly though for plane surfaces, and is not affected by changes in material properties within the object. Apparent changes in the volume properties only appear if encoded at the surface.

Because subsurface scattering and backscattering both tend to reduce the contrast on a lit object, they are sometimes confused. A backscattering object will appear black when lit from behind, while a subsurface scattering object will appear illuminated, at least at edges where the material becomes thin. A backscattering object can have sharp shadows cast on it, and points are either bright or dark depending on their view of a distant-point light source. A subsurface scattering object will not have sharp shadows cast on it, since some light always diffuses from the lit area to the unlit area.

5.8 SPATIAL VARIATIONS

The reflectance functions discussed in Section 5.7 may vary with position. Variations in reflectance parameters are often encoded in texture maps [28]. In addition, they may be coupled with small-scale surface variations. In Chapter 6, we will consider how particular scattering functions are combined with small-scale surface variations to represent particular classes of materials.

Small-scale surface variations result in masking, shadowing, and self-interreflections on a scale that is visible (rather than microscopic). Even though these are visible geometric effects, it is sometimes more convenient to represent them as a function mapped on the surface, rather than explicitly defining the geometry and computing the small-scale effects in the course of a global illumination solution. These representations include bump maps [29], normal maps [52], bidirectional texture functions (BTFs) [62], and surface light fields (SLFs) [341]. BTFs and SLFs are generally captured in a measurement process, rather than expressed as parameterized functions or computed by simulation. Obtaining BTFs and SLFs will be discussed in Chapter 7, and encoding them in Chapter 9.

effects in the course of a global illumination solution. These representations include bump maps [29], normal maps [32], bidirectional texture functions (BTFs) [62], and surface light fields (SLFs) [24]. BTFs and SLFs are generally captured in a measurement process, rather than expressed as parameterized functions or computed by simulation. Obtaining BTFs and SLFs will be discussed in Chapter 7, and encoding them in Chapter 9.

6 SPECIALIZED MATERIAL MODELS

Many materials, including some very common ones, are difficult to model with simple surface or volume models. In this chapter, we describe specialized models that have been developed for particular materials. Some of these models have been curiosity motivated—researchers seeking to replicate intriguing appearance. Some are application motivated—researchers and practitioners seeking to replicate aspects of appearance that are critical in a particular simulation or design setting. Most of the models use a subset of effects that we discussed in Chapter 5, coupled with domain-specific small-scale geometric models.

There are some common themes that run through many of these models. One is materials composed of thin fibers, including fur, hair, and textiles. Models for the materials build on models for the individual fibers that are then combined to find the bulk effect. Another theme is materials that have sparkle, such as snow and automative points, or that just occasionally reveal very-fine grain structure at the visible level. In these cases, the small features need to be included in the model in some way, even though the amount of light energy that they individually reflect is small compared to the total light scattered by the material. A third theme is the combination of thin layers and volume scattering that give materials a sense of "depth." Such as the human iris, metallic paints, plants, and some polished and coated woods. Finally, many specialized models are formulated around data that can be readily captured.

Rather than categorize the specialized material models by apparent structure or particular effects, we organize them as either natural organic, natural inorganic, or manufactured. These are not cut and dried; many materials are found naturally and then processed for achieving particular appearance effects in manufactured products. Natural organic sheep's wool is sheared and then processed to be knitted into sweaters. Natural inorganic rocks are shaped and polished to become building stones. The loose natural organic, natural inorganic, and manufactured organization is for convenience in presentation.

Valuable specialized material models appear in a wide range of publications, from electronic proceedings of small computer graphics workshops to journals in fields outside of computer science. Our listing of specialized materials is not an exhaustive survey of what exists in computer graphics. Further, many of the models we discuss here do not boil down to simple equations for bidirectional reflectance distribution function (BRDF), or bidirectional scattering surface reflectance distribution function (BSSRDF). Instead, many models involve complicated geometric structures, libraries of measured parameters, and nontrivial procedures. Our goal here is to provide an overview, with pointers to the relevant literature that provides greater detail.

6.1 NATURAL ORGANIC MATERIALS

Much more attention has been paid in computer graphics to detailed modeling of organic natural materials rather than inorganic. Within the realm of natural organic materials we consider first modeling humans and other mammals, then other animals, and finally plants.

6.1.1 HUMANS AND OTHER MAMMALS

Modeling realistic virtual humans to stand in as actors in films and games has been a long standing goal in computer graphics. The rendering of the appearance of humans is as critical as the challenging problems of shape modeling and animation of humans. In this section, we focus on humans, but include closely related techniques that apply to other mammals as well.

In human appearance rendering two areas have received the most attention: hair and skin (primarily facial skin). Models for hair and skin can be built from principles presented in Chapter 5. The details of the models are critical, however, since we are so familiar with human appearance, and are capable of discerning small discrepencies in human models. Recently, major progress has been made in these areas not only due to insights in modeling, but because computing processing power has made it possible to explicitly deal with complex models and measurement instruments have been developed that provide the detailed parameter values needed.

A common theme across modeling aspects of human appearance is the pigments that contribute to color. The pigments melanins—either black-brown (eumelanins) or reddish yellow (pheomelanins)—play a role in both hair and skin. Obviously, even though skin and hair share the same basic material substance, the geometric structure and combination with other biological substances result in a wide range of appearances.

In addition to skin and hair, modeling of other organs has received attention, and we include here the modeling of eyes and internal organs.

Hair and Fur

Hair (on humans) and fur (on animals) are studied extensively in areas outside of computer graphics. The importance of understanding hair appearance and its enhancement is obvious in cosmetology. In human and veterinary medicine hair and fur appearance can be diagnostic of health conditions. Less obvious, perhaps, is that detailed study of hair and fur geometry and spectral properties are important in studying thermal transfer in zoology and identifying the origin of artifacts archaeology and criminal forensics. The structure of fur fibers, such as wool, also is important in modeling textiles. We briefly review some properties of hair and fur and nongraphics resources for additional data, and then describe specific models proposed in computer graphics.

The structure of hair and fur is presented in great detail in references such as Robertson [275] and Blazej et al. [25]. We draw on these references to give a brief description of hair. An individual structure consists of a core medulla, cortex, and exterior cuticle. The granules of the melanin pigment, either eumelanins or pheomelanins, are in the cortex. Hair with no pigment granules appears white. The cuticle consists of lapped cells on the outside of the air. There are two different types of hairs: vellus hairs and terminal hairs. Vellus hairs are unpigmented narrow (4 microns) and short (1 mm) hairs that grow nearly all over the body. Terminal hairs are those typically found on the scalp and received the most attention in computer graphics modeling.

Terminal hairs on humans are 50 to 90 microns diameter and may be circular or ellipsoid. Hairs tend to curl with more ellipsoidal (i.e., flatter) cross sections and may twist along the axis. Terminal hairs in a beard and moustache (rather than scalp) may have triangular cross sections. Another type of terminal hair, eyelashes, are 20 to 120 microns in diameter. A person has about 175 to 300 terminal hairs per cm^2, for a total of approximately 100,000 hairs on the typical human scalp.

The fur in mammals varies from human hair in color, size, and density. Foxes and rabbits have fine, dense hair (average diameter 20 to 30 microns, and approximately 4,000 hairs per cm^2) while goats and badgers have thicker, sparser hair (average diameter 70 to 80 microns and approximately 100 to 200 hairs per cm^2) [43]. These are only average numbers, and each animal normally has a variety of different types of hair on its body. There are longer guard hairs that form an animal's overcoat, and shorter fine fibers that form the undercoat. An extraordinarily detailed collection of animal fur microstructure that was documented in Blazej et al. [25] is available online at *http://www.furskin.cz/* for the purpose of fur identification.

Individual hairs can be treated as surfaces with some subsurface scattering. However, it is normally the assembly of many hairs packed in a volume that results in the appearance we associate with hair. Simply modeling hair as a volumetric medium like a cloud or volume scattering solid is not adequate. The detailed structure of hair is apparent and affects the direction of scattering. The surface and volumetric properties of hair are combined in the *texel* data structure, originally proposed by Kajiya and Kay [169]. While texel is used often for a single entry in a texture image, a texel as defined by Kajiya and Kay is a volumetric data structure that stores a projected area density ρ, a frame bundle **B**, and a bidirectional light reflection model Ψ in each three-dimensional (3D) location. The projected area density is the fraction of the projected area of the voxel in a particular direction that is covered by hair geometry projected in the same direction. The projected area density is different from the idea of particle density in a participating medium. Unlike particle density, the effect of the projected area density value is independent of the thickness of the voxel element. The frame bundle **B** specifies the orientation with the normal, binormal, and tangent. For a hair, this frame is determine by considering a general cylinder growing from the skin surface.

The bidirectional light reflection model Ψ gives the reflected light at a point as a function of incident light, and in Kajiya and Kay, this model is a variation of the original Phong model. Like the original Phong model, Ψ is formulated to give relative values of light rather than being formed as a BRDF that is reciprocal and energy conserving. For hair defined as general cylinders, the light reflected is in terms of unit length rather than area, accounting for the light reflected from the entire circumference of the hair at a point along its length. Using the parameters K_d, K_s, and p from the original Phong model, the diffuse component Ψ_d and specular component Ψ_s of the Kajiya and Kay light reflection model ($\Psi = \Psi_d + \Psi_s$) are then:

$$\Psi_d = K_d sin\theta_i \tag{6.1}$$

$$\Psi_s = K_s(cos\theta_i \, cos\theta_r + sin\theta_i \, sin\theta_r)^p \tag{6.2}$$

where θ_i is the angle between the incoming light and the tangent to the hair, and θ_r is the angle between the view direction and the tangent to the hair.

Given the texel data, the calculation of hair lighting is then computed by adding up contributions for each texel pierced by a ray through the volume from the closest location t_{near} to the furthest t_{far}:

$$L = \Sigma_{t=t_{near}}^{t=t_{far}} e^{-\tau\Sigma_{u=t_{near}}^{u=t}\rho(u)}\rho(t)\Sigma_i L_i(t)\Psi(t) \qquad (6.3)$$

where τ is an ad hoc adjustable coefficient that is chosen to convert the projected area distributions to an attenuation coefficient, and the sum over i is over all light sources.

From a distance, the rendered texel data structure (Figure 6.1, *left*) looks like fur. In an extreme close-up, the volumetric nature of the representation is visible (Figure 6.1, *right*).

The Kajiya–Kay model works for short hair (the typical case in animal fur) only. Extensions and elaborations of the model include Goldman's approximiation for viewing fur at a distance [116], Bank's general derivation of the light reflection model for a one-dimensional object in 3D space [12], Lengyel's real-time approach [194], and Neyret's generalization of texels to other geometric structures [247].

With an increase in processing speeds, it has become feasible to consider rendering individual strands of hair as geometry. Features of the Kajiya and Kay approach have been continued along two lines: improved reflectance models to replace Ψ, and accounting for the effect of the full volume of hairs on the appearance of each hair. For example, in the production of *The Chronicles of Narnia* [147], fur on main characters such as Aslan is modeled as a set of generalized cylinders. These cylinders are passed to the renderer as ribbons of polygons. The light from each hair is computed with the Kajiya–Kay lighting model Ψ modified to include a transmittance for enhancing back-lighting effects, and using both the strand tangent and a shifted tangent to compute specular reflection to obtain secondary highlights. To account for the self-shadowing effects of the full volume of hair, a method introduced by Neulander and van de Panne [245] represents

Figure 6.1: A patch of fur rendered using the texel data structure proposed in Kajiya and Kay. *Source*: From Kajiya and Kay [169], © 1989 ACM. Included here by permission.

attenuation of light incident on each of the hairs by a normal N_o and height value h_o stored at each point. Using these values and a density ρ defined for each hair type is:

$$attenuation = e^{-\rho\left(-h_o cos\,\theta_i + \sqrt{1-h_o^2(1-cos^2\theta_i)}\right)} \tag{6.4}$$

where θ_i is the angle between N_o and the incoming light, and h_o is normalized to be less than 1.

Improved models of the light reflectance model for individual hairs continue to use the idea of a model that represents the light scattered per unit length rather than per unit area. Marschner et al. [215] formulated this approach in a rigorous form defining the bidirectional scattering function for a fiber $S(\Theta_i, \Theta_r)$ as:

$$S(\Theta_i \rightarrow \Theta_r) = \frac{d\bar{L}_r(\Theta_r)}{d\bar{E}_i(\Theta_i)} \tag{6.5}$$

where $\bar{L}$ and $\bar{E}$ are defined, respectively, as the curve intensity per unit length and curve irradiance per unit length.

Marschner et al. [215] developed a model based on the features of an individual hair strand, shown in Figure 6.2b. Essential features of the model is that it accounts for three light paths and the detailed surface of a hair, with the paths shown in two views in Figure 6.2a and Figure 6.2b. The three paths are the same as the first three paths followed in thin layer analysis in Chapter 5, except now they are followed through a

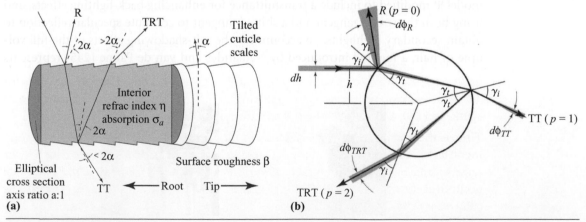

Figure 6.2: The single hair strand geometry (a) used for modeling and a cross-sectional view of paths through the strand (b). *Source*: From Marschner et al. [215], © 2003 ACM 2003. Included here by permission.

cylinder rather than a flat slab. The three light paths are reflection directly from the hair surface **R**, transmission through the hair **TT**, and internally reflected light **TRT**. The path **TT** is similar to the transmittance term added by other models, but is computed specifically taking refraction effects into account. It adds brightness to light (e.g., blond) hair when backlit. The path **TRT** results in a different shape and location of highlights over the simple reflection path **R**. The detailed hair surface is a set of scales that are tilted at an angle α from the surface of a smooth cylinder with the same axis. This tilting results in a shift of the specular peaks toward the root of the hair. The results of these three types of paths and the surface tilting are specular and transmitted peaks in light scattering by the hair, diagrammed in Figure 6.3a.

The detailed analysis of these paths on this geometry results in an impractical model. Instead, Marschner et al. [215] propose a simplified approach that is the sum of terms for the three paths. The term for each path consists of Gaussian distribution that accounts for the width in reflected/transmitted peaks due to surface roughness of the scaled surface times a term that accounts for attenuation and absorption along the path within the hair. Figure 6.3b compares the results of this extended model to the original Kajiya–Kay model as applied to dark hair.

In subsequent work, Zinke and Weber [353] have proposed a bidirectional fiber scattering distribution fuction (BFSDF) as a general framework for modeling hair and other fibers. This function defines the radiance leaving one location on an area of a cylinder enclosing the fiber as a function irradiance at another location. Both the Kajiya–Kay and Marschner et al. models are demonstrated to be special cases of the far-field bidirectional curve scattering distribution function (BCSDF) derived from the BFSDF.

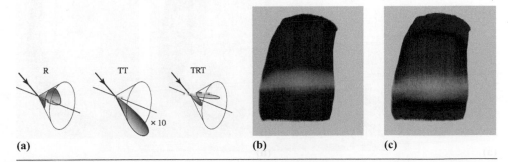

Figure 6.3: (a) The resulting reflected and transmitted lobes based on the hair geometry in Figure 6.2, and a comparison of the Kajiya–Kay model (b) with the Marscher et al. method (c). *Source*: From Marschner et al. [215], © 2003 ACM. Included here by permission.

In addition to advanced models for individual strands, alternative approaches for the self-shadowing and interreflections in collections of hairs have been developed. For self-shadowing, Lokovic and Veach [207] extended the idea of traditional shadow maps that save the depth of the closest object from each light source to saving the partial visibility at a range of depths. Similar to the N_o and h_o values described earlier, this allows more rapid lookup of the attenuation of light that reaches a strand in the hair volume. Figure 6.4a shows hair rendered with and without self-shadowing. For interreflections, Moon and Marschner [235] developed a radiance caching technique appropriate for the highly directional nature of light reflection from hair that accelerates the calculations. The images of Figure 6.4a show the effect of accounting for interreflections compared to direct lighting alone. A complete survey of hair rendering methods, together with modeling and animation techniques for hair, is given in Ward et al. [328].

Modeling hair and fur discussed so far has focussed on terminal hairs. Koenderink and Pont [178] have modeled scattering from the small vellus hairs as part of the class of "asperity scattering," which is light from small particles or features on a surface such as fine hair and dust. For these very thin, short hairs, Koenderink and Point model media as a sparse volumetric layer of scatterers, and derive a BRDF for particles with general

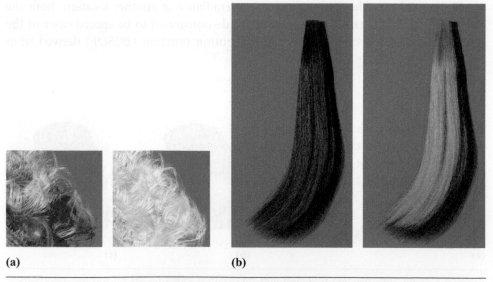

(a)   (b)

Figure 6.4: Computing key effects in hair: (a) the effect of self-shadowing (with and without)—from Lokovic and Veach [207], © 2000 Pixar; and (b) the effect of scattering between hair strands (without and with)—from Moon and Marschner [235], © 2006 ACM. Included here by permission.

scattering phase functions. In the case that the small particles are isotropic scatterers, that the thickness d of the layer is small compared to the typical path length between scattering events ($1/\sigma_s$), the BRDF is approximately given by:

$$f_r(\Theta_i \rightarrow \Theta_r) = \frac{\frac{\sigma_s d}{4\pi}}{cos\theta_i cos\theta_r} \qquad (6.6)$$

Since Eq. 6.6 goes to infinity for grazing angles, when this model is implemented, the values of θ_i and θ_r need to be limited. A thin illuminated layer is observed in this asperity scattering. This illumination results in scattering of light well beyond what would be a sharp shadow, giving a softening effect. Since the vellus hairs are normally not perceived individually, modeling the effect of vellus hairs can be thought of as one element in the realistic rendering of skin.

Skin

As a major organ of the body, and the study of a whole branch of medicine, the detailed structure of skin is well documented. Skin appearance is critical in diagnosing many diseases, and is a major preoccuppation of the cosmetics industry. A comprehensive description of skin appearance measurement and modeling would require a much longer text than this.

Basic details of human skin structure can be found in handbooks such as Walters [323]. The thickness of skin varies across the body from 0.1 to more than 0.5 cm. A simple view of the structure of skin is that it has three layers: the epidermis, dermis, and hypodermis. The epidermis is the thin outside layer that includes the exterior layer of "dead cells" (the stratum cornuem) that are sloughed away from the skin surface. The dermis is thicker, and includes the vessels that carry blood in varying amounts that affect skin color. The hypodermis connects the skin to the rest of the body. Each layer has a complex structure.

Spectral variations on the subsurface scattering may vary gradually with position, or may have easily seen edges such as freckles and age spots. Spectral variations may also change temporally—relatively gradually due to sun exposure (tanning and burning) or suddenly due to changes in blood flow (blushing). The directionality of the surface reflectance can vary with transient states such as the amount of oil on the skin. Small-scale geometric variations are due to wrinkles and pores. Wrinkles clearly change on a relatively long temporal scale, becoming more prominent with aging. Pores may change size over short time-scales with changes in air temperature. Variations in color and geometry can be caused by a wide variety of skin conditions and diseases.

Computer graphics models for skin reflectance are generally composed of a subsurface scattering model, a surface reflectance model (such as Cook–Torrance), and/or a model of small-scale spatial variations in the spectral reflectance and geometry variations of the skin surface. The basic models described in Chapter 5 coupled with data from tables in references such as Mobley and Vo-Dinh [234] or captured with methods described in Chapter 7, have been used in a variety of combinations to generate realistic skin models. For example, Marschner et al. [214] use a Lafortune model to fit directional measurements of skin reflectance, and couple this with a texture map that represents spectral variations across a person's face to generate a realistic facial model. Haro et al. [139] added measured fine geometric detail by measuring fine skin texture from polymer molds pressed against the face at different points, and synthesizing fine-scale detail across a face model. Debevec et al. [66], Georghiades [105] and Fuchs et al. [102] present systems that rapidly take multiple images of a person's face to recover both detailed shape and skin reflectance. Weyrich et al. [336] use a shape scanner, multiple images, and a subsurface reflectance measurement device to capture data to fit a skin model for faces that combine a surface BRDF and a map of spatial variations with the dipole approximation for subsurface scattering.

Models for skin reflectance can be built up from layers, using the technique first described by Hanrahan and Krueger [137] and described briefly in Chapter 5. Stam [298] extended this approach to include layers with rough surfaces. Krishnaswamy and Baranoski [181] have taken a comprehensive computational first principles approach, which they refer to as BioSpec. They define detailed models of the epidermis and dermis layers, from which a Monte Carlo simulation is used to compute skin BRDF/bidirectional transmission distribution function (BTDF). Scattering within the layers is computed from goniometric measurements from the medical literature for the epidermis, and Rayleigh scattering (Eq. 5.42) for the dermis. Absorption, essential in computing the final skin color, is computed, taking into account the density of pigmented material in each layer. In the epidermis, melanin (both eumelanin and pheomelanin) as well beta-carotene, are included. In the dermis, blood, beta-carotene, and bilirubin are included. The blood may be oxygenated or deoxygenated, with the deoxygenated absorbing light at slightly longer wavelengths on average. Using the BioSpec model, the appearance of skin based on a description of its composition can be predicted, as shown in Figure 6.5.

The modeling of wrinkles crosses the areas of appearance, geometric modeling, and animation. Boissieux et al. [34] review wrinkling models used in animation. They differentiate between the permanent wrinkles due to aging, and temporary wrinkles that are due to change in expressions. They used data provided by a cosmetics manufacturer (L'Oreal) to produce eight generic masks of wrinkle patterns, and determined a linear function of the depth of wrinkles with age. Golovinsky et al. [117] developed a method for generating realistic facial wrinkles and pores based on a database of high-resolution facial scans. The high spatial frequency variations on different parts of the face were isolated from a smooth underlying base mesh. The collection of high spatial

Figure 6.5: Changes in skin appearance predicted from skin composition in the BioSpec model presented in Krishnaswamy and Baranoski [181]. From left to right, the level of melanin pigmentation is increased. *Source*: Images © 2004, used courtesy of The Eurographics Association and Blackwell Publishing, Inc.

frequncy maps are then used as sources to synthesize detail on new smooth-base meshes to produce realistically detailed facial skin.

Details of how skin structure affects appearance is the subject of large volumes of publications that appear in journals such as the *Journal of Biomedical Optics* and *Skin Research and Technology*. Research results that could be included in skin appearance models include how stretching skin (which may be the effect of closing a wound or a surgical procedure) affects reflectance by smoothing the surface and increasing specularity [131], the mechanisms that result in color change when skin is exposed to ultraviolet (UV) radiation or pressure [300], and a device for measuring the variation of refractive index and directionality of the scattering phase with depth in skin [176]. Additional studies include the variation of lip color caused by various combinations of lip wrinkles and lipstick [282] and the design of a chart for clinicians to assess changes in skin color based on a large data set of skin spectral reflectance [64].

Eyes

In generating realistic images of humans or many other animals, we are sensitive to the appearance of eyes. Lefohn et al. [193] developed a method for modeling realistic eyes based on the methods used by ocularists to produce prostheses. The method is based on defining multiple translucent layers on a series of circular cone frustra. The multiple layers give eyes their appearance of depth. The cone geometry is shown in Figure 6.6a. The layers consist of the components shown in Figure 6.6b. Lefohn et al. identify these layers as the stroma consisting of dots or smears; the collarette, which is the inner portion of the iris; the sphincter, which is a colored ring near the pupil; the limbus between the cornea an scelra; and the pupil, which is a black dot at the center.

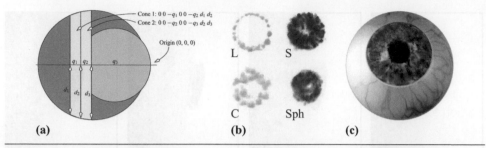

Figure 6.6: (a) Geometry, layers, and results for modeling an eye using ocularists'
methods: (a) cone geometry; (b) layers—L = limbus, S = stoma, C = collorette, Sph
= sphincter muscle; (c) a rendered synthetic eye. *Source*: From Lefohn et al. [193], ©
2003 IEEE.

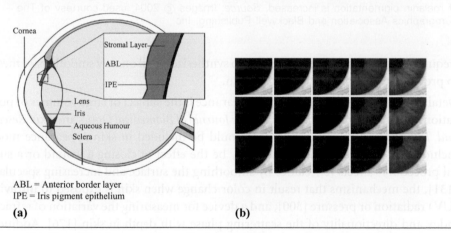

Figure 6.7: Geometry, layers, and results for modeling an eye using a biophysical
approach from Lam and Baranoski. The results (b) show the variation of eye color, as
concentrations of the pigments eumelanin and pheomelanin are varied. *Source*: From
Lam and Baranoski [186]. Images © 2006, used courtesy of The Eurographics Association and Blackwell Publishing, Inc.

Multiple translucent layers of the various types are built up to model the eye. A result
from their model is shown in Figure 6.6c.

Lam and Baranoski [186] developed a detailed predictive model called ILIT for the spectral BRDF of the iris. ILIT models the layers of tissue in the eye with accurate biophysical
data, and considers reflection and transmission at boundaries and absorption and scattering within each layer. Figure 6.7 shows the layer structure used by ILIT. Lam and
Baranoski identify the anterior border layer (ABL) and stromal layers as being primarily
responsible for iris color. The indices of refraction of the different layers and the spatial
distribution and spectra of pigmented cells (primarily eumelanin and pheomelanin)

in these layers are used in a Monte Carlo simulation to compute the BRDF of the iris. Rather than emulate the look of the eye as in Lafohn et al. [193], the ILIT model seeks to predict the BRDF for a particular description of eye tissue.

Internal Organs

An application of computer graphics realistic image synthesis is the simulation of minimally invasive surgical procedures. In minimally invasive procedures, instruments and a small light and camera are attached to small-diameter cables and inserted into a patient through a small incision. A surgeon performs the procedure while viewing the images from the light and camera on a monitor. Realistically simulating such procedures for training requires computing physical deformations and collisions. The surgeon observes such changes visually as well as using haptic cues. Realistic images of internal organs are needed for the simulations.

Neyret et al. [248] present a model for laproscopic surgery on the liver. Their method focuses on real-time rendering for the interaction speed required by surgical simulators. Their model is composed of three layers to account for the liver surface texture, for appearance changes due to blood drops, cauterization and local pressure, and for specular highlights from the mucus layer on the liver. For one layer, they use a procedural texture generated using a cellular texture basis function [343] to mimic the liver texture observed in surgery. For the layer accounting for dynamic color changes, texture sprites of red (for blood drops), yellow and brown (for cauterization), and white (for pressure) are generated. Finally, on the third layer specular highlights are generated using the graphics processing unit (GPU). Neyret et al. use a constant specular reflectance over a smooth liver model. Elhelw et al. [87] present a refinement to this approach in which a map of detailed surface normals is used to modulate the specularly reflected light to produce a more realistic appearance.

An alternative to procedurally derived textures is to measure the appearance of organs in patients. Chung et al. [49] measure the texture and BRDF of lung tissue using capture techniques described in Chapter 7, adapted for the constraints of the minimally invasive bronchoscopy procedure. They developed a simulation using the textures and BRDF they estimated, along with simulations of bronchoscopy artifacts of image blurring and noise. Chung et al. conducted a user study with medical imaging specialists using the models captured using their technique, and found that the images were rated as realistic as images obtained from physical bronchoscopoy images.

6.1.2 BIRDS, REPTILES, AMPHIBIANS, FISH, AND INSECTS

Many animals besides mammals have interesting appearances that require detailed modeling of both small-scale, yet visible to the eye, geometric structures and microscropic structures. Examples of small-scale structures that are characteristic of particular animals are the scales on fish and reptiles, and the feathers on birds. Microscopic structures on many animals are responsible for intense colors and irridescent effects.

Many types of structures, such as the scales on snakes and reptiles, have been modeled with bump and texture maps and procedures based on simple observation, rather than on detailed biological modeling (e.g., [157, 171, 231]). Detailed textures of reptiles in feature film and television are often produced by detailed hand painting by artists [88, 233].

Bird feathers are a small-scale structure that have been studied with reference to biological models [46, 61, 304]. Each of these models notes the overall structure of a feather, as illustrated in Figure 6.8. A feather has a main shaft, or rachis. At the bottom of the shaft, the calamus, there is nothing attached. The vanes of the feather are formed by barbs that are attached to the rachis. Barbs are interlocked with one another by small barbules that branch off them. The vanes may be fuzzy, or plumulaceous, such as the lower section of the feather in Figure 6.8, or stiff, or pennaceous, as in the upper section.

Dai et al. [61] parameterize the feather model, allowing the user to set values for features such as barb length, distance between barbs, angle variation between barbs, and number of barbules. They present a model for coloring, or texturing, the feather. In Figure 6.8, the texture is just a simple brown area on the right. Other bird feathers such as pheasants and peacocks have more detailed textures. Dai et al. generate these more

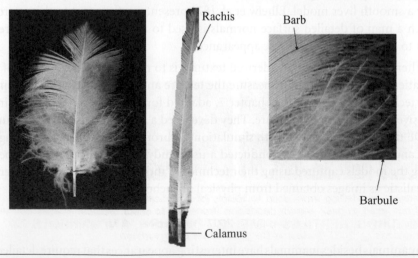

Rachis

Barb

Barbule

Calamus

Figure 6.8: Overall feather geometry from biology used in generating synthetic feathers.

detailed textures by noting their similarity to patterns formed by dynamical systems and adapting functions used in that domain.

Streit and Heidrich [304] introduce a different parameterization of the feather structure. In particular, they use the idea of key barbs that allow the modeling of the irregular gaps observed in real feathers such as in Figure 6.8. Streit and Heidrich also consider constructing a complete coat of feathers by placing key feathers. They define interpolation methods to add barbs between key barbs, and to generate feathers between the key feathers.

Chen et al. [46] take a somewhat different approach to defining the feather structure. The rachis and the left and right sides of the feather are defined by curves. They define production rules for an L-system that generates the barbs along the rachis. The rules include a random external force introduced with the generation of each barb in order to produce the irregular gaps. The result of this procedure is always a pennaceous, rather than plumeaceous, feather. Similar to Streit and Heidrich, Chen et al. produce feather coats on birds by interpolating between key feathers defined and placed by the user. Noting that the fine geometric structure along with the complicated BRDFs of individual barbules are expensive to evaluate, Chen et al. precompute bidirectional texture functions offline via ray tracing to use in rendering.

The complicated BRDFs of the barbs and barbules on bird feathers are due to their microstructure. Thin films on regular structures result in interference and irridescence on bird feathers as well as in insects. Some measured reflectance data with both wavelength and direction dependence are available for bird feathers [255]. Studying these biological structures is recently of interest even outside of biology, because they suggest structures that could be produced artificially to control light [321].

For computer graphics modeling, Sun [305] present an analysis of this type of structural color and how it can be modeled for rendering. Sun et al. [305] derive the solution for intereference in a multilayer structure such as that found on a morpho butterfly or a ground beetle. The result is a complicated expression for reflectance, which becomes even more complicated with consideration of the natural fluctuations in the structure. Sun et al. propose a simple expression that approximates this solution. The parameters of the expression for mirror reflectance R at a particular wavelength λ for a smooth layered surface at an angle of incidence θ are the thickness of the films d_{film}, the thickness of the layers of air between the films d_{air}, the index of refraction of the film η_{film}, and the number of layers, along with empirically set parameters c_{interf} and m:

$$R_\lambda = c_{interf} \left| cos(\delta_b) \right|^m, \ if \ cos(\delta_b) > 0$$

$$\delta_b = \tfrac{4\pi}{\lambda}(\eta_{film} d_{film} cos\theta' + d_{air} cos\theta)$$

(6.7)

The value of m determines the sharpness of specular peaks, and c_{interf} determines the overall magnitude of the reflectance. For the ground beetle, Sun et al. give values of 150 nm, 100 nm, and 1.5 for film thickness, air layer thickness, and film index of refraction, respectively, and values of 90 nm, 90 nm, and 1.56 nm for the morpho butterfly.

Birds may also have intensely colored, but not iridescent skin, bills, legs, and feet that are the result of microstructure and coherent scattering. Prum and Torres [269] have studied this effect and give peak wavelength values for striking colors in a wide variety of birds including ducks, pheasants, cuckoos, etc.

An interesting feature of fish, amphibians, and reptiles that has not been modeled in computer graphics is that their surface appearance, in particular their color, may change with their environment. For example, Hadley and Oldman [133] study the change of lizard color from brown to green as a function of incident illumination conditions, and Cooper et al. [57] examine the transformation from noniridescent to iridescent colors in squid.

6.1.3 PLANTS

Modeling botanical structures has long been recognized as important in portraying landscape scenery. However, these structures pose significant challenges due to their composition and appearance.

A wide variety of techniques exist for creating the overall geometry of trees and plants, as well as the geometry of leaves or needles, in particular. Two different approaches have emerged: defining branching structures primarily in geometrical terms [30], such as the lengths of branches and branching angles, or through specifying plant topology [270]. In both cases, plants are defined by a small number of rules applied repetitively to produce detailed structures. In particular, the formalism of L-systems has proved highly successful in modeling plants.

Due to its importance in rendering close-up views, leaf appearance has received considerable attention. A leaf is usually modeled by a series of layers (typically four), each with different optical properties [101, 320] (see Figure 6.9). Several researchers have studied subsurface scattering in leaves. Hanrahan and Krueger [137] modeled leaves as layered surfaces and used Monte Carlo ray tracing to evaluate the BRDF and BTDF. Baranoski and Rokne [13] proposed the algorithmic BDF model (ABM), which accounts for biological factors that affect light propagation and absorption in leaves. Baranoski and Rokne [14] later introduced the foliar scattering model (FSM), which gains efficiency over ABM by precomputing reflectance and transmittance values and applying a simplified scattering model.

Researchers have also developed leaf scattering models for botany and remote sensing applications [320]. Such models are generally based on biological information of plant

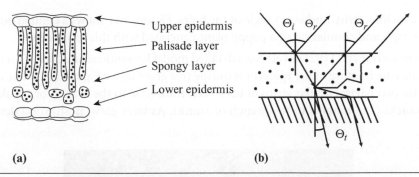

(a)   **(b)**

Figure 6.9: Leaf interior: (a) leaf interior, and (b) scattering of light in an optical layer.

Figure 6.10: Leaves rendered from captured data approach. *Source*: From Wang et al. [325], © 2005 ACM. Included here by permission.

tissues. For example, Govaerts et al. [122] explicitly modeled the 3D internal cellular structure of leaf tissues (epidermus, palisade cells, spongy cells) and used Monte Carlo ray tracing to simulate the propagation of light.

Increasingly, the appearance of leaves is modeled using data captured from real leaves. The idea is to use *measured* data acquired from real samples in lieu of *predicted* data obtained through simulation. Examples include the work of Franzke and Deussen, who introduced an approach in a which a leaf is represented by a set of textures obtained from leaves [101] and Wang et al. [325] who introduced a parametric model that describes leaves in terms of spatially varying BRDFs and BTDFs. This approach is amenable to real-time rendering; Figure 6.10 shows results rendered with the technique.

Work has also been done to model and place small-scale visual elements as part of plant modeling. For example, Fowler et al. [99, 100] proposed a method for placing and orienting spines on cacti. Führer et al. [103] describe a system for placing small hairs on a plant using an L-system framework. The system allows the specification of whether hairs are on the front, back, or edges of plant structures, and the density, length, radius, incline, twist, and wrap angle of the hairs. Figure 6.11 shows a comparison of a photograph and simulation of a poppy plant generated with this technique.

Lefebvre and Neyret [192] developed a detailed model for synthesizing bark. This model simulates the fracture of the epidermus during tree growth (see Figure 6.12). The model includes two parts: circular strips of bark (i.e., transverse to the branch or trunk) and axial cracks (i.e., parallel to the branch or trunk). As trees grow, fresh wood develops

Figure 6.11: Plant hair. *Source*: Reprinted from Führer et al. [103], copyright © 2006 Elsevier, Inc. used with permission.

Figure 6.12: Real images of tree bark: (a) fracture-based bark of various tree species (real images). *Source*: From Lefebvre and Neyret [192], © Eurographics Association 2002. Reproduced by kind permission of the Eurographics Association.

on the inside and fresh bark on the outside. In the next section, we provide a detailed discussion of wood.

Wood

Wood can be considered both a natural and a manufactured material. Wood is an important material in scenes with trees and is important in the construction and manufacture of decorative items; in nature, or when roughly split wood takes on characteristic shapes (Figure 6.13a), as an untreated or lightly treated construction material outdoors where it forms unique patterns as it ages (Figure 6.13b), both in forming dark and light

Figure 6.13: Photographs of wood, (a) shapes of natural wood, (b) aging of wood used in construction, (c) consistency of wood grain in nonplanar shapes, and (d) variety of grain and color.

areas, cracking in particular directions; and by biological growth forming in preferred patterns. Wood has a 3D structure that we expect to see consistently when it is cut into nonplanar forms (Figure 6.13c). Finally, different pieces of wood have varying textures and colors depending on the type of wood and the finish applied to it (Figure 6.13d).

The most recognizable feature of wood is its grain. Wood's directional grain is the result of the vascular system of trees that transports water and nutrients along the trunk and branches and that provides support to the tree. The cell structure of this system determines the dark and light patterns seen in wood, the directionality of reflection, and the directions where the wood will be weakest and so most likely to split. A detailed model of wood could be created by modeling the details of tree growth for various tree species, following the example of models of leaf venation [280]. More often, however, models are built from functions that have forms similar to observed wood grain, simple models of growth, or that are generated from example images of wood grain.

A simple early method for generating wood grain patterns was developed by Yessios [345]. His method is really a nonphotorealistic technique for representing wood grain in architectural drawings. The grain is represented as sets of concentric ellipses, with small perturbations introduced along each ellipse. By tilting the ellipses relative to vertical or horizontal, and drawing the ellipses with short strokes rather than thin lines, a variety of convincing wood grain patterns can be obtained (Figure 6.14).

Peachey [260] showed that solid 3D textures concentric cylinders of dark and light color tilted at an angle to a block of wood or a wooden object gave good results with greater ease than attempting to map two-dimensional (2D) wood textures to objects. Buchanan [36] developed a more detailed 3D wood model by considering a simple model of axial and radial growth of soft wood trees. A trunk and branches are distributed through a voxel volume. Tree growth is simulated by a set of rules governing the addition of voxels to an initial model in the direction of its tip and the direction of the tree walls.

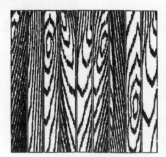
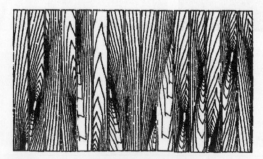

Figure 6.14: Wood grain patterns produced by perturbed concentric ellipses. *Source:* From Yessios [345], © 1979 ACM. Included here by permission.

The result of "growing" a piece of wood with these rules is a volume where each wood voxel is labeled with a time that it was added. Each time value is either part of an early growth step or a late growth step, with color varying for early and late growth. Different grain patterns are formed by using different numbers of steps for early and late growth.

Dischler et al. [71] derive a 3D model of wood grain from orthogonal 2D images of wood grain. A 3D noise volume is altered so that the statistics of slices through the volume match the statistics of the 2D images. Lefebvre and Poulin [191] combined the procedure and sampling approaches in synthesizing 3D wood texture. They define a wood procedural model in terms of nine parameters. In addition to the eight parameters shown in Figure 6.15, a turbulence intensity is estimated that indicates the perturbation from grains that are straight parallel lines. These parameters can be estimated from an image of wood. A full 3D volume of wood can be synthesized from a single 2D image, although the volume will not contain any knots.

In addition to coloration, the grain has an effect on the directional reflectance of wood. Marschner et al. [216] studied this effect and developed an empirical model for fitting reflectance measurements from finished wood. For unfinished wood (e.g., Figures 6.13a and b), they note that the irregular surface reflects light diffusely, and reflectance due to the subsurface structure is not as noticeable. Adding finish to a wood (e.g., Figures 6.13c and d) eliminates this diffuse effect, making the anisotropic scattering due to subsurface structure more evident, as well as adding refractive effects

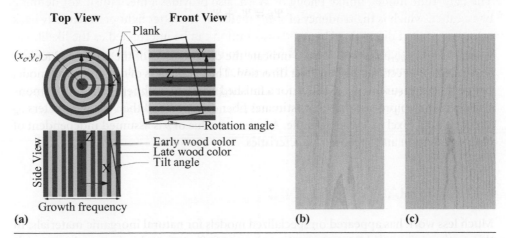

Figure 6.15: Procedural model parameters fit to sample image (a), and example synthetic results (c) obtained from a sample photograph of wood (b). *Source*: From Lefebvre and Poulin [191], © 2000 Laurent Lefebvre and Pierre Poulin.

in the finish layer. The empirical model given for the BRDF of finished wood is given as:

$$f_r(\Theta_i \to \Theta_r) = f_s(\Theta_i \to \Theta_r) + T_i T_r(\rho_d + f_f(\Theta_{fiber}, \Theta_i \to \Theta_r)) \qquad (6.8)$$

The term f_s is the BRDF of the top layer of the finish. This can be modeled with any standard surface BRDF model to account for the roughness of the top layer. The factor $T_i T_r$ accounts for attenuation of light as it enters the finish layer to hit the wood, and as it exits again. The factors T are each equal to 1 minus the Fresnel reflectance for the angle to the normal. The reflection from the wood beneath the finish layer is then the sum of a diffuse reflectance and a component that depends on the direction of the fiber Θ_{fiber}. To express the component from the fiber, the directions Θ_i and Θ_r are modified to the directions within the finish layer after refraction by Snell's law to $s(\Theta_i)$ and $s(\Theta_r)$. In the style of many previous reflectance models, the highlight is then given in terms of a Gaussian $g()$ with lobe width β:

$$f_f(\Theta_{fiber}, \Theta_i, \Theta_r) = k_f \frac{g(\beta, \Psi_h)}{cos^2(\Psi_d/2)}$$
$$\Psi_i = sin^{-1}(s(\Theta_i), \Theta_{fiber})$$
$$\Psi_r = sin^{-1}(s(\Theta_r), \Theta_{fiber}) \qquad (6.9)$$
$$\Psi_d = \Psi_r - \Psi_i$$
$$\Psi_h = \Psi_r + \Psi_i$$

where $s(\Theta_i), \Theta_{fiber}$, and $s(\Theta_r), \Theta_{fiber}$ indicate the dot products of the adjusted incident and reflected directions and the fiber direction. The parameters of this empirical model can be fit to measurements of BRDF for a finished wood. Marschner et al. [216] demonstrate a two-step process that first estimates fiber direction and then the parameters ρ_d and k_f at each pixel in a wood sample. A constant value of β is assumed independent of fiber orientation and spectral characteristics.

6.2 NATURAL: INORGANIC

Much less work has appeared on specialized models for natural inorganic materials. In this section, we consider two important classes of effects found in inorganic materials such as rocks: the effect of pores and the effect of water entering into materials. We also briefly consider the appearance of snow.

6.2.1 POROUS MATERIALS

Natural materials such as rocks (and indeed many manufactured materials such as ceramics) cannot be adequately modeled as a surface that is a set of randomly oriented small facets. Within the faceted surface there may be many deeper pits or pores. These pores are generally larger than the wavelength of light, but are not visible to the eye. They are generally smaller than the pores that are often visible in human skin. Merillou et al. [225] studied the effects of pores in inorganic materials. The pores may have complex faceted shapes, as shown in Figure 6.16. Merillou et al. note that the effect of pores can be viewed as modifying the diffuse and specular coefficients for any BRDF modeled as a facet distribution (i.e., Ward, Cook–Torrance, etc. model).

Referring to Figure 6.16a, the path of a ray may be affected in two ways by the presence of a pore: a ray may be absorbed, or redirected. The absorption or redirection of a ray that would be specularly reflected reduces the specular coefficient. The redirection of specular rays increases the diffuse coefficients, but the absorption of rays that would have been reflected reduces it. Merillou et al. do Monte Carlo simulations following the paths of rays in pores to calculate the appropriate modifications of diffuse and specular components for specific pore size, distribution, and shape. Figure 6.16b shows how the distribution of the BRDF changes, and Figures 6.16c and d show how this translates into a rendering.

6.2.2 WATER IN OTHER MATERIALS: WET/DRY APPEARANCE

Wetness is an important factor in the appearance of many materials [162, 211]. Wet materials often look darker, brighter, and more specular, depending on the type of material and the viewing conditions. For example, most rough or powdered materials, such as sand, asphalt, and clay, become darker when wet. Other materials, such as

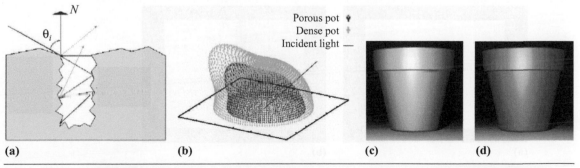

(a)   **(b)**   **(c)**   **(d)**

Figure 6.16: (a) Geometry of a porous surface. (b) Effect of modifying a surface facet BRDF for the effect of pores. (c) Rendering comparing facet BRDF without pores and with (d). *Source*: From Merillou et al. [225], © 2000 IEEE.

paper and cloth, become more transparent. This is due to a combination of the presence of liquid on the surface and within the material.

The effect of the liquid that enters into a material is to alter the paths of light within cavities and pores, as discussed in Section 6.2.1. If the pore is filled with a fluid of a higher index of refraction, total internal reflection at the surface when rays are traveling from the higher to lower index fluid results in both more rays being absorbed (causing darkening) and rays undergoing more internal reflections. More internal reflections accentuate the effect of spectral variations and results in changes in hue and saturation. That is, if a material reflects long "red" wavelengths more than short "blue" wavelengths, the reflected distribution of light after two reflections has a greater percentage of energy in the long wavelenghs than the short, and will appear to have shifted in hue and have a more saturated color.

One method for computing the effect of wetness on materials would be to do the simulations outlined by Merillou et al., taking into account the change of index of refraction in the pore, to estimate the modifications of the specular and diffuse components. However, this approach does not account for the increased specularity resulting from a layer of water on top of the surface, or increased transparency of thin materials.

Jensen et al. [162] demonstrated a combined surface and subsurface model to capture the appearance of wetness on the surface of and within a material. The surface model is a thin layer model, with a thin layer of water between the external air and the denser material. The dense material is modeled as a scattering volume, which shifts from near isotropic to strongly forward scattering as the amount of water in the material increases. Figure 6.17 shows how changing the scattering phase function for the wet area of a material results in higher transparency.

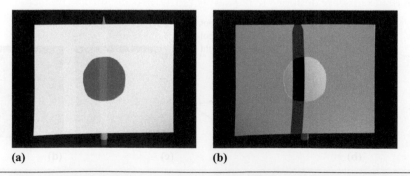

(a)   (b)

Figure 6.17: Modeling the effect of wetness as a change in volumetric phase function. A spot on a piece of paper: (a) front lit, and (b) back lit. *Source*: From Jensen et al. [162], © 1999 Springer-Verlag.

An important application of modeling wet and dry appearance is in driving simulators. Nakamae et al. [239] classify areas of road surfaces as dry, wet, puddled, or drenched. Dry surfaces are modeled with a Cook–Torrance reflectance model. Wet surfaces are modeled by increasing the specular and decreasing the diffuse components of reflection by an order of magnitude each. Puddled areas are modeled by ray tracing through cloudy water, modeling as a scattering voume, on an opaque surface. Drenched areas are a weighted average of wet and puddled reflectance.

As discussed in Chapter 7, the variation of material appearance with wetness can also be found by measurement (see Figure 7.14).

6.2.3 SNOW

Nishita et al. [253] have proposed a model for rendering snow. Snow is a volumetrically scattering medium, and Nishita et al. present a rendering system that treats the snow as a dense medium with a value of 0.85 for albedo, strong forward scattering, and a Henyey–Greenstein parameter of g equal to 0.95. In addition to being a denser medium than atmospheric clouds, the appearance of snow is distinguished by the appearance of small glints from crystals in the snow. Nishita et al. model this effect by embedding small prisms in the snow volume and computing a specular reflection when light hits one of these prisms.

6.3 MATERIALS IN MANUFACTURED GOODS

Three major areas of materials that are synthesized or processed for manufacture have received a lot of attention in computer graphics modeling: fabrics, paints and coatings, and gems. Most interest in these materials has been driven in creating predictive models for product design.

6.3.1 FABRICS

The modeling of knitted and woven fabric shares common elements with fur and hair modeling, since the basic unit of the material in both cases is a thin fiber, and a large number of such units need to be considered together to form the material. Similar to fur and hair models, paths through cross sections of fibers are considered to compute scattering for individual threads. Also similar to fur, volumetric representations are used to model the bulk behavior of groups of fibers.

In the synthetic fiber industry, fiber cross sections have been designed using ray tracing, following large numbers of paths of incident light through the fiber to find the variation of spectral scattering as the result of the shape and dye distribution in the fiber.

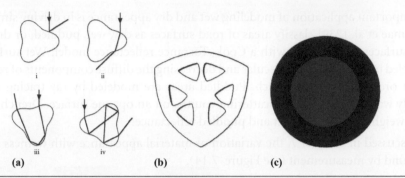

Figure 6.18: Thread cross sections for synthetic fibers are designed for specific properties. The three-lobed cross section (a, shown with various possible ray paths) has a higher glitter than the more complex fiber in (b)—from Rubin [277], © 1998 Wiley-VCH Verlag GmbH & Co., KGaA. Reproduced with permission. The cross section shown in (c) produces an iridescent effect because the ray paths have different lengths through the two colored dyes depending on view direction.

Rubin [277] describes ray tracing round, three-lobed, and complex cross sections containing holes. Key quantities of interest are the overall level of light reflection and the variation of the reflected radiance with view for a particular angle of incidence known as the fiber glitter. A clear thread circular cross section has a very low value of glitter. A three-lobe cross section, shown in the center in Figure 6.18, has a much higher glitter value. In Rubin [278], fiber with a core full of one color dye surrounded by a sheath of another color, shown on the right in Figure 6.18, can be designed to exhibit an irridescent look. Because light entering from different directions travels different relative lengths in the differently dyed sections, the fiber appears different colors when viewed from different directions.

Bundles of fibers forming threads show detailed structure, particularly in knitted garments with relative large diameter yarn such as that typically used in scarves and sweaters. Groeller et al. [125] propose using a volumetric, texel-based structure to represent yarn in these cases. The volumes representing the yarn follow a centerline defining the stitch structure used to form fabric. Xu et al. [348] built on this idea to define a volumetric structure specifically for yarn called the *lumislice*. The lumislice is built on the observation that the 2D cross section of yarn is a similar cross section of small fibers, as shown in Figure 6.19, twisted around a central axis that follows the stitch shape. Enclosing a section of yarn with a set of voxels, the light scattered in each exitant direction for each incident direction can be precomputed for a 2D slice of voxels representing the lumislice.

This data structure is repeated and oriented according to the twisting for a particular yarn along the stitch centerline. Figure 6.19 shows the complete system for defining a

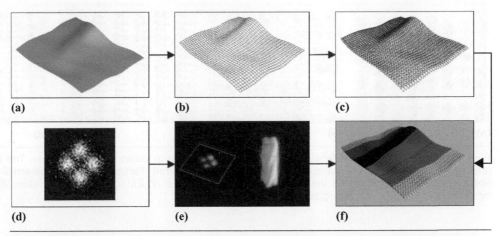

Figure 6.19: Figure from Xu et al. [348] illustrating the lumislices for knitwear modelling. At the macroscale, a scape (a) and control points (b) guide the definitions of the yarn centerlines. An individual yarn strand has multiple threads defined in cross section (d), with a volume defined by twisting the cross section (e) used to define the light leaving the yarn for each incident direction in order to render the knitted fabric (f). *Source*: © 2001 ACM. Included here by permission.

piece of knitted fabric. At the largest scale, surface of the fabric is defined (Figure 6.19a), control points are placed in the surface (Figure 6.19b) and the stitch pattern is defined by curves along this surface (Figure 6.19c). At the smallest scale, the fibers in the yarn are defined in cross section (Figure 6.19d). The extension of the cross section into a volume by twisting is shown in (Figure 6.19e). The resulting rendered knitted fabric is shown in (Figure 6.19f).

The appearance of woven, rather than knitted, fabric has been modeled by Adabala et al. [2]. Woven fabric is generally manufactured from thread, in which the fibers are more tightly wound together and do not exhibit the fluffy appearance modeled by volumetric approaches such as the lumislice. The model of woven fabric is based on the weave pattern that describes how a variously colored set of weft threads pass over and under a set of variously colored set of warp threads that are held in parallel. For computing the appearance of woven material when viewed from a distance, Adabala et al. use a BRDF microfacet model based on the weave pattern. This microfacet model takes the approach proposed by Ashikmin et al. [9] to generating a shadowing function, rather than using the V-groove solution. The facet distribution used is a weighted average of the visible warp and weft distributions. The facet distributions for both warp and weft are cylindrical Gaussians. The width of the cylinder is determined by the thread width.

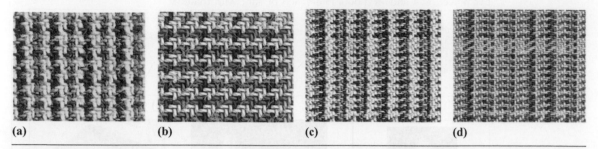

(a)   **(b)**   **(c)**   **(d)**

Figure 6.20: Figure, from Adabala et al. [2], illustrating close-up views of woven fabric. The (a) and (c) photos are of physical fabric samples; (b) and (d) are synthesized. Particularly in (b), the small randomly placed fibers are visible on top of the warp and weft threads. *Source:* © Eurographics Association 2003. Reproduced by kind permission of the Eurographics Association.

For close-up views, Adabala et al. use the Cook–Torrance model for the individual thread (Figure 6.20). They use a procedural model to define the twisting of fibers within a thread, and use that as the basis of the microfacet distribution in the model. They also model transmission of light through each thread based on the fiber density.

In the close-up views, in addition to the individual models of threads, individual fibers that are an order of magnitude thinner than threads are included. Individual fibers often come loose on a fabric at random locations. The individual fibers are rendered with a combination of light of the same color as the light source and light that is the same color as the thread beneath the fiber.

6.3.2 PAINTS, COATINGS, AND ARTISTIC MEDIA

Paints, clear coatings, inks, crayon, and pencil are applied to surfaces to achieve various appearance effects. Paints and inks may be, in particular, designed to have particular directional variations. When used as artistic media paints, inks, crayons, and pencil produce distinctive small-scale spatial distributions that are desirable to reproduce in simulations. Paints, and more generally coatings including shellac or clear coats, may also act as to physically protect an underlying material as well as having an effect on appearance.

Two different types of applications have driven work in simulating these materials. In one type of application the end product is an image that has the appearance of being produced by a specific physical medium, that is, the image should look like it was produced by physical pen and ink or a crayon rather than by a computer. In the second type of application the end product is the design of a physical product, with the simulated image only being a means of evaluating a design. An example of this is the design of automotive paints that will ultimately be used in manufacture. This second class of applications obviously has more stringent requirements as far as producing results that correspond to the results of physical experiments.

Artistic Media

Many models for reproducing the effects of watercolor, ink, thicker paints, and crayon have produced characteristic spatial variations in appearance by simulating the process of the application of the medium to a paper or canvas. A great deal of work in this area has been inspired by models developed by Guo and Kunii [129], Small [293], and Cockshott et al. [51]. A popular method for simulating the interaction is to use the framework of cellular automata to track the flow of the liquid carrying the ink or pigment particles. Various rules are used at each cell to account for effects such as gravity, absorption, and evaporation at each step in the process.

In the work described in Small [293], different pigment particles can be carried at different rates and the end colors are computed with simple subtractive color rules. Different patterns are formed by the interaction of the flow and the spatially varying paper properties. In Cockshott et al. [51], the height of the paint is tracked as it dries, so that the small-scale geometric variations in surface normal orientation can be simulated.

Increasingly, accurate simulation methods for paint and ink flow have been proposed. Curtis et al.[59] used the more accurate shallow-water model from fluid mechanics in place of the simpler rules used at each cell in earlier models. Rather than simple subtractive color calculations, Curtis et al. used Kubelka–Munk theory to estimate the color resulting from multiple overlapping strokes of watercolor. An even more faithful fluid model was demonstrated in the "Moxi" ink simulation system [48]. Rather than using the shallow-water model, recently developed lattice Boltzmann equations are used in Moxi to solve for the fluid flow of the ink. Appearance effects achieved by the Moxi system are shown in Figure 6.21.

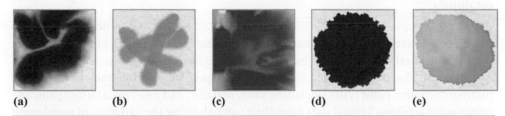

(a)   (b)   (c)   (d)   (e)

Figure 6.21: Examples of the appearance effects, as classified by Chu and Tai, achieved using the Moxi system to simulate ink flow: (a) feathering, (b) light fringes, (c) branching, (d) boundary roughening, and (e) boundary darkening. *Source*: From Chu and Tai [48], © 2005 ACM. Included here by permission.

Modeling the appearance of crayons, Rudolf et al. [279] also follow a simulation approach. In this case, the fluid flow simulation of the deposition of wax on the paper is simulated as a function of the force on the crayon, the viscosity of the wax, and the frictional force that breaks the wax from the crayon. After computing the spatial distribution of the wax deposited, the color resulting from the combination of the crayon and underlying paper is computed using a simplified Kubelka–Munk model.

Designing for Manufacture

Automotive Paints Appearance is a significant factor in the marketing and sales of automotive vehicles. Complex coatings have been developed for the automotive industry, and are tuned to emphasizing a particular look when coupled with shape styling. Two types of models have evolved in computer graphics; models that provide a good fit to measured paint data so that vehicles in the design stages can be visualized with a variety of different coatings, and models that allow the design of paint appearance to be used in testing paint formulations.

A convincing early demonstration of the importance of accurate paint formulation to examine car designs was given by Takagi et al. [309] from Toyota. Takagi et al. used measured data to define coatings in order to take into account the influence of the lighting environment that the car will be seen in on perceived color. They used a specular plus imperfect diffuse model, with the specular term given by the Fresnel reflectance. They used tabulated measured data for imperfect diffuse reflectance as a function of aspecular angle, that is, the angle between the reflected light and the direction of specular reflectance for a particular incident angle. They made detailed spectral measurements in order to get the correct spectral distribution of specular reflection, reflection of direct sunlight, and light from the sky and ground. In estimating the specular term from the Fresnel equations, they included polarization effects, since skylight is polarized. Their results showed that accurate predictions of vehicle appearance were obtained by giving side-by-side synthetic images of numerical models of cars using their paint model and photographs of the physically manufactured cars in the same weather and lighting conditions.

A question left by Takagi et al. [309] is at how many aspecular angles and measurements of reflectance are needed. It is clear that performing large numbers of measurements is a difficult method to quickly characterize a large number of paints. In recent work, another group led by Takagi et al. [310] analyzed aspecular reflection measurements for many automotive paint types (including solid, metallic, and pearl mica) using principle component analysis. Typical data from their work showing the variation of wavelength and angular dependence for different types of car paints are shown in Figure 6.22. They found that measurements at just five aspecular angles—10, 18, 28, 40, and 90 degrees—can be used to model the reflectance.

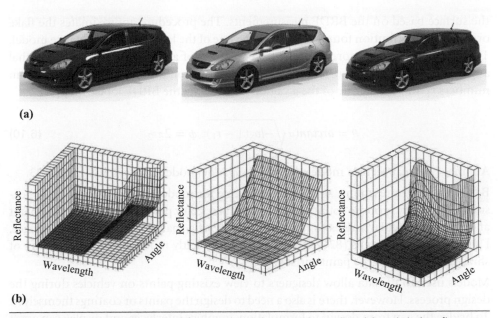

(a)

(b)

Figure 6.22: Images showing different types of automotive paints (a) and their reflectance values (b), relative to a white Lambertian surface, for different wavelengths and aspecular angles. *Source*: From Takagi et al. [310], © 2005 Wiley-VCH Verlag GmbH & Co. KGaA. Reproduced with permission.

Dumont-Bècle et al. [80] describe a modeling approach for automotive paints used in in Renault's P2V (Presentation of Virtual Vehicle) system. In addition to using measured data for a series of incident and reflected light pairs, Dumont-Bècle et al. add a bump map layer for the top varnish or clear coat layer that models spatial variations in the surface known as "orange peel" in the paint industry. They also introduce a layer of fine-grained noise that gives the effect of "sparkle," the tiny bright spots resulting from specular reflection from small flakes in the paint.

Günther et al. [128] also considered the problem of selecting a model to represent measured paint data. Using a measurement technique invented by Marschner (discussed in Chapter 7), they obtained measurements at closely spaced incident and reflected directions. They found that the data could be fit to a multilobe Cook–Torrance model. That is, the sum of distributions of the form given in Eq. 5.16 with three different values of α is used in place of a single distribution defining the specular lobe. This is the result of different scales of roughness in the paint surface.

For close views of the paint surface, in addition to the multilobe reflectance, Günther et al. model sparkle. To model sparkle, rather than hand tuning a noise function, they proposed using a procedural map for the orientation of the flakes at each point on the surface based on the BRDF measurements. The procedure approximates the flake orientation distribution found for computing one of the lobes in the reflectance model. The orientation of the normal of the flake in terms of a polar angle θ and azimuthal angle ϕ relative to a local surface coordinate system is computed from pseudo-random numbers r_1 and r_2 and one of the α values determining the BRDF lobe using:

$$\theta = arctan(\alpha\sqrt{-log(1-r_1)}), \; \phi = 2\pi r_2 \tag{6.10}$$

An image of a car section modeled with this sparkle model is shown in Figure 6.23.

Baba et al. [10] present an alternative technique for modeling sparkle based on measurements. They propose counting sparkle and base color pixels in an image of the paint at different aspecular angles to find a probability of a sparkle appearing on a surface. Durickovic and Martens [82] model sparkle by explicitly modeling the distribution of shiny metal flakes in the paint surface.

Models used to fit data allow designers to view existing paints on vehicles during the design process. However, there is also a need to design the paints or coatings themselves. To bridge the gap from design to formulation, graphics interfaces and display can assist the user in specifying paint characteristics appearance terms, such as face, flop, travel, glitter, and sparkle, and translate these into a formulation or paint recipe.

Considering just metallic paints, Meyer et al. [230] describe a model and interface for specifying metaling paints in terms of colors in the face (specular) direction, flop

Figure 6.23: An image of a close view of paint rendered using measured data fit to a model for BRDF and "sparkle." *Source*: From Günther et al. [128], © 2005 Max Planck Institute.

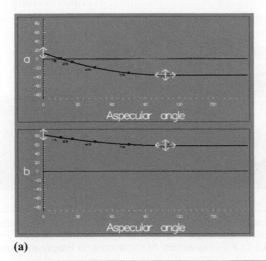

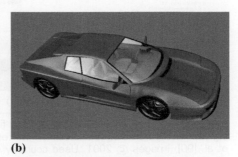

(a)   (b)

Figure 6.24: (a) Curves showing the variation with aspecular angle for the a and b components of reflected color in lab space. (b) Visualization of a paint defined by such curves on an automobile. *Source*: From Shimizu and Meyer [286]. Reprinted with permission, © 2003 The Society for Imaging Science and Technology, sole copyright owners of *IST/SID Eleventh Color Imaging Conference Proceedings*.

(far-off specular) direction, and travel direction (angular distance between the two colors). This model is based on earlier work by Westlund and Meyer [335] on modeling reflectance with measurements from simple industry-standard instruments. The simple metallic paint model and interface allow the user to specify and view paint on a vehicle by specifying a small number of parameters. Interactive formulation and application of metallic paints in this form facilitate assessing how paint and form will work together [286]. A particular combination of face, flop, and travel may produce an appealing color variation accentuating the form of a vehicle, or may be perceived as uneven application of paint. The formulation approach has been validated by Meyer et al. [230] by taking the color specification and using industry-standard methods to mix a physical paint. Figure 6.24 shows the interface and a visualization of the paint applied to a car.

Ershov et al. developed a first principles multilayer method [90], and in subsequent work a method for inverting the model for paint microstructure design [89]. The detailed model and parameters to be specified are shown on the left in Figure 6.25. Figure 6.25 in the middle and right shows images rendered with this paint model.

Ershov et al. [89, 90] use the thin layer doubling and adding approaches described in Chapter 5, and present complete models for layers containing flakes and pigment particles. They also derive a "simple" model for a two-layer model with one layer containing mirrorlike flakes in a clear binder and the other an opaque substrate coating. For flakes

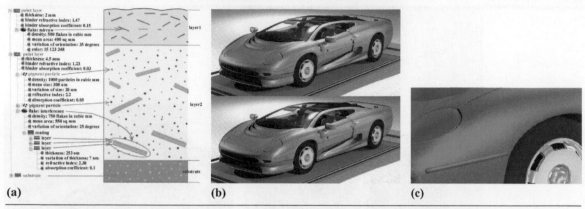

(a)   (b)   (c)

Figure 6.25: (a) Detailed geometry for a first principles car paint model, (b) variations predicted by changing just one parameter (thickness of interference coating on flakes), and (c) sparkle. *Source*: From Ershov et al. [90]; images © 2001. Used courtesy of The Eurographics Association and Blackwell Publishing, Inc.

characterized by reflectance r, transmittance t, orientation distribution $P(\beta)$ (β is the angle between flake normal and surface normal), parameterized by a disalignment parameter δ, density D, and average area $<S>$, embedded in a layer of binder h thick, roughness giving a specular peak width w, and with index of refraction n and average Fresnel reflectance $\bar{F}$ over a substrate with diffuse reflectance (albedo) a, the BRDF model is given by:

$$f(\Theta_i \to \Theta_r) = \frac{F(\theta_i)}{2\pi w^2} e^{\frac{\cos\theta_{vs}-1}{w^2}} + (1 - F(\theta_i))(1 - F(\theta_r))\frac{R_{eff}P(\beta)}{4n^2\cos\bar{\theta}_i\cos\bar{\theta}_r}$$
$$+ (1 - F(\theta_i))(1 - F(\theta_r))a_{eff} \tag{6.11}$$

$$R_{eff} = \frac{1 - e^{-2\tau h}}{2\tau h}D<S>hr \tag{6.12}$$

$$a_{eff} = a\frac{n^{-2}e^{-2h\tau}}{1 - 0.5a(1 + e^{-2h\tau}[2\bar{F} - 1])} \tag{6.13}$$

$$\tau = D<S>(1-t) \tag{6.14}$$

$$P(\beta) = \frac{1}{2\pi\delta}e^{\frac{\cos\beta-1}{\delta}} \tag{6.15}$$

where θ_{vs} is the angle between the view and mirror reflection directions, $\bar{\theta}$ is the direction after refraction at the air binder boundary, R_{eff} is the effective bulk reflectance of the flakes, and a_{eff} is the effective reflectance of the substrate as seen through the flake layer. A model for sparkle is added to this BRDF for close viewing.

Inks for Printing A number of models have been proposed to predict the appearance of ink on paper for specific applications in the print industry. In Power et al. [268], the problem of selecting the two best inks to use for reproducing an image in a two-pass, rather than standard three- or four-pass, printing process. Also in Power et al. [268], the resulting colors are modeled using the Neugebauer model for computing the additive color results of printing many small dots with different inks in a small area coupled with the subtractive color results of printing with inks covering the same area on the page. In a related paper by Stollnitz et al. [302], a more sophisticated extension of the Neugebauer model is used to consider the problem of choosing more than three custom inks for reproducing an image.

Beyond predicting the spectral properties of combinations of inks, Hersch et al. [146] consider a printing problem that includes directional effects. Metallic inks have a directional reflectance, showing a strong specular highlight. Using metallic and conventional inks together, it is possible to have different designs appear on a printed documented depending on the observers point of view. This is an interesting artistic effect, and also provides a useful security mechanism to make counterfeiting of documents more difficult. To accurately predict appearance for specular and nonspecular view angles, Hersch et al. present extensions of the Kubelka–Munk and Neugebauer models that take into account interreflections of light within ink layers, including layers of traditional inks on top of metallics inks.

6.3.3 GEMS

Gems, whether from inorganic minerals or biological sources, are selected and processed specifically for appearance. The raw material for gems may occur naturally, or may come from crystals formed under controlled conditions in a laboratory. As noted in Chapter 2, specialized vocabularies have been developed to describe important attributes of these materials. Because different light/material interactions are important for different gems, one model does not suit all of them. Of the hundreds of types of gems, simulations of only a few have been reported.

As a material, diamond is characterized by a relatively high index of refraction compared to glass. This results in a higher percentage of light rays undergoing total internal reflection and a more pronounced dispersion in diamond than in glass. While ray tracing is ideally suited to simulating the appearance of a diamond, the effect of dispersion is the creation of large numbers of ray paths to be followed. Yuan et al. [349] describe a method for efficiently following the paths of dispersed rays with diamonds as an example. Sun et al. [308] describe a complete spectral rendering framework that includes dispersion. Figure 5.41 is an example of a diamond rendering produced with their system.

The desirable appearance qualities of a diamond are referred to as brilliance, the amount of light returned to the viewer; fire, the colors produced by dispersion; and scintillation, the flashes of light produced when the diamond moves. Researchers in gemology have used ray-traced visual simulations of diamonds to form metrics for brilliance [145] and fire [273]. With metrics for these qualities, visual simulations can be used to compare the effectiveness of different diamond cuts.

Guy and Soler [130] extended the simulation of gems beyond refraction and disperson that are dominant effects for diamonds. For other stones, such as tourmaline, rubies, sapphires, and andalusite, polarization, birefrigence, and pleochorism are important. Guy and Soler detail the two-by-two coherency matrices (see Section 5.6) required for simulating these effects in gems. They also offer simplifications that allow real-time hardware rendering of these effects in gems. Specifically, they note that for the small length scales involved, using the same angle of refraction for rays in both states of polarization results in small errors for common birefrigent gems. The Fresnel coefficients in the two-by-two coherency matrices can be computed more simply with this approximation. An example of the ability of their method to render birefrigent gems with different orientations is shown in Figure 6.26.

One effect seen in rounded, rather than faceted, gemstones is chatoyancy. Chatoyancy is the appearance of ellipsoidal light streaks such as the bright lines in a cat's eye or the stars in sapphires. Yokoi et al. [346] model this effect by modeling the stones as ellipsoidal volumes with small cylinderical inclusions. The inclusions have rough surfaces. The difficulty in computing the image of such stones is integrating the effects of scattering from all the small inclusions along a ray through the material. Yokoi et al. present

(a)   **(b)**   **(c)**

Figure 6.26: For gems that are birefringent, these simulations From Guy and Soler [130], illustrate that the orientation of the gem crystal with respect to the cut makes a difference in the observed color: (a) axis toward eye, (b) updown axis, (c) left=to=right axis. *Source*: © 2004 ACM, Included here by permission.

two approximations for efficiently computing the line integral needed to account for the scattering from the volume of oriented occlusions.

Opals are another stone generally rounded rather than faceted. Imura et al. [156] studied the "play of color" observed in opals. They modeled spectral variations in opal with location and direction as the result of effects at two length scales. At the microscopic level, opal has a regular structure that produces diffraction/interference effects similar to the colors seen in compact discs, discussed in Section 5.5. At the macroscopic scale, clusters of the microstructures are organized with random locations and orientations, and with voids in the overall material volume. This combination of regularity at a microscale and randomness at the macroscale produced results similar to real opals.

Nagata et al. [238] studied the appearance of pearls, with the goal of building a practical simulator for evaluating pearl quality. They identified three key features of pearl appearance and their sources: the sense of depth due to interference effects, the sense of brightness due to specular reflection, and the sense of grain due to texture. They modeled interference effects by modeling the multiple thin crystallized layers that make up a pearl. An interesting feature of pearl appearance is that the color variations due to interference are only a function of the position of the viewer, not the light source. They attribute this effect to the spherical pearl shape, and tailor their model to reproduce the view-dependent changes. For the specular highlight they use the Cook–Torrance model.

The various types of surface textures of pearls are obtained by processing images of real pearls and extracting the spatial frequency of the intensity variations. These spatial variations are used to modulate a diffuse component of reflectance for the pearl. The sum of the interference results, the Cook–Torrance reflectance, and the textured diffuse component produce the full pearl model. Nagata et al. conducted observer experiments to validate the model. Observers evaluated pearl qualities based on photographs of real pearls. Synthetic images using the pearl model were then rated with respect to the pearl like qualities identified in the observation of real pearls. The synthetic images were successfully identified as pearl like.

Many of the models discussed in this chapter depend on measurements. In Chapter 7, we consider the devices and processing methods that have been developed to measure materials for computer graphics applications.

7   MEASUREMENT

One way to specify materials is to select from a library supplied with a software package. Some software packages come with extensive libraries that have been collected by measurement from the manufacturers of various products. In this chapter, we consider how such measurements are made, and how material descriptions can be obtained if they are not found in a standard library.

As discussed in Chapter 6, specific values of material parameters for special materials can be found in the detailed graphics literature. Basic material properties, such as the relative magnitudes of diffuse and specular reflectance, can often be estimated from tables of standard values for classes of materials. For example, Larson and Shakespeare [187] give typical values for common materials in their text on modeling with the Radiance software system. Larson and Shakespeare also suggest simple techniques such as comparing the lightness of a material with a standard gray card (Figure 7.1) to estimate reflectance values. Spatial variations can be captured from a uniformly lit image of a surface texture.

When properties need to be measured, we need to measure the light that reaches a sensor after scattering by an object composed of the material. As noted in the Chapter 2, the light leaving an object depends on the incident illumination, object shape, and object material. The various methods of measuring materials have different approaches to either controlling or measuring the incident illumination and shape so that the sensed light can be interpreted to give the material properties.

Figure 7.1: A simple method for estimating reflectance is to photograph objects with a standard grayscale card.

Since material properties vary with wavelength, position, and direction, a very large number of measurements may be necessary. The various measurement techniques vary in trying to reduce the number of measurements needed to characterize the material, or in trying to gather data for as many variations in wavelength, position, and direction as possible in parallel.

We begin with some traditional methods for measuring materials that predate computer graphics. We follow with new methods that have been developed in the area where computer vision and computer graphics overlap.

7.1 TRADITIONAL MEASUREMENT

Measuring how materials scatter light was a topic of interest long before computer graphics realistic image synthesis evolved in the 1970s and 1980s. Broadly speaking, two classes of measurement systems had developed: high accuracy gonioreflectometers and industrial spot measurement devices. Both of these classes of device can produce data of use in computer graphics, although their use has been superseded in the past 10 years by digital camera–based methods. Understanding a bit about their design and usage, however, gives some useful insight into material measurement. In particular, high accuracy systems give an idea of the magnitude of uncertainty that can be expected from even carefully constructed systems. Industrial spot measurement systems give an idea of how powerful relatively simple measurements can be.

7.1.1 GONIOREFLECTOMETERS

Accurate measurement of reflectance or scattering is necessary for high-performance materials. Understanding the reflectance of, for example, a mirror used in a satellite or a coating used on a military vehicle, is essential design. Accurate measurement is also necessary in studies of the relationship between material microstructure and reflectance that produced the first principles reflectance models in use in many disciplines today.

Examples of precision reflectance measurement devices are those described in publications from the U.S. National Institute of Standards and Technology (NIST) [16, 108]. A detailed account of a gonioreflectometer adapted for computer graphics applications is given Sing-Choong Foo's Master's thesis [98]. A typical setup is shown in Figure 7.2. Essentially, a system consists of a light source, positioning system to hold a sample of the target material to be measured, and a sensor that records the quantity of light scattered from the target. Since extraneous light reflecting from the target to other surfaces in the setup is a source of error, a room with everything coated in black is used for measurements. Since accurate positioning is needed, the system is generally mounted on a heavy optical table to prevent vibrations from movements in the room affecting the positions of the source, target, and sensor.

The definition of the bidirectional reflectance distribution function (BRDF), is in terms of infinitesimal cones of incident and reflected angles, and an infinitesimal area on the target surface. Since the components of any system will be finite in size, some

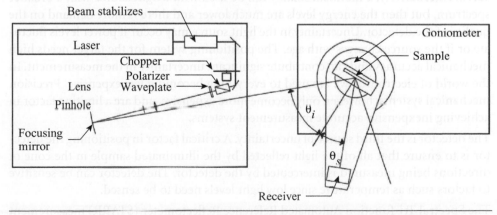

Figure 7.2: A typical setup for measuring BRDF includes a light source with focusing optics, a positioning stage holding a material sample, and a detector to sense the scattered light. *Source:* From Germer and Asmail [108].

uncertainty is inherent in the process. The incident and reflected angles and target illuminated area can be made very small, but this results in very low quantities of energy being scattered that are difficult to measure accurately.

To obtain the absolute value of the BRDF, the detected light from a sample has to be compared to the incident. A typical way of doing this is to compare the detected light to that from a known sample. For an imperfectly diffuse object, the known sample might be a material such as Spectralon for a specular material like a front surface mirror.

Two terms to characterize a system are its precision and its uncertainty. Specific terms in metrology are defined by the ISO (International Standards Organization): "International vocabulary of basic and general terms in metrology." Roughly speaking, precision is the repeatability of the measurement. If you took the same measurement with the same equipment the same way a second time, how close would the result be to the first measurement? This characterizes the measurement system reliability, but it does not give how close the measurement is to the true value. Uncertainty is the interval within which the true value of the measurement is known to be with some level of confidence. For example, an uncertainty level for measuring a reflectance could be established by obtaining a reference standard with known reflectance (from NIST or another national standards body) and finding the difference in measured value from the established true value for multiple trials of the measurement. An uncertainty is associated with each element of a measurement system, and the combined uncertainty accounts for all factors acting together (i.e., not just taking the uncertainty of the element with the highest level of uncertainty).

For the light source, a laser may be used to provide a relatively high quantity of light at a particular wavelength. The disadvantage of this is that only that wavelength can be measured. Alternatively, a monochromator can be used with a light source with a broader spectrum, but then the energy levels are much lower and there is more demand on the quality of the detector. Uncertainty in the light source may occur if power levels fluctuate or if the source changes with age. The positioning system for the target needs high mechanical accuracy and can contribute significant uncertainty in the measurement. In the world of electronics, we are used to everything becoming less expensive. Precision mechanical systems, however, only become more expensive, and are a limiting factor in achieving inexpensive accurate measurement systems.

The detector is the third source of uncertainty. A critical factor in positioning the detector is to ensure that all of the light reflected by the illuminated sample in the cone of directions being measured is intercepted by the detector. The detector can be sensitive to factors such as temperature since low light levels need to be sensed.

The Spectral Tri-function Automated Reference Reflectometer (STARR) measurement device at NIST is constructed with an uncertainty of less than 1 percent, the result of combining the uncertainties in the full measurement system. The measurement capabilities of other systems can be seen in the results of a "round-robin" measurement conducted in 1999. The same sample of vacuum-deposited aluminum on a ground aluminum surface was sent to several labs to be measured [85]. The percent differences in measurements at different laboratories compared to the NIST standard were as high as 4 and 6 percent in some cases (see Figure 7.3). This is consistent with the stated

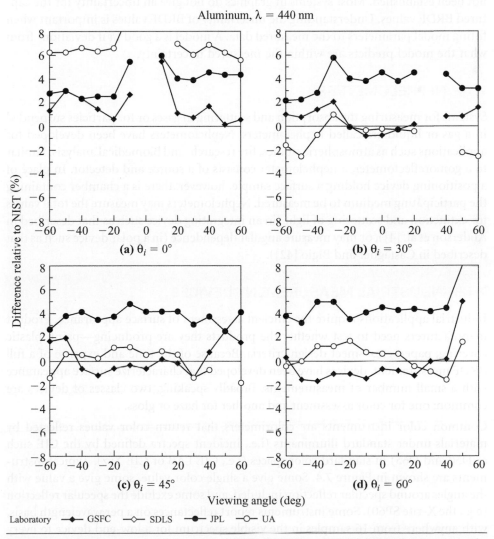

Figure 7.3: Measurements of the same BRDF sample by several laboratories in terms of difference from known standard value. *Source*: From Early et al. [85]. Reprinted courtesy of the American Meteorological Society.

uncertainty of the facilities based on the analysis of the uncertainty of individual components in their systems.

The key observation we can make for graphics applications is that absolute measurements of BRDF with very low (less than 5 percent) uncertainty are extremely difficult and expensive to obtain. Fortunately, graphics applications do not have this high a requirement for accuracy, although exact standards for what accuracy is needed have not been established. Most systems in graphics do not give an uncertainty for the captured BRDF values. Understanding the uncertainty of BRDF values is important when fitting model parameters to the measured data. A model is a good fit if deviations from what the model predicts are within the measured uncertainty.

7.1.2 NEPHELOMETERS

Systems for measuring the absorption and scattering in gases or for particles suspended in a gas or liquid are called nephelometers. Nephelometers have been developed for applications such as atmospheric studies, fire research, and biomedical analysis. Similar to a gonioreflectometer, a nephelometer consists of a source and detector. In place of a positioning device holding a surface sample, however, there is a chamber containing the participating medium to be measured. Nephelometers may measure the total values for extinction and scattering of light (in an integrating device such as that described in Anderson et al. [4]), or may measure angular dependence (in a polar device such as that described in Castagner and Bigio [42]).

7.1.3 INDUSTRIAL MEASUREMENT DEVICES

Industrial applications require the efficient assessment of surface appearance. Product manufacturers need to test whether the products they are producing—paint, plastic covering, paper, etc.—meet design criteria. Because of the time and expense of a full BRDF measurement, devices have been developed that characterize surface appearance with a small number of measurements. Broadly speaking, two classes of devices are common: one for color assessment and another for haze or gloss.

Common color instruments are colorimeters that return color values reflected by materials under standard illuminants (i.e., incident spectra defined by the CIE such as D50 and D65) in standard color spaces (i.e., CIE LAB or CIE Xyz). Typical instruments are shown in Figure 7.4. Some give a single color value, some give a value with the angles around specular reflection included, and some exclude the specular reflection (e.g., the X-rite SP60). Some instruments report reflectances on a per wavelength basis, with anywhere from 16 samples in the visible spectrum for a low-end device to every 10 nanometers at the high end. Some devices are designed for very special-purpose applications, such as the Minolta BC-10 for measuring the color of baked goods.

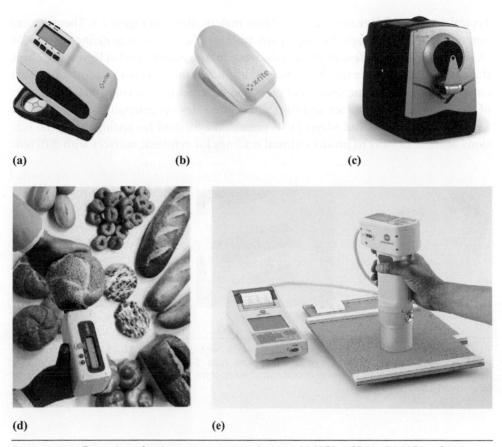

Figure 7.4: Examples of color measurement devices: (a) X-Rite SP60, (b) X-Rite CA22, (c) X-Rite F400, (d) Minolta BC-10, and (e) Minolta CR-400. *Source*: (a) through (c) courtesy of X-Rite Incorporated; (d) and (e) pictures courtesy of Konica Minolta Sensing Americas, Inc.

Because of the demands for accuracy and reliability in industrial applications, colorimeters typically cost in the range of $1,500 to $10,000 U.S.

Intuitively, since successful models such as Ward and Cook–Torrance characterize directional variations in reflectance with a single surface roughness parameter, it should be possible to estimate this parameter with a small number of measurements. Industrial devices designed to measure qualities such as gloss and haze take suitable measurements for this purpose. Westlund and Meyer [334] brought such devices to the attention of the computer graphics community, and devised a method for relating industrial measurements with BRDFs used in graphics.

Typical directional devices are gloss and haze meters, shown in Figure 7.5. These devices measure reflectance at specific angle pairs with specific apertures as defined by ASTM (American Society for Test and Materials) standards, as enumerated in Figure 7.6. These standards were set as the result of experiments finding the best spot measurements that correlate with human perception of gloss and haze. Similar to colorimeters, because of the demands for accuracy and ruggedness, these devices generally cost in excess of $1,000 U.S. Westlund and Meyer [334] presented a method for setting up virtual versions of these devices to produce virtual readings for synthetic surfaces with different

(a)   **(b)**   **(c)**

Figure 7.5: Examples of gloss and haze measurement devices: (a) Novo-Haze gloss measurement, (b) Novo Curve, and (c) Wave-scan dual. *Source*: (a) and (b) pictures courtesy of Rhopoint Instruments (*www.rhopointinstruments.com*); (c) photos courtesy BYK-Gardner USA (*www.byk.com*).

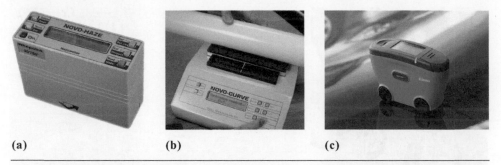

Gloss	ASTM Standard	Specular Angle	Aspecular Angle	Aperture Field (in degrees) Source	Receptor
Speular gloss	D523	20°	0°	0.75 × 2.5	1.8 × 3.6
Speular gloss	D523	60°	0°	0.75 × 2.5	4.4 × 11.7
Speular gloss (sheen)	D523	85°	0°	0.75 × 2.5	4.0 × 6.0
Speular gloss	E430	30°	0°	0.44 × 5.0	0.4 × 3.0
Distinctness of image	E430	30°	±0.3°	0.44 × 5.0	0.14 × 3.0
Haze	E430	30°	±2°	0.44 × 5.0	0.4 × 3.0 or 0.5 × 3.0
Haze	E430	30°	±5°	0.44 × 5.0	0.4 × 3.0 or 0.5 × 3.0

Figure 7.6: ASTM measurement standards. *Source*: From Westlund and Meyer [334], © 2001 ACM. Included here by permission.

roughness parameters for common computer graphics BRDFs. By relating these virtual readings and parameters, the readings from the physical devices can be used to set material parameters.

7.2 IMAGE-BASED BRDF MEASUREMENTS OF SAMPLE MATERIALS

The increasing availability of inexpensive consumer digital cameras in the 1990s launched interest in new methods of measuring materials specifically for computer graphics applications. Digital cameras are used as the sensing elements. Because a camera consists of a two-dimensional (2D) array of sensors, a single image capture can collect data for many directions or spatial locations in parallel. The trade-off in this parallel capture over traditional gonioreflectometry is speed at the cost of increased uncertainty in the light measurement.

Many recent image-based methods described in the computer graphics literature are measurements only in the sense that they provide numerical values for the BRDF. An important caveat in using data from many of these devices is that the precision and accuracy of many systems have not been characterized. From the point of view of the discipline of metrology, many of these systems would be best referred to as "capture," rather than "measurement," systems.

7.2.1 CAMERAS AS SENSORS

Essentially, cameras contain arrays of sensors that produce signals dependent on the light incident on the sensors. The individual sensors may be CCD (charge-coupled device) or CMOS (complementary metal oxide semiconductor). At a high level each type of sensor converts energy to a voltage that is subsequently converted to an integer that can be stored in a relatively small number of bits (8 or 10). Traditionally, CCD sensors have been viewed as higher quality and CMOS as less expensive and requiring less power. Which type of sensor is better depends on overall system design, and is a topic of debate in the optics/photonics design community [204]. To produce images that look correct to people and that are stored efficiently, a great deal of processing occurs in a camera between light failing on one of the camera sensors and storing a standard image in tiff or jpeg format. The 0–255 value in an image pixel cannot be read out directly as the radiance of light that fell on the pixel. The following issues need to be considered in using camera images as measurements:

- *Energy versus radiance:* The radiance that we are interested in for measuring BRDF is a rate, an amount of energy per unit time. Camera sensors don't measure rates though; they collect the incident energy over some time period, called the exposure (i.e., 0.1 second). We can change exposures on a camera (holding the shutter open different lengths of time) and get different 0–255 values for the same incoming radiance. In combining different images taken of an object, the different exposures need to be taken into account.

- *Spectral variations:* Cameras convert the incoming light that has a general spectrum using red, green, and blue (RGB) filters that each allow some subset of the visible spectrum to pass through. Different cameras can use different filters and thus produce different RGB values for the same incoming light. Furthermore, cameras perform a "white balance." Different light sources (i.e., sunlight versus indoor fluorescent light) have different spectra that affects the spectra of the light reflected from a material. If the light reflected from a white card was measured for different light sources, it would vary in appearance to appearing shades of red, yellow, green, or blue. Cameras have built-in white balance that factors out the known spectra of common light sources so that white will look white. The same camera will give different RGB values for the same incoming light if the white balance is set differently.

- *Physical versus virtual pixels:* There is not a one-to-one relationship between the physical sensor elements and the array of pixels in the image produced by a camera. Sensor elements recording RGB are staggered in position in many cameras. The Bayer pattern is often used, and it alternates green sensors with red or blue, with overall twice as many green sensors in the camera. The output of these sensors is interpolated to give a value of RGB for every pixel in an image array that may have greater or fewer pixels than there are camera sensor elements.

- *Nonlinearity:* To efficiently store values in equal perceptual, rather than physical, steps, gamma correction is applied the output of the sensors. That is, the 0–255 values correspond to the actual energy detected raised to power. This output has to be converted to linear values when used as a measurement.

- *Dynamic range:* The dynamic range of light, that is, the ratio of the greatest quantity of light to the smallest, is likely to be much larger on the object we are measuring than what can be recorded in a single exposure. A higher dynamic range can be obtained by capturing a series of images at different exposures. Capturing high-dynamic range images is considered in depth in Reinhard et al. [272].

Several of these issues are becoming simpler to deal with with the evolution of a common "raw" format that gives linear values for the actual sensor pixels. The availability of raw values to people doing measurement is a byproduct of the needs of digital photographers. The raw formats are useful to photographers who want the same control over digital photographs that they had in dark rooms doing traditional wet photography.

7.2.2 MEASURING PREPARED HOMOGENEOUS MATERIAL SAMPLES

A number of systems have been built to measure the BRDF of materials on simple shapes. The systems vary in the geometry used for a camera, target, and light source. Different shapes of target materials or camera systems using different shapes of mirrors are used in these systems to capture values for multiple incident and/or exitant values in parallel.

A simple system demonstrated by Karner et al. [170], is shown in Figure 7.7. A flat sample of the material is placed next to a diffuse reflectance standard material. A light source that has a symmetric output pattern shines on both the sample and the standard, and a digital camera records both. The BRDF is calculated from the ratio of the

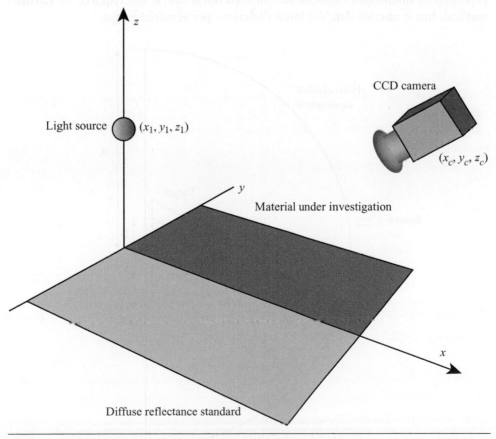

Figure 7.7: Measurement geometry. *Source*: Redrawn from Karner et al. [170], © 1996 The Eurographics Association and Blackwell Publishers.

light reflected from the sample and the diffuse standard. Different incident/reflected directions are sampled by moving the camera. The data values were then fit to a Ward anisotropic reflectance model. While a very simple concept, this system produced values that compared well to measurements from a traditional gonioreflectometer.

A somewhat more complex but earlier system was proposed by Ward [326] and is diagrammed in Figure 7.8. A small, flat material sample is illuminated by a light source located outside of a hemisphere that is a half-silvered mirror, with the silvered side facing the object. The light source can be repositioned for different angles of incidence. The sample reflects light into the hemisphere. A camera is located next to the sample and takes an image of the hemisphere with a fish-eye lens. The BRDF is measured by taking the ratio for each direction of the reflected light for the material sample and the light reflected from a diffuse standard. The system depends on a more expensive to obtain and calibrate half-silvered dome that is not required by Karner's method, but it obtains data for more directions per acquired image.

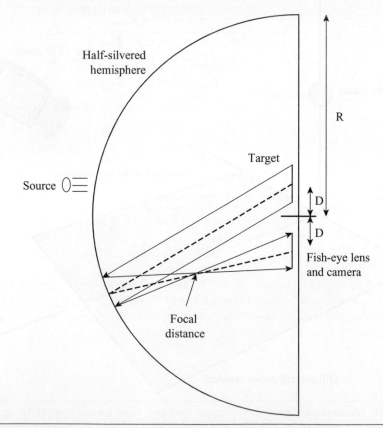

Figure 7.8: Measurement geometry. *Source*: Redrawn from Ward [326].

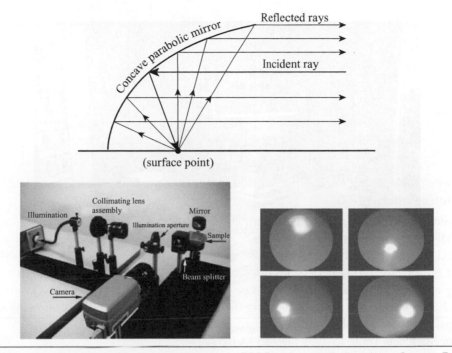

Figure 7.9: Examples of a system to measure BRDF with a parabolic mirror. *Source*: From Dana and Wang [63]. Image © 2004, used courtesy of the Optical Society of America.

A more recent design for obtaining data for multiple directions developed by Dana and Wang [63] uses a parabolic mirror (Figure 7.9). A parabolic mirror focuses on a particular point on a sample target. The direction of incident light is easily varied by just translating the light source. The translation becomes a change in direction when reflected off the parabolic mirror. The light from the sample is reflected back on to the parabolic mirror, and an image of the mirror simultaneously records light reflected in many different directions.

An alternative to using different shaped mirrors to capture multiple directions, is to use sample materials on different geometric shapes.

Lu et al. [210] describe an experimental setup for measuring the BRDF of velvet that uses the fabric wrapped around a cylinder. In his dissertation, Marschner [213] details a system for measuring BRDFs from spheres and cylinders. Convex objects need to be used to avoid self-interreflections from affecting the light incident on each point. With appropriate filtering of light and geometric calibration, Marschner demonstrates measurements from nonplanar samples that compare well with measurements from a traditional gonioreflectometer (Figure 7.10). Matusik [218] built a system using the same idea of using spherical samples. The sample shape allows the capture of multiple

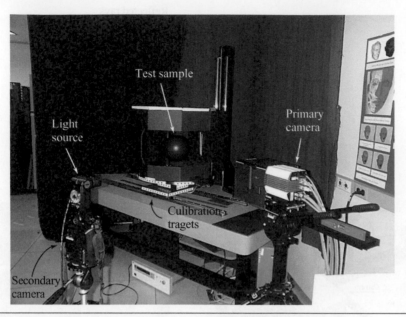

Figure 7.10: Example of a system to measure BRDF with nonplanar targets. *Source*: From Marschner [213], © 1998 Stephen Marschner.

directions quickly, and a light source is mounted on an arm attached to a turntable to automatically acquire high-dynamic range images (using multiple camera exposures) for different incident angles.

Matusik captured data for over 100 materials. With so large a database, he proposed that rather than pursuing first principles models of light reflection, a system of specifying and modifying reflectance functions can be built on the analysis of measured data. He also proposed a method for more efficient measurement based on the analysis of the data collected for his dissertation [220].

7.3 MEASUREMENT OF EXISTING OBJECTS

In many cases, it is desirable to measure materials from existing objects rather than from specially prepared material samples. This is clearly the case when capturing digital models of existing physical objects for reuse in rendering. For example, in cultural heritage applications a physical artifact may be captured to be re-rendered in an historical setting. Alternatively, a physical object might be scanned to be used as a realistic digital prop in a film or game. It may also be desired to capture the material from an existing object because it is the only exemplar a user can find of the material they want to use in constructing a new synthetic object.

Three-dimensional (3D) shape may be acquired by a variety of techniques, with a wide range in the cost of the hardware and in level of detail of the geometry obtained. On the high-cost end, an object can be imaged using devices that use radiation transmitted through an object, as in computer-aided tomography (CAT) scanning. Tomographic methods provide data for the complete internal structure of an object. A detailed object surface is obtained with isosurface extraction techniques. On the low-cost end, sparsely sampled geometric models can be constructed from simple passive systems such as video streams by exploiting structure from motion [266] or by observing silhouettes [217]. However, systems for capturing both shape and appearance generally use devices that capture range images that are an array of depth values for points on an object from a particular view point.

Two types of range scanners dominate: triangulation scanners for small (tabletop-size) objects, and time-of-flight scanners for large (building-size) objects. Triangulation scanners work by emitting a light spot or line from a known position and direction, observing the spot from a sensor with a known position (Figure 7.11a), and solving for the 3D spot position knowing two angles and one side of a triangle. Time-of-flight

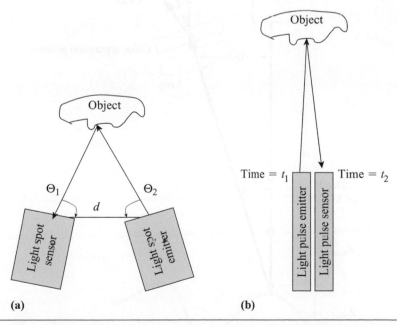

Figure 7.11: (a) Triangulation scanners measure position using the distance d between the emitter and sensor of a small spot, and the angles Θ_1 and Θ_2 between the lines of sight from emitter and sensor to the baseline between them. (b) Time-of-flight scanners measure position using the time difference $t_2 - t_1$ between when a pulse of light is emitted and its reflection is sensed.

scanners work by emitting a light pulse and measuring the time it takes the pulse to travel to an object and reflect back to the scanner (Figure 7.11b). In both cases the scanners typically sample a regular rectangular array, forming an image where each point in the image is a depth or 3D point location rather than an RGB color. More detail about range scanner operation and accuracy can be found in the survey by Blais [23]. Issues in forming full models from sets of range scans are reviewed by Bernardini and Rushmeier [22].

Shape and material measurements may be made simultaneously with the same instrument or in sequence with different instruments. An example of a device for measuring material and shape simultaneously is the polychromatic laser triangulation scanner developed by the National Research Council of Canada (Figure 7.12). Light from three

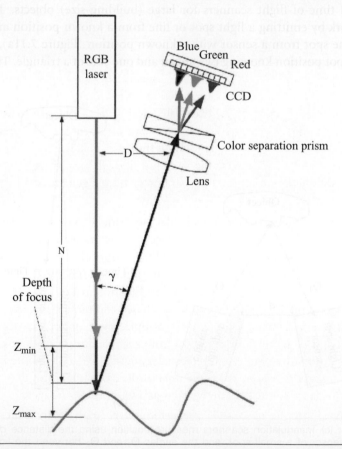

Figure 7.12: Example of a system to simultaneously measure object shape and color. *Source*: From Blais et al. [24].

lasers with wavelengths in the RGB ranges of the spectrum are overlaid and projected on to an object to illuminate the same spot. A sensor receives the light after a prism has spatially separated the three wavelengths. Measuring the magnitude of reflection for each wavelength provides data for computing the spectral reflectance at the same spot. The data for one spot, however, only provides an estimate of the BRDF for one incident/exitant direction pair. Baribeau et al. [15] describe how this data can be used to estimate the full BRDF of a material when an object with spatially homogeneous surface is scanned.

More often, rather than using multiple lasers, data for material measurement is typically acquired with a digital camera. The digital images need to be registered with the acquired 3D model. One way to do this is to capture digital images at the same time as the range images, and to calibrate the camera position and orientation in the scanner coordinate system. This can be done using standard calibration algorithms and physical calibration artifacts such as cubes and checkerboards [315, 350]. In addition to finding position and orientation (i.e., extrinsic camera parameters), camera calibration is also performed to compute intrinsic camera parameters such as focal length and lens distortion.

When images are acquired by a camera that is not coupled to the shape scanner by calibration, the image-to-geometry registration is usually performed after the range images have been integrated into a full model. Essentially, the full model plays the role of the calibration artifacts in the camera-to-scanner calibration. Each image has to have a separate camera calibration. Correspondences between each image and the model are found by a user picking points, or by automatic feature detection.

Images that are captured and aligned to the model need to be processed to estimate the material properties from the reflected light. For objects that are near Lambertian, some systems are designed to eliminate or reduce the processing needed by appropriate lighting design. For a Lambertian surface, the major variations in the light reflected from a surface are due to surface orientation. Inexpensive scanning systems that do not acquire high-accuracy geometry attempt to minimize the effect of surface orientation by using large-area light sources to approximate illumination from the full hemisphere. While not perfect, for capturing spatially varying diffuse material properties to be used in re-rendering the object, this approach can be very effective.

When high-end systems that capture very accurate geometry are used with calibrated, near-point light sources, the geometric information is used to adjust for variations in angle and distance to convert linearized image pixel values into BRDF data. For objects with a spatially homogeneous surface, all of the pixel values can be regarded as data points for a single BRDF model. Unlike the methods that use specially prepared spheres, adjustments should be made to discard or correct values from concave

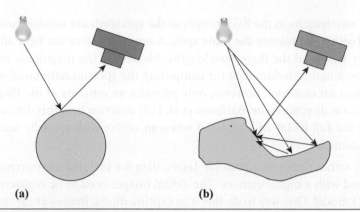

Figure 7.13: Capturing material properties from existing objects is complicated by concavities. For a convex shape (a), all light reflected to the camera came directly from the source. For a concave shape (b), some of the light reflected to the camera may have undergone one or more interreflections.

portions of the surface that are illuminated both by the calibrated light source and by self-interreflections, as diagrammed in Figure 7.13.

One way to account for the effects of interreflections is to iteratively estimate the BRDF, simulate the interreflections, and then revise the estimate [68]. Alternatively, illumination patterns that have fine spatial variations to produce closely spaced points with illumination and indirect illumination only can be used to estimate and remove the effect of indirection illumination from measurements [243].

For spatially varying materials on existing objects, the difficulty is sampling enough directions for each point on an object. For a spatially varying BRDF, Kay and Caelli [174] used images captured from the same view-point for many different incident light directions along with a range image of the object. Because the directional sampling was still sparse, they fit the data to a Torrance–Sparrow reflectance model. They shared data across pixels where the directional sampling missed potential specular peaks.

Sato et al. [283] presented an alternate method for obtaining an estimate of BRDF for a full object. They used range and color images to measure an object, with the sensor and light source registered by calibration by moving the object with a robot arm manipulator. They also used a Torrance–Sparrow model to fit the data. They simplified the parameter fitting by separating diffusely and specularly reflected light in each image based on color. Assuming nonwhite, dielectric materials, the diffuse component is assumed to be any nonwhite color reflected and white areas are assumed to be due to the specular component. Because the specular component is sampled sparsely along the surface, the estimate of specular reflectance parameters are interpolated over larger areas of the object.

Rather than depending on color alone, the state of polarization of light can be used to separate diffuse and specular components. In general, the diffuse reflection from a dielectric will be unpolarized, but the specular reflection will be polarized (as illustrated in the plot in Figure 5.45). An example of exploiting this in measurement is shown in Figure 7.14. The figure shows the wet surface of a stone. In Figure 7.14a, the surface is imaged with a polarization filter in front of the camera that is oriented to maximize the light to the camera. The specular reflection of light from the smooth film of water on the surface is visible. In Figure 7.14b, the surface is imaged with the polarization filter and is turned so that the polarized light reflected from the smooth water film is blocked, and only the diffusely reflected light from the surface is visible. The use of polarization state and color to separate components of reflection is discussed in detail by Nayar et al. [242].

Rather than attempt to separate diffuse and specular components, Lensch et al. [196] take an approach that begins by treating an object as spatially homogeneous. After this global BRDF is computed using data from all scanned points, two groups of pixel values are formed based on the distance between their measured values and their values computed from the global BRDF. This splitting process is repeated until the distance of samples in a group from the BRDF computed from them falls to some threshold. Point-by-point variations are computed by computing each BRDF for each point on the final model as a linear combination of the set of BRDFs formed from the groups.

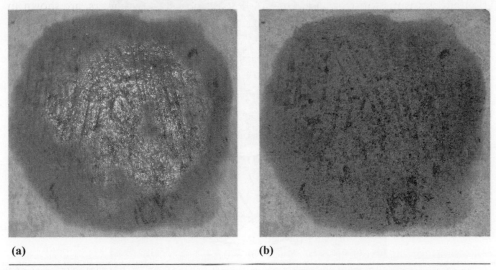

(a)   (b)

Figure 7.14: A wet surface imaged with a polarizing filter oriented to maximize light (a), and minimize it (b).

Capturing data for many light sources and view directions can take a substantial amount of time, much longer than the time a person can be expected to sit without moving. For scanning the shape and appearance of people the acquisition time needs to be reduced. Data for multiple light source directions or multiple view directions can be obtained efficiently using a dome arrangement, such as that shown in Figure 7.15. For each node the dome may have one light source. Using photographic flashes, for example, and a video rate camera, multiple lighting conditions can be captured for objects that may move (e.g., a human face). Similarly, multiple cameras can simultaneously capture the result of one light source. This type of arrangment was used to capture the facial images for various view and lighting directions for several of the facial skin modeling efforts mentioned in Chapter 6 (i.e., [66, 105, 336]).

To create full models of existing objects with materials, the last step in processing is to create one or more layers of texture images that give the material parameters over the surface of the object. Details of converting material parameters into texture maps on scanned models are discussed in Rocchini et al. [276] and Bernardini et al. [21]. The mapping process requires flattening and/or segmenting the 3D geometry into a 2D domain. The individual processed textures are then projected onto the 3D geometry, and maps are formed for each geometry segment by combining all processed images that project onto the segment. A variety of techniques are used to combine the images,

Figure 7.15: Example of a dome measurement device used in Georghiades [105], © 2003 Yale University.

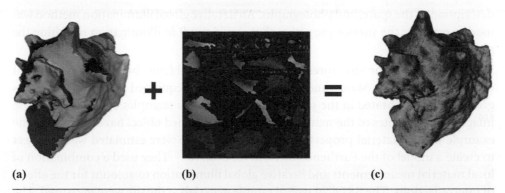

(a)   (b)   (c)

Figure 7.16: To create a full model of an object, the geometric model must be partitioned into segments that each have a 2D parameteriziation (a). The textures for each segment are computed from the acquired images and packed into a single texture image (b). By specifiying the 2D coordinates in the texture image for each 3D vertex in the geometry, the texture data are associated with the shape for a full model (c).

such as choosing the best texture for a region [276], forming a weighted average of all the textures [21], or using different weighting techniques for the different spatial frequency channels in the textures [17]. Figure 7.16 shows a scanned seashell that has been partitioned, with the accompanying texture map computed from images captured of the shell.

A specialized case of modeling existing objects, described in Chapter 6, is the appearance of organs for surgery simulation. Chung et al. [49] captured the BRDF and texture of lung surfaces using the same basic pipeline of capturing geometry, capturing images, aligning images to geometry, processing images, and reprojecting results onto segmented geometric models. In this case, the geometry was captured by taking computed tomography (CT) scans of patients. Images were subsequently captured using a bronchoscope. Registration was performed using a specialized technique for endoscope tracking. The texture and BRDF were estimated taking into account the specific characteristics of the capture, most notably the colocation of the light and camera and interreflections in the airway passages.

7.3.1 LARGE OBJECTS AND BUILDINGS

Capturing materials for interior spaces (i.e., rooms, caves, or vaults) rather than individual objects presents challenges because of the quantity of data and the need to account for interreflections. Yu et al. [347] considered the problem of capturing spatially varying diffuse reflectances and specular reflectances that were constant over large areas in an interior space. Input to their model was a simple geometric description of the space, and photographs. An iterative global illumination method was used to estimate the surface properties that would result in illumination matching the photographs.

Materials on outdoor structures pose even greater problems, because of the lack of control over lighting. Many time-of-flight scanners are equipped with digital cameras geometrically calibrated in the scanner coordinates. Few examples of processing these images into estimates of the material properties of scanned object have appeared. One example where material properties for a large structure were estimated was a project to create a model of the Parthenon by Debevec et al. [68]. They used a combination of local material measurements and iterative global illumination to account for the effects of interreflections. The BRDF of typical sample materials at the site were measured. The geometry of the site was captured with a time-of-flight scanner. Photographs were then taken of the full structure, along with images of probes to estimate the incident skylight and sunlight. An iterative global illumination solution was then used to estimate the BRDF of points on the structure as linear combinations of the locally measured typical materials.

In large interior spaces or exterior structures, estimating the illumination using sparse measurements obtained by imaging sample spheres or shadows may not be adequate. A number of different light sources with different spectral characteristics may be important in different areas of the scene. An additional source of data is the return intensity that is provided by many range scanners with each 3D point scanned. Umeda et al. [317] demonstrated how the return intensity could be calibrated to estimate Lambertian reflectance for the wavelength used by the range scanner for a small-scale triangulation scanner. Xu et al. [344] used Umeda et al.'s method with a time-of-flight scanner. They further used the correction factors used to compute Lambertian reflectance for the scanner wavelength to segment objects in regions illuminated by different sources to be color adjusted separately.

7.4 SIMULTANEOUS SHAPE AND REFLECTANCE CAPTURE

Some systems have been designed to capture both shape and reflectance from the same image data. One approach is to make some assumptions about both shape and reflectance. For example, Georghiades [105] estimates shape and reflectance from a small number of images taken from the same camera position, but from a variety of unknown lighting directions. Georghiades assumes a form for the reflectance function (Torrance–Sparrow), limitations on the angle between the view and surface normal (to minimize Fresnel effects), and the smoothness of the shape (shape formed as a sum of smooth basis functions). The coefficients of the reflectance function and the shape can be estimated on a pixel-by-pixel basis. These assumptions are valid for instances such as measuring a human face.

Zickler et al. [352] consider capturing more general objects. They exploit the reciprocity of the BRDF to eliminate the effect of the BRDF on captured pixel values. Specifically, consider two images obtained with a single light source and camera. The two images are the same, except the positions of light source and camera are switched. The reciprocity of the BRDF implies that a relationship can be stated between captured pixel intensities in the two images that depends only on the object geometry—the distance from the camera and the orientation of the surface normal. By capturing several such image pairs the geometry can be estimated from the pixel intensities. Once the geometry is known, estimates of the BRDF can be made from the images. This technique, referred to as Helmholtz stereopsis, does depend on the illuminated and imaged areas being carefully controlled so that the reciprocity conditions hold for finite areas of the object being sampled.

7.5 SMALL-SCALE GEOMETRIC STRUCTURES

Capturing the spatially varying BRDF of a material may not be adequate to characterize it. Small-scale—on the order of millimeters or fractions of millimeters—features such as grooves and bumps are important for many common materials such as orange peels or corduroy. Extremely high-accuracy scanners would be needed to capture this geometry by measuring the surface point by point, so alternative means have been developed to capture the effect of small-scale features on appearance without completely reconstructing the geometry.

7.5.1 NORMAL AND BUMP MAPS

Many methods are based on the concept of photometric stereo, invented by Woodham [342] for computer vision applications. Photometric stereo uses M images of an object from a single camera view point with lighting from M different directions. For many classes of materials photometric stereo can be used to estimate surface normals.

Assuming a Lambertian surface and small light sources of uniform strength, an equation for the surface normal N_p visible through each pixel p in each image m for each light source in direction $L_{m,i}$ is given by:

$$(L_{m,i}, N_p) = sG_{m,p} \qquad (7.1)$$

where $G_{m,p}$ is the image grayscale value p in m after correction for nonlinear gamma values, $(L_{m,i}, N_p)$ is the dot product, and s is a scaling constant that includes the light source radiance, surface reflectance, and solid angle subtended by the light source. Since N_p has unit length and thus represents only two independent variables, given at least three equations we can solve the equations for N_p and s. By omitting very bright pixels (likely to be caused by specular highlights) and very dark pixels (likely to be in shadow), reasonable estimates of surface normals can be obtained from surfaces that are not purely Lambertian. The spatial resolution of the normals computed is limited only by the resolution of the digital camera used. Images captured at a range of 1 meter with megapixel digital cameras can be used to compute normals at a spatial resolution of 0.1 mm.

Rushmeier et al. [281] demonstrate this for capturing detailed bump or normal maps. Bump maps, originated by Blinn [29], are texture maps that store a perturbation of the underlying geometric surface at each pixel. A normal map, originally described in Cohen et al. [52], is an image that has the full surface normal stored at each pixel, not a perturbation of the normal of the underlying geometric surface. Both bump and normal maps exploit the fact that the intensity variations on a surface are more strongly affected by surface orientation than by distance variations for small surface features. An example of using a captured normal map is shown in Figure 7.17. In addition to using captured normals as maps, they can also be used to improve the accuracy of scanned 3D points [244].

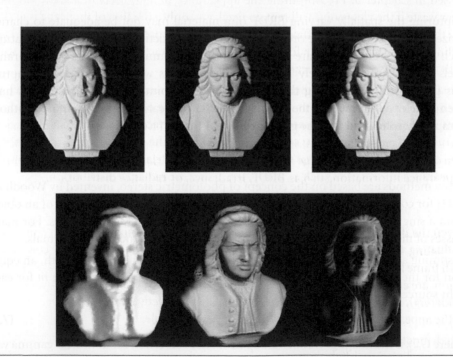

Figure 7.17: Using captured normal maps. Images (*top row*) taken with three different light source directions. (*Bottom row*) A low-resolution geometric model (*left*) is augmented with a normal map derived from the captured images and is relit from two new directions.

Alternative hardware systems can be used to capture normal or bump maps. Malzbender et al. [212] designed a small dome of light sources, similar to the dome used to capture faces, to capture sample materials. The multiple lighting directions give the data necessary to apply photometric stereo. Beyond bump or normal maps, they also propose storing a biquadratic polynomial at each captured pixel to encode the appearance at each point for the full range of lighting directions. Gardner et al. [104] designed a scanner for nearly flat objects that uses a linear light source that translates over the surface to efficiently scan. The linear light source scanner measures reflectance, shape, and detailed normals. Rather than using the diffuse component of reflectance, as in photometric methods, the linear light source uses the appearance of the specular peak during two passes of the light source to estimate the normal orientation.

As noted in the measurement of BRDF, interreflections need to be accounted for in using photometric stereo to estimate normals. Nayar et al. [243] demonstrate the difference in surface shape estimation from photometric normals when the effects of interreflection are removed by using an illumination sources with high spatial frequency variations.

7.5.2 BIDIRECTIONAL TEXTURE FUNCTIONS

Detailed normals, in the form of bump maps, and spatially varying BRDFs, are ideas that predate the capture of materials with digital camera systems. Dana et al. [62] observed that even full BRDF and normals maps are not adequate for capturing the change in detail surface appearance with lighting and view for surfaces with fine-scale geometric complexity such as bread and velvet. Such materials can be imaged from multiple views under different lighting conditions. Dana et al. developed the concept of bidirectional textures that include all the effects of BRDF and small-scale geometry including self-shadowing, occlusion, and interreflections. The bidirectional texture function (BTF) data structure was a breakthrough because it enabled the modeling of complex structures like bread that were impossible to capture as geometry and normals plus BRDF.

Conceptually, the BTF records the light scattered at each 2D point on a hypothetical flat surface over the material as a function of the direction of light incidence and view. It is different from a spatially varying BRDF, however, because the 2D location in each view of the surface may correspond to a different 3D point on the actual surface, as shown in Figure 7.18.

In this synthetic example, the material consists of irregularly yellow-surfaced cylinders sitting on a bumpy blue base plane. The left-most column shows the geometry in wire frame from two different views. The radiances for different illumination and view direction will be stored in a 2D plane of pixels, as shown in the second column from the left. The second column from the right shows the geometry lit by a light coming

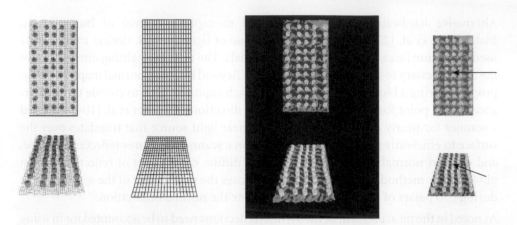

Figure 7.18: The BTF is defined on a flat surface over the material. The two rows show a detailed geometry and the 2D plane the radiance data are recorded for two views with the same lighting. The same 2D point on the flat surface may correspond to different 3D locations on the material. The arrows in the last column of images point to the same 2D location on the BTF images stored for these two views.

from the right from the same two views. The BTF maps for this lighting condition for these two views are shown in the right-most column. The arrow points to the same pixel location in the two maps. From the top, the background blue is visible through the pixel, so a dark blue color is stored for this location. From the other view, the side of one of the cylinders is visible, so a yellow color is stored for the same location in this view. Because the values stored in the map at a particular pixel don't all correspond to the same 3D geometric location, BRDF models do not necessarily do a good job of fitting BTF data.

BTFs are captured by positioning cameras and lights in a manner that is similar to a BRDF sample. Instead of capturing a reflected radiance for every light direction and view direction pair, an image of a flat surface covered with the material is captured. Dana's original setup used flat target samples positioned by a robotic stage relative to a source of parallel light and a video camera (Figure 7.19). As an alternative, Han and Perlin [135] designed a system in which multiple images of different views are captured in one camera shot by using a kaleidoscope arrangement of mirrors (Figure 7.20). Additional kaleidoscope geometries have been examined in simulation by Bangay and Radloff [11].

Using BTFs on arbitrary surfaces is more difficult than assigning a BRDF to a single point. Work by Liu et al. [205] and subsequent research has considered how texture synthesis techniques can be used to apply BTFs over arbitrary surfaces. A complete survey of BTF acquisition and processing has been prepared by Müller et al. [237].

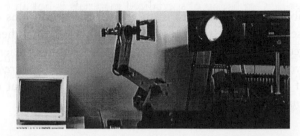

Figure 7.19: Example of a system to measure BTF with robot positioning arm. *Source*: From Dana et al. [62], © 1999 ACM. Included here by permission.

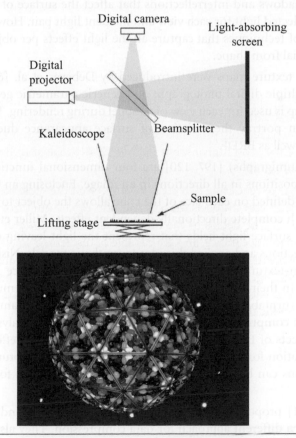

Figure 7.20: Example of a system to measure BTF with a kaleidoscope arrangement of mirrors. *Source*: From Han and Perlin [135] © 2004 ACM. Included here by permission.

While it is possible to compute BTFs from numerical descriptions of objects [71], captured databases of BTFs are the most common form for using them. The CURET database of bidirectional textures is maintained by the Computer Science Department at Columbia University at *http://www1.cs.columbia.edu/CAVE/software/curet/index.php*. A different set of BTFs are maintained at the University of Bonn at *http://btf.cs.uni-bonn.de/index.html*.

7.6 ALTERNATIVE REPRESENTATIONS

No scanning method has been developed to truly capture bidirectional textures for complete objects. That is, a technique has not been developed for "undoing" the effects of larger-scale shadows and interreflections that affect the surface of an object while capturing the reflected light for each view and incident light pair. However, there have been a number of techniques that capture all the light effects per object, rather than separating material from shape.

View-dependent texture maps were introduced by Debevec et al. [67] for building models from multiple digital photographs and generic parametric geometries. A different texture map is used for each view of a model during rendering. View-dependent texture maps can portray the variation of surface appearance due to changes in self-occlusion as well as BRDF.

Light fields (or lumigraphs) [197, 120] are four-dimensional functions of the light leaving from all positions in all directions in an image. Enclosing an object in a cube with a light field defined on each face of the cube allows the object to be viewed from any direction with complete directionally dependent effects. Miller et al. [267] developed the idea of surface light fields that represent the light leaving each point on a surface in all directions and applied this idea to synthetic models. Nishino et al. [252] created the Eigen-texture system to capture and represent surface light field from physical objects. In their method, a light is fixed to an object and multiple views are obtained using a turntable. The series of M small texture maps obtained for each part of the surface are compressed by performing an eigenstructure analysis. The textures represent the effects of BRDF, self-shadowing, and self-occlusion effects for the single lighting condition for that particular object. Eigen-textures captured for different lighting conditions can be combined linearly to generate textures for novel lighting conditions.

Wood et al. [341] proposed an alternate method for capturing and storing surface light fields using a different approach for data compression. They also demonstrated how small changes could be made in an object represented by surface light fields while maintaining a plausible, if not completely accurate, appearance.

Many subsequent systems have been developed for capturing surface light fields and view-dependent textures. In general though, these result in representations of a particular object, rather than a representation of a material that can be applied to a new digital object.

7.7 SUBSURFACE SCATTERING AND VOLUMETRIC MEDIA

Obtaining parameters for surfaces with significant macroscopic subsurface scattering poses additional challenges. Point light sources that illuminate multiple areas on a target at once cannot be used, because the effects of subsurface scattering from one position are mixed with the direct surface reflection of another. Isolated areas need to be illuminated. In particular, to measure the subsurface scattering properties of materials, Jensen et al. [163] propose the measurement configuration shown in Figure 7.21. A pair of lenses are used to focus light on a small area of a target. Assuming strong multiple scattering, the diffusion approximation for subsurface scatter is used to find values of the scattering attenuation and scattering coefficients that would produce the observed lit area.

In their system for measuring facial skin (Chapter 6), Weyrich et al. [336] use a specialized fiber-optic spectrometer to measure subsurface scattering. In their device,

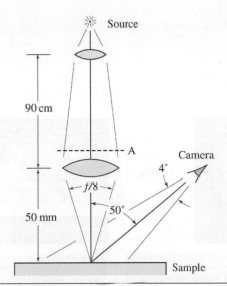

Figure 7.21: Example of a system for measuring subsurface scattering parameters. *Source*: From Jensen et al. [163], © 2001 ACM. Included here by permission.

one optical fiber carries the source light, and an array of additional fibers located around the source carry the scattered light back to a camera for recording.

Goesele et al. [114] invented a system for capturing surface light fields for objects with subsurface scattering. Similar to the colored laser triangulation system, three lasers are used with wavelengths in the RGB ranges. The lasers are driven to sweep out points over the complete object. For each illuminated spot, the light existing on all other locations on the object are captured. The spatial nature of subsurface scattering, that is, the relationship between the positions where light enters and exits the object, are captured. Directional variations at each point are not. Similar to other light field systems, the system captures the characteristics of the specific object rather than the material.

Hawkins et al. [141] presented an image-based nephelometer for measuring the albedo and phase function of particles suspended in air (Figure 7.22b). The medium is introduced into a clear-sided chamber, and the scattering from a laser beam passing through the medium is observed. Directional measurements are obtained from a single photograph of the medium at low density (so that single scatter can be assumed) by using a conical mirror. For measuring the extinction coefficient of the medium, a high-density medium is used so that the spatial rate of the beam extinction can be easily captured. Effects of multiple scattering are removed from the extinction measurement by taking advantage of the sharp spatial cutoff of the beam, and subtracting the average intensity

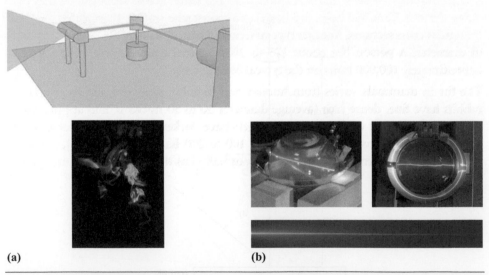

(a)   (b)

Figure 7.22: Measuring participating media: (a) spatial distribution captured by illuminating planes of media, and (b) angular scattering and extinction measured by introducing media into a clear-sided enclosure. *Source*: From Hawkins et al. [141], © 2005 ACM. Included here by permission.

of scattering from indirectly illuminated sections of the medium just next to the beam. Hawkins et al. also demonstrate the measurment of the spatial distribution of a participating medium using rapid imaging of a light plane sweeping through the medium (Figure 7.22a).

For measuring the scattering properties of liquids or particles suspended in liquids, Narasimhan et al. [240] developed an alternative image-based nephelometer. Dilute liquids, with particle densities small enough that single scattering can be only approximated, fill a rectangular tank and are illuminated by a lightbulb immersed in the medium and imaged through antireflection-coated glass. Knowing the geometry of the tank holding the fluid and the imaging device, high-dynamic range images can be interpreted to estimate the absorption and scattering of the suspended particles.

7.8 ADDITIONAL DIMENSIONS

For many materials we think in terms of modeling appearance variations over a 2D surface. Textiles, paints, and other coatings are essentially 2D. However, many interesting materials are useful to model fully in three dimensions. Stone and wood are examples of common materials that are useful to model in 3D. The BRDF and small-scale structure of any surface cut from these materials need to be consistent with a 3D model. Ideally, tomographic methods would be used to collect data from these materials. The expense of such an approach has prevented this. Capture methods for 3D textures have been limited to capturing 2D slices of materials and using texture synthesis [110, 143] or stereological techniques [158] to infer the full 3D structure.

Time is the other dimension to consider in modeling materials. The various measurement techniques that have been discussed so far can be used to capture data for the same sample or object for several time periods. In Chapter 8, changes in materials that occur over time will be considered, and examples of measurements used to model these changes will be discussed.

8 AGING AND WEATHERING

In the previous chapters, we described materials in idealized form. However, real materials frequently change in appearance with time as a result of their interaction with the surrounding environment. For a particular object composed of a given material, the rate and extent of change are dependent on the shape of the object, its exposure to the surrounding environment, and the properties of the material of which it is composed.

Much of the visual richness of natural scenes is due to the patinous action of the environment, resulting in such looks as lichen-covered stonework or silver-gray cedar boarding. Such changes in appearance are generally termed *aging* or *weathering*. Figure 8.1 shows several examples of weathered materials. Modeling appearance variations associated with aging is critical to generating input for realistic scenes.

This chapter begins with a taxonomy of aging effects. Next, we look at the two primary ways to generate weathering effects: simulation and replication. The chapter concludes with a survey of recent work on capturing real aging effects and transferring them to synthetic shapes.

8.1 WEATHERING TAXONOMY

There are three broad categories of mechanisms for weathering: *chemical*, *mechanical*, and *biological*. In this section, we discuss these categories in detail and describe a variety of representative weathering effects.

(a)   **(b)**

(c)   **(d)**

Figure 8.1: Examples of real weathering effects: (a) biological growth on clay pots, (b) silver-gray cedar shingles, (c) corroded metal gears, and (d) weathered seashell. *Source*: Photograph (d) by Nancy Bea Miller, © 2007.

8.1.1 CHEMICAL

Chemical processes transform an original material into a substance with different composition and physical characteristics. The new substance is typically much softer and more susceptible to weathering than the original material.

Corrosion

Corrosion is the destructive chemical attack of the intrinsic properties of a material by atmospheric agents. This type of damage usually affects metallic materials and typically produces oxide(s) and/or salt(s) of the original metal. Metals may corrode merely from exposure to moisture in the air, but the process can be strongly affected by exposure to certain atmospheric pollutants. The corrosion process forms a complicated system of reacting layers, consisting of the metal, corrosion products, surface electrolyte, and atmosphere.

Although the chemical changes of a metal that occur during corrosion generally imply a wearing, or eating, away of the metal, this is not strictly the case. Corrosion changes can be divided into two classes: those that produce a solid film, or *patina*, and those that produce a porous layer. The former usually performs a protective function, that is, once the film forms, corrosion of the underlying metal is impeded. While in the absence of a film formation, corrosion generally proceeds until a reactant has been exhausted. The latter case also generally involves a loss material (Figure 8.2).

Corrosion can be concentrated locally to form a pit or crack, or it can extend across a wide area to produce general deterioration. (Representative varieties are shown in Figures 8.3 and 8.4.)

Tarnish

Metals exposed to the atmosphere quickly develop tarnish, a thin layer of corrosion that forms on aluminum, brass, copper, silver, and other metals as they undergo oxidation. Tarnish is similar to rust, but with a slower rate of development.

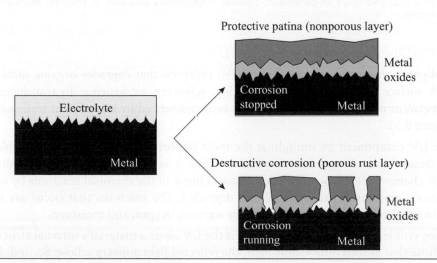

Figure 8.2: Types of surface corrosion.

Figure 8.3: Examples of patination. *Source*: Photographs courtesy of Michael Marsland, © 2007 Yale University.

Fading/Changes Due to Ultraviolet Light

Sunlight is the source of ultraviolet (UV) radiation that degrades organic materials. Such surface degradation includes fading, yellowing, or wearing. In translucent or transparent materials, these effects may be characterized by loss of light transmission (Figure 8.5).

The UV component of sunlight is the most important single factor responsible for the breakdown of organic compounds, while it is also responsible for producing color changes. Ultraviolet radiation initiates many of the chemical reactions by which organic compounds are oxidized and degraded. The reactions that occur are often chain reactions, which are accelerated by warmth, oxygen, and moisture.

Three visible changes may occur. First, if the UV alters a material's internal structures to those that absorb blue visible light, the reflected light appears yellow. Second, if the

Figure 8.4: Examples of rusty/corroded surfaces.

Figure 8.5: Samples of deteriorated paper and fibers due to ultraviolet light: (a) comparison between papers before and after discoloring, (b) bindings of a book published in 1966, and (c) a book covered by the same fibers but published in 1987.

Figure 8.6: Examples of a charred material.

colorant used in the material is affected by UV, even if the polymer itself is not, fading results. Third, mechanical or physical changes, such as cracking or crazing, are possible due to chemical reactions.

Combustion/Charring

Combustion or burning is a rapid reaction between a substance (the fuel) and a gas (the oxidizer), usually oxygen, that releases heat and usually light. Of particular importance in appearance modeling is *charring*, the process of slight or incomplete burning that occurs when a material, particularly an organic one, is subjected to heat (Figure 8.6). The resulting mattter is termed *char*. Charring removes hydrogen and oxygen, so char is composed primarily of carbon.

Phase Changes

A phase change (or transition) is the transformation of a substance from one state—solid, liquid, or gas—to another, which is characterized by an abrupt change in one or more of a material's physical properties (Figure 8.7). Such changes are often due to variations in pressure or temperature.

Figure 8.7: Phase changes: (a) Melting (from solid to liquid); (b) solidification/freezing (from liquid to solid); (c) evaporation/drying (from liquid to gas); and (d) deposition (from gas to solid). *Source*: Images courtesy of: (a) © 2007 Wendy Crone, University of Wisconsin; (b) © 2007 Phil Medina; (d) far left image © 2007 William D. Bowman; remaining images © 2007 Guillaume Dargaud (*www.gdargaud.net*).

Examples of phase changes include:
- *Melting* is the solid to liquid transition.
- *Solidification* or freezing is the liquid to solid transition.
- *Evaporation* or drying is the liquid to gas transition.
- *Deposition* is the gas to solid transition.

8.1.2 MECHANICAL

Mechanical processes involve the disintegration of a material into fragments and/or the transport and deposition of material, such as dirt or salts.

Figure 8.8: Peeling examples. *Source*: *Left* photograph by Nancy Bea Miller, © 2007.

Peeling

Continued exposure of paint, or other thin layers, on surfaces to the elements reduces the strength of layers and often leads to peeling and cracking (Figure 8.8). As a paint film embrittles, it becomes increasingly incompatible with the underlying material until it is eventually stressed to failure. The rate of change depends on a variety of factors, including the surrounding atmosphere, the type of paint, and the character of the underlying surface. As paint loses its adhesion—the ability to attach itself to a surface—it either peels or curls away and eventually falls off.

Cracking

Cracking or fracture is the separation of a material into multiple pieces as a result of stress (Figure 8.9). The causes of stress are many and extremely complex, for example:

- Uneven stress due to material irregularities (fracture lines).
- Uneven stress due to different expansion and contraction (paint layers).

Materials are rarely homogeneous and, therefore, vary in their properties with respect to stress.

Compaction

Compaction is the process by which a material becomes more closely packed together due to the application of an external applied force (Figure 8.10). This process generally occurs differentially on a surface over a long period of time, resulting in an array

Figure 8.9: Cracking examples. *Source*: Photographs by Mayang Adnin, © 2004.

Figure 8.10: Compaction examples. *Source*: Middle photograph by Michael Marsland, © 2007 Yale University.

of dents or scratches. Walking or dropping of objects are common causes of surface impacts.

Delamination

Delamination is a type of failure associated with laminates or composite materials. Cyclic stresses due to impacts can cause layers to separate, leading to a significant loss in a material's mechanical integrity. Delamination often occurs inside a material, only manifesting itself when the material fails.

Deposition and Erosion

Material appearance, particularly in exterior environments, is often affected by the effects of water and air. Water and air may add to a surface through *deposition* (Figure 8.11), or substract from a surface through *erosion* (Figure 8.12).

Rain The flow of rainwater is one of the most important and pervasive natural forces contributing to the weathering of materials, producing distinctive surface patterns. Water may clean some areas by washing dirt away, while staining other areas by depositing dirt and other substances.

Figure 8.11: Deposition examples. *Source*: From Dorsey et al. [76], © 1996 ACM. Included here by permission.

Figure 8.12: Erosion examples. *Source*: *Middle* image from Dorsey et al. [74]. Included here by permission. *Right* image © 2007 by Shawn Phelps.

Such solutions, containing dirt and contaminants, may also be absorbed into porous materials, where they can then transform the original materials into claylike substances that are soluble in water. After recrystallization at the surface or subsurface, a weak crust may form at the surface. Parts of this weakened crust often break off or wash away, leading to erosion.

Air Wind, like water, is more generally an agent that transports abrasive materials and, in so doing, contributes to the mechanical weathering process. The effect of wind action can be pronounced on loosely adhering, or relatively soft, materials. This can lead to dust deposition on materials, or natural sand blasting, as has been the case of the Sphinx in Egypt.

8.1.3 BIOLOGICAL

Biological processes involve the development of patterns on surfaces due to living organisms. In addition, biological processes may also include lifecycle changes to the materials themselves.

Growth

Patterns on surfaces due to biological growth are ubiquitous in exterior scenes. Examples include algae, fungi, lichen, mold, and moss. These plant forms exhibit a rich variety of color and form (Figure 8.13).

The growth of biological organisms is dependent on the presence of nutrients, moisture, light, and heat. Biological organisms require moisture to start and progress.

Biological agents may also play a role in mechanical weathering, either by binding surface materials together or pulling them apart, primarily through root action.

(a)   (b)   (c)

Figure 8.13: Various types of biological growth on materials: (a) lichen on rocks, (b) moss on a stone wall, and (c) algae on a stone pedestal.

Lifecycle

Leaves Changing Color The leaves of most broadleaf, or deciduous, trees change color in autumn (Figure 8.14). Pigments present in leaves determine a leaf's color and play an important role in the autumn coloration process. During the growing season, leaves are green because of the formation of chlorophyll. Yellow and orange pigments, called carotenoids, are also present but are masked by the larger concentrations of green pigments. During autumn, chlorophyll degrades, thereby unmasking the carotenoids. Red and purple colors are due to anthocyanins, a group of pigments that develop in the sap of some species. Leaf coloration is due to a complicated series of interactions involving such factors as pigments, sunlight, moisture, chemicals, and genetic traits.

(a)   (b)

(c)   (d)   (e)

Figure 8.14: Autumn leaf coloration. *Source*: Photographs (c) through (e) by Michael Marsland, © 2007 Yale University.

Skin Aging/Wrinkling/Spots An outstanding example of lifecycle change in appearance is the aging of human skin (Figure 8.15). Changes in the appearance of skin are due primarily to the aging of the connective tissue of the *subcutis*—deep part of the dermis. Notably, younger skin displays a denser and more complex arrangement of underlying fibers, which, as aging progresses, lose their density and regular alignment. The aging process is affected by many factors, including exposure to sunlight, environmental toxins, and harsh soaps, in addition to diet and genetics. Effects include wrinkles (Figure 8.16), freckles, and spots. The aging of skin is of particular interest to the cosmetics industry.

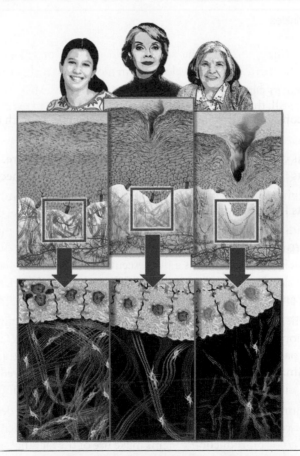

Figure 8.15: A schematic cross-section through the layers of skin for three individuals of increasing age. *Source*: © 2007 Cognis Gmbh (from *Skin Care Forum* 39—*scf-online.com*).

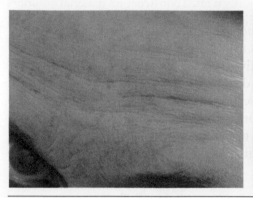

Figure 8.16: Wrinkles.

8.1.4 COMBINED PROCESSES

Processes often combine to produce complex weathering effects, such as the following:

- Flow deposits chemicals that react and cause mechanical fracture.
- Flow deposits fluid in porous material that freezes and causes mechanical fracture.
- Flow deposits fluid that promotes biological growth.

Representative effects are shown in Figure 8.17.

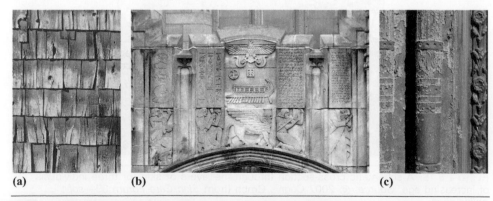

(a)　　　　　　　　　(b)　　　　　　　　　(c)

Figure 8.17: Examples of weathering processes in combination.

8.2 SIMULATION OF WEATHERING EFFECTS

One way to generate appearance variations over time is through simulation. A wide variety of different simulation techniques have been developed, which we discuss in the sections that follow. We classify by the type of process in the context of the weathering taxonomy presented in the previous section.

Table 8.1 summarizes weathering effects for which simulation models have been proposed, along with information on model parameters, performance, and validation. To date, only a small subset of weathering effects has been modeled. Most existing simulation methods are limited to a single effect, such as peeling or rusting, whereas in the real world, effects develop in complex combinations. Clearly, much work remains to be done in broadening the range of effects that can be generated and the scale at which they can be applied.

8.2.1 PATINATION

Metals often develop a patina over time. The patination process involves atmospheric corrosion, or the chemical alteration of a surface resulting in changes in color. This process forms a system of thin surface layers. Dorsey and Hanrahan [75] and Chang and Shih [44] describe approaches for simulating patinas on metallic materials. Patination is affected by the exposure of a surface to the environment. To model this interaction, or tendency of a surface to weather, both techniques precompute an accessibility map, which is then used to modulate the spatial development of the patina.

Dorsey and Hanrahan [75] represent a surface as a set of thin, homogeneous layers (Figure 8.18). Patinas are developed by applying a series of procedural operators, such

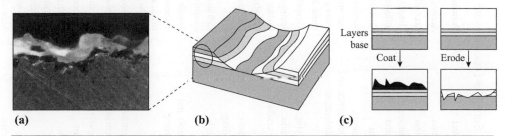

(a)   **(b)**   **(c)**

Figure 8.18: Metallic patinas—a surface patina as a stack of layers. (a) Micrograph of a copper surface showing the layers, (b) abstraction of the layered structure, and (c) the coat and erode operators. *Source*: From Dorsey and Hanrahan [75], © 1996 ACM. Included here by permission.

Table 8.1: Survey of previous work on synthesizing aging effects, including information on parameters, performance, and validation

Paper	Effect	Parameters[a]	Time	Data Size	Validation
[75]	Patina	Accessibility, surface inclination, orientation	n/a	n/a	Rendering only
[44]	Patina	Accessibility, gravity, curvature, moisture in soil	n/a	n/a	Rendering only
[227]	Rust and patina	"Imperfection factor," layer protection, object collision, aeration	n/a	n/a	Prediction of rate and spread of corrosion
[45]	Rust	Curvature, accessibility, orientation, current, salts	n/a	n/a	Rendering only
[74]	Erosion, efflorescence, and discoloration	Mineral concentration, solubility, decay index, exposure map, maximum saturation, permeability, water pressure, density, fluid velocity, porosity, stone density, viscosity	24 hr. 3 hr.	2.2M tri. 1.3M tri.	Rendering only
[208]	Drying	Accessibility, distance to wet/dry boundary	n/a	n/a	Ground-truth comparison
[149]	Cracks	Spring constant, mean and variable of maximum strain, surface layer depth, contraction ratio, material density, timescale	24 hr. 8 hr. 20 hr.	20480 tri. 1000 cu. 540 cu.	Rendering only
[150]	3D cracks				Density of cracks; speed of formation
[112]	Cracks	Resistance, stress	3 hr.	2017 tri.	Rendering only
[113]	Peeling	n/a	11 min.	1.8M cells	Rendering only
[5]	Cracks	Cell size, spring constant, maximum strain, moisture, content, diffusion constant	8 hr. 1 hr.	8000 cu. 700 cu.	Temporal development of cracks
[258]	Cracks and peeling	Tensile stress, break strength, crack strength, deformation, elastic relaxation distance, shearing stress, adhesion strength, crack width, adhesion width	78 min. 23 min. 6 min.	400K poly. 150K poly. 130K poly.	Visual quality
[226]	Scratches	Surface type	n/a	n/a	Scratch appearance
[35]	Scratches	Material hardness, tool shape, orientation, force	n/a	500 scratches	Scratch appearance
[259]	Impacts	Tool shape, hit path	2 hr.[b]	n/a	Impact size and density
[151]	Dust	Surface slope, stickiness, exposure, dust source	n/a	n/a	Rendering only
[76]	Flow	Material roughness, rate, capacity of absorption; deposits adhesion rate, solubility rate; water particle mass, position, velocity, soluble materials; rain, sunlight	3 hr.	450 poly.	Rendering only
[69]	Lichen	Accessibility, light, moisture (from simulation)	n/a	n/a	Rendering only
[340]	General	Sources; surface exposure, accessibility, curvature	n/a	n/a	Rendering only

[a]For more information about the model parameters, please refer to the original publications.
[b]Time spent on user interaction, not on simulation or rendering. *Source*: From Lu et al. [210], © 2007 ACM. Included here by permission.

as "erode," "coat," and "polish," to the layered structure. By sequencing these operators, a wide variety of effects can be generated. Surface growth models enhance the layers by adding the variations and richness of detail present in the real aging process. To model the reflectance and transmission of light through the layered surface, they use the Kubelka–Munk model, which is discussed in Section 5.7.2.

Figure 8.19 shows the development of a patina on a small statue of a buddha. The various stages of the development of the patina are modeled with a three-layered surface: base copper, a layer of tarnish, and a layer of patina. Parameters related to the thickness of the layers as a function of time are shown in Figure 8.20

Chang and Shih [44] focus in particular on modeling the patination process on objects buried underground, such as Chinese bronzes, which have been buried for thousands of years. Beginning with a set of random surface points, they use an L-system to simulate the patination process taking the environment map and local geometry into account. They use a two-layer model: a tarnish layer that adheres to the surface and an upper layer that contains the green patina. A solid texture surrounding the object is used to simulate the role of soil in the corrosion process.

Figure 8.19: A sequence of images showing the aging of a statuette. *Source*: From Dorsey and Hanrahan [75], © 1996 ACM. Included here by permission.

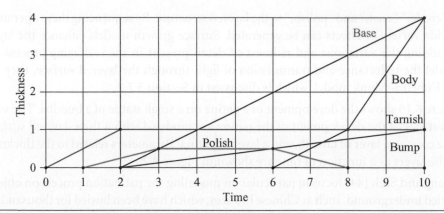

Figure 8.20: Time chart, showing the development of patina on the buddha statue shown in Figure 8.19. *Source*: From Dorsey and Hanrahan [75], © 1996 ACM. Included here by permission.

Rust

Patination, an instance of the more general process of corrosion, generally involves visible changes only to the color and reflectance of a material. Corrosion, more generally, can lead to additional changes (loss of material), particulaly holes, that involve the geometry of objects. Merillou et al. [227] introduced a model for the simulation and rendering of corrosion on metals. Specifically, the corrosion process is simulated on a thick plate or corrosion map, which is in turn applied to an object. The user indicates a set of starting points to initiate the corrosion process. They account for real-world time and different atmospheric conditions using experimental data. The evolution of corrosion over time can then be specified (Figure 8.21).

Chang and Shih [45] extended their L-system-based patination simulation approach to generate rust on metals in seawater. Here, a four-layer model accommodates pits, cracks, and blisters. An enhanced environment model, which includes the effects of seawater, is used to simulate the interaction between water and metallic surfaces.

8.2.2 IMPACTS

A common form of aging is the deformation of an object caused by repetitive impacts over long time periods, such as due to walking or the dropping of an object. Changes due to compaction often involve only a narrow region close to the surface, adding small depressions. Paquette et al. [259] developed an approach to consider such surface-level impacts (Figure 8.22).

In this approach, dynamic objects, or tools, are used to hit static objects. Each impact corresponds to a simulation step in which the system computes the surface deformation caused by the user-controlled tool.

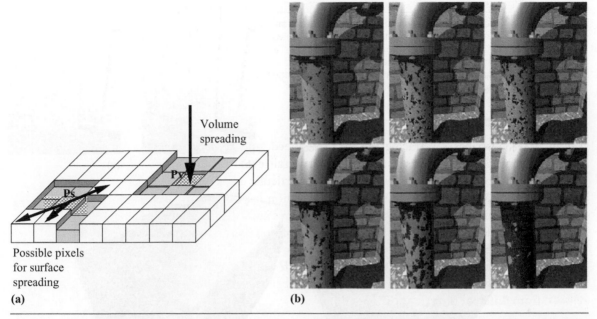

Figure 8.21: Rust: (a) different spreading cases and (b) pitting corrosion (*top*) compared to uniform corrosion (*bottom*). *Source*: From Merrillou et al. [227], © 2001 S. Merrillou, J.-M. Dischler and D. Ghazanfarpour.

The approach employs an empirical simulation to modify an object so that its surface reflects the many small depressions caused by individual impacts. To begin, the user initiates the simulation by selecting a tool, and setting its properties from user-specified values or statistical distributions. The tool is intersected with the object surface to find the area that will be potentially modified. The object surface, expressed as a mesh, is adaptively refined in regions where it is hit by important tool features. The refinement proceeds until the impact effect can be represented on the mesh. The object surface is updated by modifying the affected mesh geometry. This is done by moving the mesh vertices. This process is repeated for each impact. The mesh is then adaptively tesselated such that it can represent the impact compaction. The surface geometry is updated to reflect the effect of the impact.

8.2.3 SCRATCHES

Scratching is a common form of weathering. Scratches result from deliberate machining, such as etching or brushing, or through everyday use. Merillou et al. [226] and Bosch et al. [35] have proposed models for simulating surface scratches. They distinguish between microscratches and individually visible scratches. The former are not perceptibly visible as individual marks but instead have a homogeneous appearance. They are usually modeled with anisotropic BRDF models. Isolated scratches are

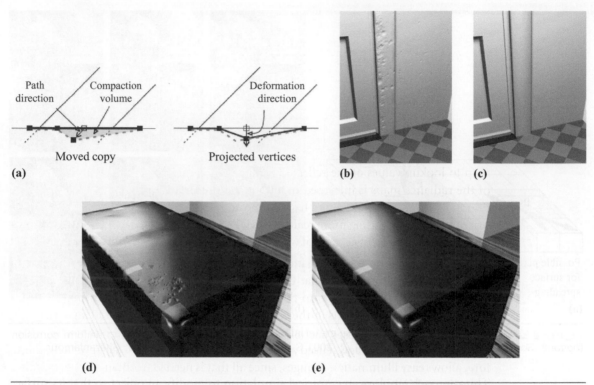

Figure 8.22: Examples of impacts: (a) adaptively refining a mesh to reflect an impacted region, (b) a synthetic door frame with aging, (c) a synthetic door frame without aging, (d) a synthetic trunk with aging, and (e) a synthetic trunk without aging. *Source*: From Paquette et al. [259], © 2001 E. Paquette, P. Poulin, and G. Drettakis.

generally described by a texture, to represent the scratch's path or extent, and a geometric cross section.

To generate scratches on synthetic shapes, Merillou et al. [226] measured real surfaces to acquire geometric models of scratches. Bosch et al. [35] simulate the formation process of scratches, using a tool, penetration forces, and material properties of an object (Figures 8.23 and 8.24).

8.2.4 CRACKING AND PEELING

Surface Cracking

A variety of methods have been developed for simulating surface crack patterns. Hirota et al. use a mass-spring model to model surface [149] and volumetric cracks [150]. Gobron and Chiba generate surface cracking of layered materials and peeling of surfaces using cellular automata [112, 113]. Iben and O'Brien [153] introduced a model for

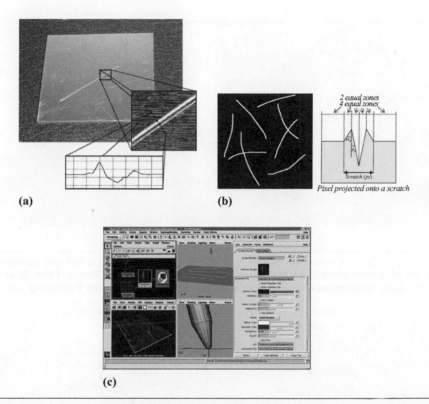

Figure 8.23: (a) Real scratched aluminium plate with a close-up view of the micro-geometry of the scratch; (b) scratches are defined by their paths (defined by a texture) and the geometry of their cross sections; and (c) simulating scratches with a Maya plug-in. *Source*: From Bosch et al. [35], image © 2004; used courtesy of The Eurographics Association and Blackwell Publishing, Inc.

generating surface crack patterns that closely resemble the look of those found in real materials such as mud, paint, and ceramic glazes. The model works by defining a stress field over a triangle mesh and evolving the field over time with the crack-generation process. Cracks are introduced as free boundaries that affect the relaxation process and stress field (Figure 8.25). A useful aspect of the model is the incorporation of user control: the appearance of the cracks can be varied by means of a small set of parameters. As cracks form and evolve, the stress field is updated; the process repeats until cracks can no longer be added, or the user achieves a desired result. Representative results are shown in Figure 8.26.

Paint Cracking and Peeling

Paquette et al. [258] introduced a model for cracking and peeling. Previous approaches deal with either the propagation of cracks, without considering multilayered

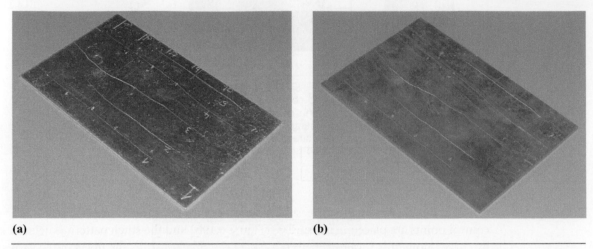

(a)   (b)

Figure 8.24: Scratch result: (a) real aluminium plate scratched with a nail and applying different forces along the paths of scratches; and (b) the corresponding synthetic image. *Source*: From Bosch et al. [35]; image © 2004, used courtesy of The Eurographics Association and Blackwell Publishing, Inc.

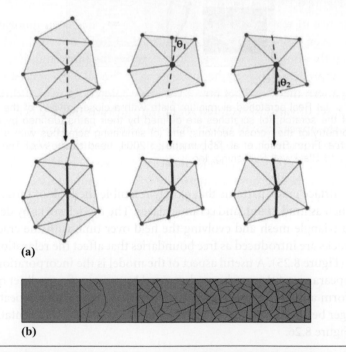

(a)

(b)

Figure 8.25: Cracking simulations: (a) simulating surface crack patterns; (b) an animation of mud drying. *Source*: From Iben and O'Brien [153]. Image © Eurographics Association 2006. Reproduced by kind permission of The Eurographics Association.

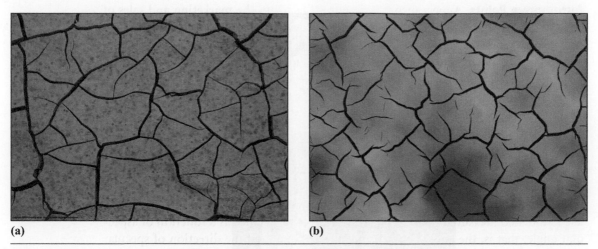

(a)   (b)

Figure 8.26: Two renderings of dried mud. *Source*: From Iben and O'Brien [153]. Images © Eurographics Association 2006. Reproduced by kind permission of The Eurographics Association.

phenomena and peeling, [112, 149], or tools to control the location of detached paint areas, without treating the crack formation process; [340].

The simulation model operates on a planar surface, which is defined by two layers: a base layer and a paint layer. A two-dimensional (2D) grid provides access to local surface properties, which can be represented procedurally, as a constant, or as a texture. Cracks form on the surface, based on the simulation of tensile stress in the paint layer. When the tensile stress is too high, compared to the paint strength, a crack can appear and expand on the paint layer. In addition to crack propagation, peeling and curling paint occur based on the adhesion between layers. As the paint shrinks, cracks reduce the tensile stress in the paint layer, which results in an increase in shearing stress and can cause adhesion to the base layer to be lost. Thereafter, the paint is free to peel away from the base layer.

8.2.5 FLOW AND DEPOSITION

To simulate the flow of water and deposition processes on materials, Dorsey et al. [76] developed a simple particle model of water flow. Each particle represents a drop of water. The motion of each particle is controlled by factors, such as gravity, friction, wind, roughness, and constraints, that keep the particles in contact with the surface (Figure 8.27). A set of equations governs the chemical interaction of the water and the surface materials. The equations describe the rate at which the surface absorbs water and the rate of solubility and sedimentation of deposits on the surface. Figure 8.28

Figure 8.27: Simulated flow. *Source*: From Dorsey et al. [76], © 1996 ACM. Included here by permission.

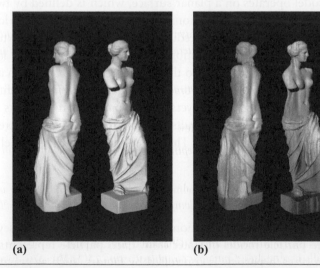

(a)   (b)

Figure 8.28: Washing and staining patterns due to simulated flows: (a) rendering without flows; and (b) rendering with flows. *Source*: From Dorsey et al. [76], © 1996 ACM. Included here by permission.

shows the result of applying the model to a digital version of the classic Venus de Milo statue.

A geometric model has a collection of texture maps attached to it that are used to represent a variety of parameters. For example, a *saturation map* stores the amount of water absorbed by the surface. In addition to water, the system also models other materials. Each patch represents a surface of a solid object made from a base material that is coated with a mixture of loose deposits. The concentration of each loose deposit is stored in a texture map attached to the surface. Each type of material has an associated set of rendering properties (e.g., diffuse and specular colors, shininess, and roughness).

8.2.6 DUST ACCUMULATION

Dust accumulation is a common process that affects appearance. Blinn [27] modeled the appearance of dusty surfaces, given the thickness of the dust layer. More recently, Hsu and Wong [151] introduced an empirical method for simulating dust accumulation on object surfaces, which takes into account surface texture, inclination, and exposure. Determining the amount of dust accumulation occurs in two parts.

First, the *normal dust amount function* is computed based on a surface's inclination and stickiness properties. Second, external factors that affect the amount of dust, including surface exposure and the removal of dust by other objects, as well as the contribution from multiple dust sources, are used to modulate the accumulation. The dust accumulation pattern is then stored as a texture map and applied during rendering.

8.2.7 WEATHERING SYSTEMS

Work has also been done on the integration of several weathering processes into individual, consistent aging systems.

Geometry-Dependent Imperfection Modeling Framework

Wong et al. [340] described a framework for applying imperfections to surfaces by first computing a geometry-dependent tendency distribution and then applying patterns generated from abstract sources. While this approach yields a range of interesting effects, it cannot handle changes due to complex environment-surface interactions, because it does not contain realistic weathering sources.

Stone Weathering

Dorsey et al. [74] introduced a system for simulating the chemical weathering of stone, which can be used to model erosion and other effects that involve changes to the shape and appearance properties of an object (Figure 8.29).

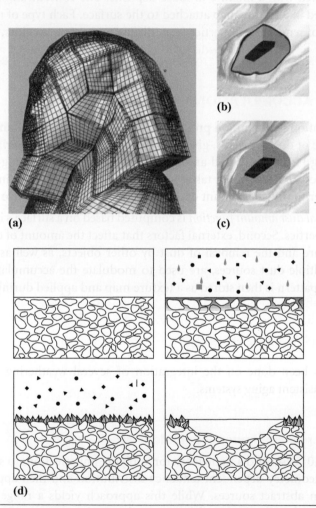

Figure 8.29: Stone weathering. Slab data structure: (a) slabs on a scanned mesh; (b) water diffused into the surface; (c) iron distributed in grains of mica; and (d) overview of the simulation model. *Source*: From Dorsey et al. [74] , © 1999 ACM. Included here by permission.

Figure 8.30: Before (a) and after (b) results. *Source*: From Dorsey et al. [74], © 1999 ACM. Included here by permission.

Stone objects are represented with a *slab* data structure, a surface-aligned volumetric grid, which is confined to a narrow band around the object. The thickness of this band can be varied according to the extent of the simulation: A narrow band is used for relatively minor indentations, while a thicker band is used for deeper cuts.

The weathering model includes the simulation of the flow of moisture and the transport, dissolution, and recrystallization of minerals near the surface. In addition, the simulation model controls the amount of surface erosion. To render the optical effects of translucency and coloration of stone, due to light interacting with the surface and subsurface, a general Monte ray tracer was employed. Figure 8.30 shows the results of simulations on a white marble statue.

Procedural Application of Simulation

Cutler et al. [60] describe a procedural approach to creating layered, solid models of weathered materials (Figure 8.31). By means of a scripting language, the internal structure of a volume is generated from one or more input meshes. A key insight is that the internal structure of an object can be inferred from a representation of its primary interface. In this framework, models are represented with tetrahedral meshes; however, the basic framework is independent of a specific geometric representation and could, therefore, support other geometric representations.

```
DIRT {
  model = GARGOYLE
  color = { 0.5 0.5 0.5 } }
WASH {
  model = GARGOYLE
  num_particles = 200000
  particle_life = 1.0 }
HAMMER {
  model = GARGOYLE
  position = { -0.78 1.22 0.77 }
  orientation = { -0.23 -0.47 0.85 } }
HAMMER {
  model = GARGOYLE
  position = { -2.53 1.03 1.06 }
  orientation = { 0.56 -0.19 -0.80 } }
ERODE {
  model = GARGOYLE
  num_particles = 2000 }
LICHEN {
  model = GARGOYLE
  num_particles = 40000 }
```

(a)

(b)

Figure 8.31: Procedural solid models; (a) Script describing the gargoyle's weathering over time; (b) sequence of images showing the application of the script via a series of simulations and interactive operations. *Source*: From Cutler et al. [60], © 2002 ACM. Included here by permission.

To modify the model, sculpting or simulation operators are applied within the context of the scripting language. The novelty of this approach lies in the use of simulation as a means of controlling the shape and appearance of an object. In addition, the system allows a variety of simulation and sculpting operators to be combined in a common framework.

8.3 REPLICATION OF AGED APPEARANCE

An alternative to simulation is to instead replicate the effects of various physical processes.

8.3.1 MANUAL APPLICATION

The most commonly used technique for applying aging effects to models is direct, highly interactive, three-dimensional (3D) painting [136]. In 3D painting, an artist applies simulated paint onto a 3D shape. The paint's properties determine the material's appearance, and patterning is obtained by applying different strokes on different parts of the shape. Because the 3D painting metaphor is natural and intuitive to an artist, and because such systems give the user immediate feedback by instantly displaying changes, they are widely used in the entertainment industry.

Although this approach is very powerful, it has several limitations. First, the process is very time consuming and tedious. Second, as the use of computer-generated images becomes more widespread, a greater range of appearances must be simulated. Ad hoc techniques that work for specific objects and applications soon run up against their limits. The desire to go beyond these limits has spurred a new focus on appearance modeling in computer graphics.

8.3.2 ACCESSIBILITY SHADING/AMBIENT OCCLUSION

An alternative to altering the actual surface is to simply adjust the shading, so the surface looks as though it has been aged.

Accessibility

Miller [232] introduced a set of algorithms for accessibility shading. This type of shading yields visual effects that resemble tarnish on surfaces. Rather than modifying the surface, accessibility shading simply resembles the appearance of a surface that has been tarnished and then cleaned.

The notion of surface accessibility was introduced in molecular modeling, as chemical reactions often depend on what parts of one molecule are accessible to the surface of another. Miller [232] developed the idea of *tangent-sphere accessibility*, which, for a surface point, is defined as the radius of a sphere that may touch that point and not intersect any other part of the surface. By varying the sphere radius, the appearance of the surface may be modulated so that material such as dust or varnish accumulates in small, inaccessible regions such as cracks and crevices.

In modeling the local variations of surface materials, accessibility is useful for modeling processes such as dirtying, cleaning, aging, or polishing.

Ambient Occlusion

Accessibility gives a coarse approximation of how accessible a surface is, and fails in some cases, for example, in regions that are occluded by a tiny object or in crevices that are long, narrow, and partially occluded.

Zhukov et al. [301, 351] introduced the concept of *obscurances*, which is commonly known as *ambient occlusion* (Figure 8.32). The obscurance of a surface point is a measure of the empty space above the surface point, taking into account only the geometry

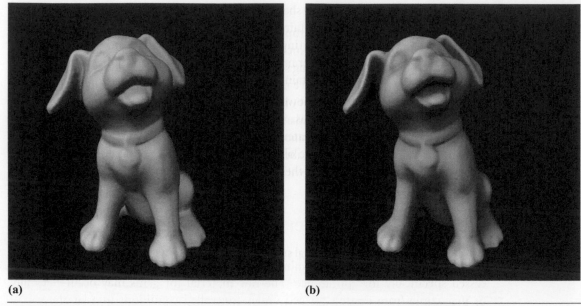

(a)   **(b)**

Figure 8.32: Rendering without ambient occlusion (a), and rendering with ambient occlusion (b).

with a certain distance of the surface point (i.e., the fraction of the surrounding hemi-sphere that is occluded by other parts of the surface). Because the calculation of ambient occlusion involves sampling in directions outward from the surface point to estimate the amount of unoccluded surface, it overcomes the problems of accessibility shading.

Often, accessibility and ambient occlusion are computed for surface points and stored in a texture map for use during simulation or rendering.

8.4 CAPTURE, ANALYSIS, AND TRANSFER OF EFFECTS

Simulating the processes that cause changes in material appearance over time is extremely time consuming or, in some cases, impossible, because some processes are not understood from first principles. Moreover, each simulation technique is generally applicable to only a single type of process or material.

8.4.1 CONTEXT-AWARE TEXTURES

As an alternative to developing a single algorithm applicable to a single phenomenon, Lu et al. [106, 208, 209] have recently introduced an approach that involves *capturing*

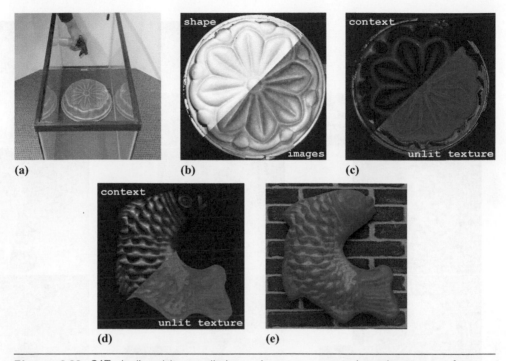

Figure 8.33: CAT pipeline: (a) controlled experiments to capture how the texture of an object changes as the result of external agents; (b) captured shape and texture history under controlled illumination; (c) calculated unlit textures related to the context parameters; and (d) and (e) transfered texture history onto a new object. *Source*: From Lu et al. [209], © 2007 ACM. Included here by permission.

and *transferring* time-varying changes in material appearance. Through a series of controlled experiments, they capture material variations on real objects as a function of key parameters that affect appearance. By using captured data and parameters, they are able to generate images of synthetic objects that change in a manner similar to the observed, or captured, objects, but with spatially varying time variations that are unique to the synthetic objects. Figure 8.33 gives an overview of the capture-and-transfer pipeline.

Figure 8.34 shows an example of patination that is captured and transferred to two different complex geometries.

In other related work, Koudelka [180] considered time-varying textures limited to static lighting with a fixed view and introduced time-varying texture synthesis. Gu et al. [126] extended this framework to include images with varying lighting conditions and multiple views, which enables the synthesis of appearance with arbitrary lighting and viewing.

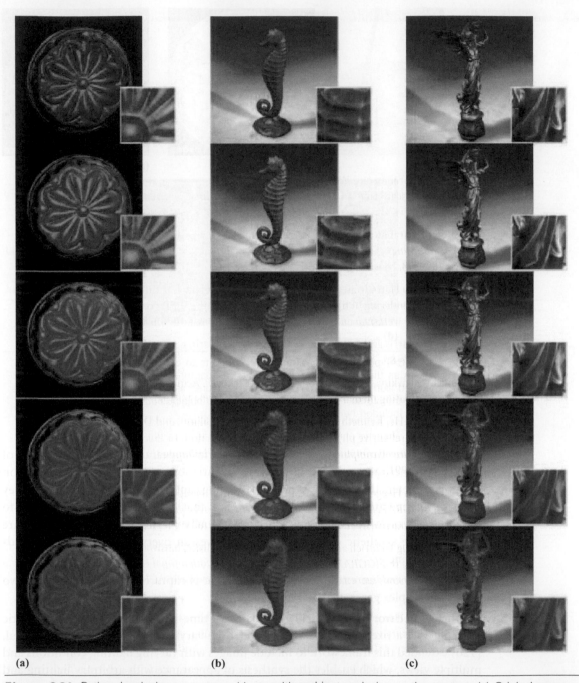

(a)   (b)   (c)

Figure 8.34: Patina developing on copper objects with ambient occlusion as the context. (a) Original appearance history from a copper kitchen mold; (b) patina transferred to a seahorse; and (c) patina transferred to a fairy. *Source*: From Lu et al. [209], © 2007 ACM. Included here by permission.

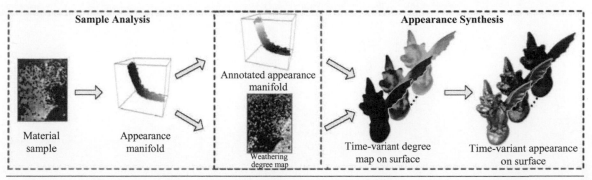

Figure 8.35: Overview of the appearance manifold technique. *Source*: From Wang [324], © 2006 ACM. Included here by permission.

8.4.2 APPEARANCE MANIFOLDS

Wang et al. [324] introduced an alternative approach for modeling time-varying surface appearance based on data captured, not as a time series, but instead at a single instant in time. This approach builds on the observation that the spatial variations in the weathered appearance of an object at a given time include varying degrees of weathering. These appearance variations form the basis of an *appearance manifold* that approximates an underlying subspace of weathered surface point appearances for a material. By arranging these appearance variations in a way that reveals their relative order with respect to weathering degree, this method infers spatial and temporal appearance properties of the material's weathering processes that can be used to convincingly generate its weathered appearance at different points in time. Figure 8.35 provides an overview of this approach.

9 SPECIFYING AND ENCODING APPEARANCE DESCRIPTIONS

Given the extreme diversity of appearance models and materials, it is not surprising that material and appearance specification remains one of the most difficult tasks in numerical modeling. In this chapter, we review the various approaches to such specification, and discuss how material properties can be represented in the computer for efficient processing and rendering.

9.1 PRACTICAL TECHNIQUES FOR APPEARANCE SPECIFICATION

Most of the general and specialized models from Chapters 5 and 6 control appearance using a set of parameters—some may be linked to the actual physical properties of the underlying material (e.g., index of refraction, surface roughness), some are geometric (e.g., direction of anisotropy), while others are purely numerical and rather arbitrary (e.g., the Phong exponent for specular highlights). Therefore, the specification of a homogeneous material can be thought of as defining a vector of parameters. Most three-dimensional (3D) modeling packages, such as Maya/3dsMax/Lightwave, offer a graphical interface with sliders to set all numerical parameters, usually with some sort of visual feedback; that is, a simple shape is rendered using the currently specified material under simple lighting.

Such direct parameter specification has a number of drawbacks. First, parameters are generally not intuitive in terms of their effect on appearance. In this respect, both physically-based and numerical parameters are often totally arbitrary for computer graphic (CG) artists and designers. This results in the massive usage of trial-and-error strategies to arrive at a desired effect. In addition, these parameters can have very nonuniform value ranges: A typical example is the Phong highlight exponent, for which a variation from 5 to 10 has a dramatic effect, whereas a variation from 100 to 105 is hardly noticeable.

Another difficulty comes with the spatial variations of appearance. Most objects are not carved in a homogeneous block of matter, and exhibit patterns and aspect variations. The common answer to this issue in modeling software is to use texture maps for spatially varying parameters. While this solution works in practice, it also has several problems: First, it creates difficulty by requiring an underlying parameterization of all surfaces; second, it is not intuitive for designers to create textures (that is, two-dimensional (2D) parameter maps) that suffer from distortion when mapped onto a 3D object. Furthermore, manipulating and consistently editing multiple texture maps to represent all relevant parameters is a tedious task.

We review the most common approaches to the specification of complex appearance characteristics next. A first group of techniques relies on interactive tools and visual inspection by users, while others use the power of composition and programmability to define shaders and assemble complex appearance behavior from simple building blocks.

9.1.1 VISUAL INTERFACES FOR ANALYTIC MODELS

The question of selecting the adequate parameters of a given appearance model, in order to achieve a desired look, remains a major difficulty for CG artists and designers. Users typically form a mental image of the appearance they want to obtain, and find it extremely difficult to infer the parameters that will let them achieve it. Furthermore, it may be the case that a desired look simply cannot be obtained using a particular reflectance model, and that another model should be chosen.

Recent advances for parameter selection include the introduction of visual interfaces for analytic models. In these systems, users work with images, presenting the appearance of a shape for a given set of parameters, and can alter an image or indicate what should be changed. The system then automatically computes the associated parameter changes. This technique is not yet integrated in mainstream modeling packages but is likely to gain acceptance since it frees users from the very difficult mapping from parameter space to "how things look," effectively using the computer processing power to invert the process.

The BRDF-Shop system [54], for instance, is based on the assumption that artists understand materials mainly through highlights. The system lets users "paint" highlights created by a simple light source on a sphere, with control over their size, strength, anisotropy, and orientation. This simple set of operations actually goes a long way toward visually controlling intuitive notions such as gloss and gloss contrast [263]. The BRDF-Shop system automatically provides a full, physically correct bidirectional reflectance distribution function (BRDF) corresponding to the chosen highlights, and displays a complex shape illuminated by natural lighting for better visual inspection (see Figure 9.1).

Pushing the assistance of a computer even further, it is possible to automatically compute possible variations on a given BRDF, and free users from actively defining their desired visual appearance. Instead, the modification of a BRDF is achieved by selecting from a small set of possibilities. Ngan et al. [250] present a navigation system based on this idea, inspired by the Variations interface of Photoshop where different instances of an image are proposed based on changing color balance, contrast, or brightness. The system relies on the finding that users can judge a BRDF using a single image of an object under natural lighting (a fact also used in the complex object visualization of the BRDF-Shop system) [96].

First, this observation justifies the use of a picture showing a simple object under natural illumination to judge a proposed BRDF. Second, it leads to the definition of an image-based difference metric that is more or less perceptually uniform. This allows the computation of several images of an object, each created by varying a single

(a)   (b)

Figure 9.1: BRDF definition in the BRDFshop system. In each example the user works on the sphere model and models the desired highlights. A valid BRDF is automatically constructed (a) and its appearance on a 3D model under complex illumination is shown in (b). *Source*: From Colbert et al. [54], © 2006 IEEE. Included by permission.

parameter of the underlying model, that are all about the same perceptual distance from the original. Users then simply choose one of the variations and continue their navigation. This system is extremely easy to use since a single parameter—controlling the "distance" of the proposed variations—is specified by the user. In a typical session, a user would start with a large distance value to quickly browse through possible appearances, and gradually reduce the distance to fine-tune the BRDF.

Another related approach consists in transforming a candidate BRDF by adding or removing relevant "traits," or features, such as glossiness, diffuseness, or metallic-like appearance. Traits do not correspond to parameters of a computational model but rather to more intuitive properties of materials, which are then automatically mapped to parameters. This approach was demonstrated by Matusik et al. [219], where a large number of measured BRDFs are arranged in a low-dimensional space (see Section 9.2.3). A given BRDF can then be moved in this reduced space along appropriate "trait directions," and the modified point is then transformed back into a meaningful, physically valid BRDF. This technique is perhaps less "visual" in that it does not necessarily involve direct visualization by users in order to drive BRDF selection, but relies on visually meaningful traits to determine the possible modifications to the BRDF.

9.1.2 3D PAINTING

Let us now consider the issue of specifying the variations of aspect across the surface (or volume) of an object. As mentioned above, most objects and materials are not homogeneous, and exhibit spatial variations of some sort. Most modeling and rendering systems capture these variations using a number of texture maps to encode the varying parameters. Given the already user-intensive process of selecting adequate reflectance properties (as discussed in the previous section), it appears that efficient tools are needed to assist a user in the specification of these parameter textures.

Following the general improvement in human-computer interfaces in recent years, innovative material specification techniques have appeared based on the *direct manipulation* metaphor, as well as instant visual feedback. As noted in Chapter 8, these techniques extend the "painting" tools common in image processing software to operate directly on 3D shapes [136].

Painting tools have become quite common and most graphically-oriented users have some knowledge of the basic painting notions, such as the use of a brush of varying size, or the ability to apply layers of semi-transparent paint to blend between colors, etc. These tools are commonly used to create the texture maps associated with spatial

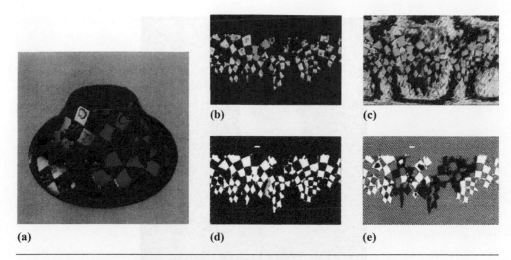

Figure 9.2: Example object (a) after painting, and associated texture maps: diffuse color (b), specular color (c), roughness (d), and displacement (e). *Source*: From Hanrahan and Haeberli [136], © 1990 ACM. Included here by permission.

variations of appearance. The idea of 3D painting is to free users from having to build a mental image of the underlying parametrization of an object, by operating on the 3D shape itself. In essence, a 3D painting system creates all the required 2D textures, representing the spatial variations of all the relevant appearance parameters based on the user's manipulations, see Figure 9.2.

Direct painting on a shape offers a series of benefits:

- Although surfaces must be parameterized internally to the system, in order to map the textures, this parameterization is never apparent to the user. Typical issues such as texture deformation (local compression, expansion, or shearing), or seams between patches with independent parameterizations, are automatically handled by the system.
- A variety of painting operations are available and can be devised to correspond to a user's intuitive or usual ways of thinking. For instance, different brush types can be defined to (a) assign a given material (changing all relevant parameters in a single operation); (b) modify a material (for instance, achieving a wet look by simultaneously reducing the diffuse reflection, making its color more saturated, and increasing the specular reflectance); or (c) selectively modify a single parameter (say a roughness value).
- The painting effect can also modify geometrical attributes, such as normal maps or displacement maps.

Lady Bird
by Peter Fendrik

Figure 9.3: Surface geometric detail (displacement and normal) painted on a surface using BodyPaint 3D from MAXON Computer GmbH. Included by permission.

- Common painting tools, such as airbrushing, controlling blending modes, and using layers, can be adapted to material specification, and let a user perform subtle mixtures and effects.
- Different effects can be obtained by changing the brush operation from image-space (similar to spray-painting) to object-space or tangent-space (similar to touching the surface of the object with a brush).

3D painting has become the method of choice for the specification of spatially variant appearance characteristics, and specialized products are now available as plug-ins for mainstream modeling packages (for instance, DeepPaint [274], BodyPaint [221], or Zbrush [265]); see Figure 9.3.

9.1.3 TEXTUAL AND PROGRAMMING INTERFACES

The simplest mechanism for specifying a set of appearance parameters for digital processing is, at least from a computer's point of view, by means of a computer file. At the opposite end of the spectrum from interactive, direct-manipulation approaches, manually editing a catalog of parameter values is an effective, if tedious, way to control appearance. The Radiance lighting simulation system, which became a reference tool in professional lighting engineering in the 1990s, used this technique for handling material and light descriptions [187] (see Figure 9.4).

Radiance material files use a fixed syntax modeled after the BRDF and lighting models used internally by the simulation program, and all parameter values are explicitly indicated. However, this system is not entirely monolithic since it also uses a simple form of programmability: Procedures (external programs) can be invoked to generate data such as patterns. The radiance system, therefore, offers a computer-oriented view of appearance specification, with a set of possible operations (programs) invoked using manually specified parameters.

A slightly more general approach was introduced by Cook [55] in the form of "shade trees," which are an algorithmic encoding of the shading formula for a given material. While the overall architecture (and data flow) of the shading calculation is restricted to be in the form of a tree (traversed and evaluated in postorder), the ability to specify each stage of a calculation as a separate, self-contained operation, as well as the separation of shading trees (describing a material) and "light trees" (describing the light sources), were significant advances on the path to greater specification freedom as well as reusability. In addition, the mixture of the two formerly separated stages of parameter calculation and model evaluation into a single "formula" opened the way to new possibilities such as displacement mapping.

```
void plastic gargoyle_lambert
0
0
5 .8 .5 .2 0.0 0.0


void metal gargoyle_metal
0
0
5 .8 .5 .2 1.0 0.0
```

The keywords plastic and metal specify the color of the specular highlights (white for plastic, same as diffuse component for metal). The tokens gargoyle_metal and gargoyle_lambert allow the definitions to be applied by name to any geometric model. Five parameters are needed for the specification: RGB reflectance (.8 .5 .2), a value for fraction specular reflection (0 or 1 here), and the surface roughness (0 indicating both are smooth). The void modifier and additional zeros allow the application of other types of descriptions.

Figure 9.4: Specification of the parameters of the Ward reflectance model that defined the materials *ideal diffuse* and *isotropic* applied to the gargoyle in Figures 5.17 and 5.18.

This trend was continually pushed in the last two decades, with the introduction of full-featured shading languages offering elaborate constructs (looping, conditionals, etc.). Such languages, of which the most famous is Renderman [318], offer a flexible means to describe the appearance of an object as a combination of shape, lighting, and material properties. This combination is described in a shading procedure, or "shader," invoked by the rendering system to compute the appearance properties of a given point on a shape [138]. Note that this generalizes the notion of procedural textures or procedural modeling tools such as the ones in the Radiance system [86, 187]. Shaders have been developed for a myriad of situations, including specific materials or objects [229, 200], and can be incorporated in most rendering packages.

The development of programmable graphics hardware in the 2000s has further justified the model of individual shading procedures for each material of an object. Most shading languages are sufficiently general that they can be used with both batch and real-time renderers, however, the question of performance remains a potential limitation to the complexity of procedural shaders, especially for applications that should run on a variety of hardware configurations (e.g., consumer applications and games) [3]. One possible avenue for increased performance is useful in situations where the final rendering will be performed as an offline process, but interactive manipulation is required to fine-tune the appearance specification using the shader parameters. In this case, the shader can be "specialized," that is, automatically transformed into a set of very fast shaders, each allowing a simple manipulation [127]. Another approach, well suited to GPU architectures allowing fast texture lookups, consists in presampling the procedural shader into a texture. This simple strategy seems ideal for real-time applications, but requires large amounts of data for all but the simplest shaders. We shall discuss this option in more detail in Section 9.3.2.

9.1.4 COMPOSITION FROM BASIC BUILDING BLOCKS

Shaders have offered a tremendous flexibility in the representation of appearance, however, their development is by nature performed by *programmers*, rather than end users. Achieving a balance between generality (or expressiveness) of a shader and easy control by the user is a particularly difficult task. In this respect, the notion of a shade tree, despite its limitations, had the advantage of presenting a fixed and easy-to-understand view of the calculations (in the form of a binary tree). The notion of visual programming can be similarly employed to assemble and connect simple shaders, thereby exposing the complexity of the overall shader in an easily understandable manner [1, 115].

In this visual programming approach, simple building blocks are represented with handles that can either receive input or produce output of a certain type. The user

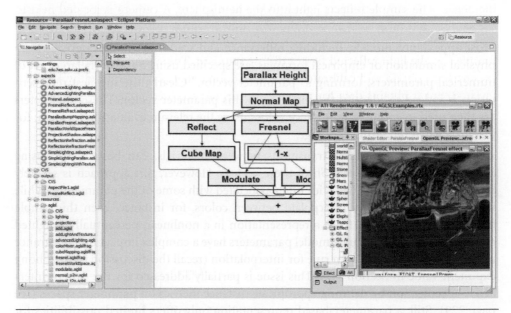

Figure 9.5: Specification of a shade tree using a graphical interface to connect simple components and shading operations. *Source*: From McGuire et al. [223], © 2006 ACM. Included here by permission.

constructs a complex behavior by appropriately linking inputs and outputs (see Figure 9.5). This idea is pushed even further in "abstract shade trees," where inputs and outputs are not strongly typed, and an advanced code generator produces the final shader procedure from the abstract diagram created by the designer [223].

9.2 ENCODING LOCAL APPEARANCE ATTRIBUTES

Let us now turn to the digital representations of appearance data that are created for computer processing. In some sense, the difficulties found in encoding this data are dual from those found in the specification of appearance, in particular, for what concerns the immense amounts of data that have to be manipulated. However, there are key differences, since user specification involves a human user whereas appearance encodings are created for the computer.

In this section, we deal with the representation of appearance data at a given point of an object. Most often the key point is the representation of the reflectance (and transmittance, or general scattering) characteristics, which is not necessarily tied to a precise point, but is defined for a given material.

9.2.1 PARAMETERIZED MODELS

Most appearance models, including reflectance and scattering models derived from physical simulation or empirical formulas, are specified using a (possibly large) set of numerical parameters, forming a "parameter vector." Clearly, the simplest representation is indeed to identify the model with this parameter vector. These parameters are then used to compute reflectance values using the relevant evaluation formula, for instance, when rendering an image.

Appearance variations, and transitions between materials, can be achieved using interpolation and extrapolation of these vectors. However, this approach is severely limited by the nonlinear behavior often associated with some of the parameters. While it is common to linearly interpolate between colors, for instance, even this simple operation would benefit from a representation in a nonlinear, perceptually weighted color space. Most reflectance model parameters have a complex impact on appearance and would require their own rule for interpolation (recall the discussion of the Phong exponent value in Section 9.1). This issue is partially addressed for the case of interactive specification by defining appropriate distance metrics on parameter spaces (see page 229). Still, a parameter-based representation only offers limited possibilities for interpolation. In addition, it is only applicable in the context of a given reflectance model; mixing the appearance behavior of different models cannot be done at this level when they are driven by different parameters.

9.2.2 TABULAR DATA

The direct use of measured or computed values to represent either reflectance or radiance data is probably the easiest possible encoding. Values for the function of interest are gathered for a number of situations (typically sampled directions, for incoming light or viewing situations, and possibly also sampled parameter values) and arranged in multidimensional tables. A reflectance or radiance value is then extracted using an interpolation scheme (ranging from the simplest nearest-neighbor value to more elaborate polynomial fittings on nearby data).

The advantage of this direct approach is that interpolation only occurs on similar data, making the mixture of different materials potentially easier, since light combination is linear in terms of radiance. Obviously, however, the volume of data is immense because of the large dimensionality of the tables (four dimensions for a general BRDF, without even changing any material parameters), and the need for fine sampling in direction space in order to capture important effects like specularities.

Compression techniques can somewhat reduce the storage needs, but the frequent access to BRDF values for arbitrary angular conditions make it necessary to have fast random-access decompression techniques. Some of the techniques developed for light field representations can be applied to four-dimensional BRDF data.

9.2.3 BASIS FUNCTIONS

Rather than directly manipulating the huge amounts of data produced by the measurement techniques from Chapter 7, or by sampling parameterized models, intermediate representations have been devised to allow both a faithful reproduction of the appearance characteristics of all materials and tractable or efficient processing.

A first approach consists in using a finite set of basis functions to represent appearance data (reflectance or radiance distributions). This essentially amounts to restricting the function of interest to a linear combination of predefined prototypes, which should therefore be carefully chosen. Decompositions of BRDF data into spherical harmonics, for instance [37, 290, 333], reduce the volume of data by making an assumption on the frequency content of the function to represent. A commonly used decomposition in computer graphics is Lafortune et al.'s combination of Ward lobes [185], which has the advantage of being very simple to compute at rendering time. However, it is not easy to transform a given model or measurement in this representation. More recent techniques use principal component analysis (PCA) to identify a small set of prototypical BRDFs that span the space of physically realizable BRDFs. Using nonlinear dimensionality reduction, Matusik et al. [219] showed that a large number of measured BRDFs can be well reproduced using as few as 15 basis functions. The resulting model encodes a BRDF with a 15-dimensional point in a reduced space, which can be back-projected to an actual BRDF for numerical calculations. As mentioned in Section 9.1.1, such a reduced space can be navigated by following particular directions associated with intuitive material features such as metallicness or glossiness.

In subsequent work, Ngan et al. [249] used Matusik's database, augmented with measures of anisotropic materials (velvet, satin, and brushed steel) wrapped on a cylinder, to examine the performance of standard BRDF models discussed in Chapter 5 (Ward, Blinn–Phong, Cook–Torrance, Lafortune, Ashikhmin Shirley, and He) in fitting experimental data. In each case, a single specular lobe, plus diffuse reflectance component form of the BRDF model, were used. The best performance for fitting isotropic BRDFs with low error were for the He, Cook–Torrance, and Ashikhmin–Shirley models. Signficantly, these models take into account Fresnel effects. In some cases, more than one specular lobe was needed to fit data, probably because of multiple roughness scales in the material. Consistently poorer fits were found with the Lafortune model. Ngan et al.[249] hypothesize that this is because of the dot product between the view and reflected angle to compute specular lobes, rather than the dot product between the half-angle and surface normal. None of the models performed well on the anisotropic data.

Another approach aims at providing an efficient computation technique for arbitrary BRDFs by expressing them as products of simpler functions that can be efficiently evaluated, represented, and sampled. These factorization techniques have the advantage that each factor typically depends on a single parameter of a model, making it both easy and efficient to interactively change parameters [144, 172, 222]. This approach has been extended to represent lighting functions in addition to BRDFs, allowing fast visualization of complex materials under arbitrary lighting [188].

9.3 ASSOCIATION OF MATERIAL AND SHAPE

Until now we have considered the specification of material properties at a given point of an object, primarily in the form of a BRDF. We now turn to the question of associating such specification to all locations at the surface of an object. Most objects are not composed of homogeneous materials—all natural materials, and most man-made ones, exhibit some variations in composition and aspect, at different scales. Even in the rare cases of homogeneous materials, manufacturing processes often create some structure or patterns, such as in a woven fabric. This *mesostructure* (i.e., structure at a scale that is intermediate between microscopic and macroscopic) would be extremely costly to model explicitly, yet accounts for many interesting appearance properties since it allows for some intricate lighting interactions on an object.

A first issue lies in the parameterization of a surface in order to precisely describe spatial variations of material properties. More generally, we also consider practical representations of space-variant material descriptions with their intrinsic complexity due to their high dimensionality.

9.3.1 DISCUSSION OF SURFACE PARAMETERIZATION

We have seen several cases where texture maps are used to describe the spatial variations of some appearance parameters. However, in general, texture mapping requires a surface parameterization, allowing the transformation between any surface point and the associated point in texture space. The two main exceptions, which do not require an explicit parameterization of the object surface, are procedural textures and solid textures. In both cases, the 3D location of a surface point is all that is required to compute the appearance properties [41]. This naturally makes them particularly suited to the description of objects carved from a solid piece of material, such as wood, stone, or marble. However, when surface appearance is mostly the result of surface processes (surface finish, weaving, coatings, etc.), one can rarely escape the need for a continuous parameterization of the object.

Surface parameterization is a difficult problem, since conflicting properties are often desired. Parameterizations should be continuous across a surface to avoid introducing seams and visual artifacts, they should preserve angles to avoid annoying visual deformations, they should preserve scale to avoid zooming effects, and so on. The best techniques in terms of compromise between user control and parameterization quality are based on texture atlases, or collections of local parameterizations [198, 199, 332]. Such atlases can be created semi-automatically (user intervention is generally needed to remove local inconsistencies) and fine-tuned for precise feature placement, such as positioning a surface defect or a particular piece of material exactly on the associated piece of geometry—think for instance of placing a color texture over a face and making sure the ears and lips fall exactly in place. Figure 7.16 showed an example of an automated parameterization generated in a data capture process.

When a surface parameterization is available, the spatial behavior of appearance properties can be modeled as a function of surface parameters using, for instance, texture mapping to modify BRDF parameters. In addition, more elaborate appearance models can be used. Recall from Chapter 7 the definition of the bidirectional texture function or BTF (Section 7.5). This six-dimensional function extends the BRDF to 2 spatial dimensions, and can be acquired using image-based techniques. A fairly intuitive view of a BTF is a series of images of a material sample, taken under varying illumination conditions (typically parallel illumination from a single direction), and viewed from a chosen observation direction (acquired images are rectified and oriented to make sure that all BTF images represent the same area of the sample). Figure 9.6 shows such a representation, as well as an alternative view as a set of BRDF images.

An interesting alternative to full BTF acquisition is the application of texture synthesis techniques, in which an acquired color image or BTF sample is used to synthesize a texture or BTF over an entire object. This synthesis can be done by assigning RGB or BTF pixel vector data to densely sampled vertices [316, 331] or by synthesizing the full texture on an object's texture atlas [119].

9.3.2 REPRESENTATION OF LIGHT AND VIEW DEPENDENCE

Let us consider a BTF consisting of many images, each taken for a given incident light direction and viewing direction. Such data sets require at least hundreds of megabytes (more commonly gigabytes) of storage, and cannot be practically manipulated as such; rather, their efficient use requires compression techniques. These range from fitting

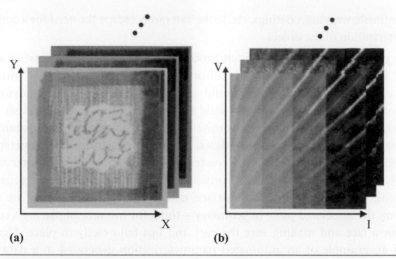

Figure 9.6: Two different views of the same array of BTF data. In both cases, the data is organized in 2D slices that appear as color images. The stack of slices in (a) represents images of the sample under different lighting conditions (for a given viewing direction). The stack in (b) represents apparent BRDF images (for a fixed point on the sample). *Source*: From Müller et al. [237]. Image © 2005, used courtesy of The Eurographics Association and Blackwell Publishing, Inc.

simple analytical BRDF models at each "texel" to per-texel or per-view matrix factorization. A complete survey of BTF representation techniques can be found in Müller et al. [237].

Of particular interest for appearance modeling are two somewhat dual cases of reduced dimensionality, where either the lighting conditions, or the viewpoint, remain fixed.

Let us first consider the case of fixed viewing conditions. The entire radiance field leaving an object can be represented as a *light field* as described in Section 7.6 of Chapter 7. The original light field and lumigraph representations are based on a parameterization of the set of rays in space, not well suited to the description of a particular object. A more geometry-based representation consists in the use of view-dependent textures [67]: By acquiring, or computing, views of an object from different angles, an approximate color value can be rendered for any point and any viewing direction using a simple linear interpolation of the closest texture directions.

A more general description of the light field leaving an object is realized by a *surface light field*. The underlying data structure is simple and flexible four-dimensional, consisting of a hierarchically subdivided base mesh (following the shape of the object)

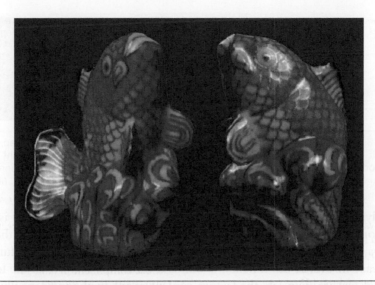

Figure 9.7: A surface light field encodes the radiance field leaving all points of the object, including localized highlights such as the gilded stripes on the fish's tail. *Source*: From Wood et al. [341], © 2000 ACM. Included here by permission

supporting "lumispheres" (i.e., directional radiance distributions represented by hierarchically subdivided octahedra). The acquisition of a surface light field is performed by recording many views of an object, resampling these data in the lumispheres, and compressing the data using variants of either principal component analysis or vector quantization [341].

As shown in Figure 9.7, surface light fields can capture important details of surface variations, such as the golden highlights on the object. The associated algorithms and data structures are fairly complex; for instance, the lumispheres should be carefully parameterized to align specularities as much as possible, allowing efficient compression. This probably explains the slow diffusion of this representation in commercial products, despite the extreme quality of the radiance representation.

An almost symmetric case to the fixed illumination is that of a fixed view point. In this case, and also in the common case of nearly diffuse materials, lighting-dependent textures can be used to model the intricate appearance variations due to the interaction of light in the neighborhood of the surface. In particular, local shadowing effects on the surface often account for dramatic contrast changes depending on the angle of incidence of the main light direction. The idea of view-dependent textures can be directly adapted to light-dependent textures. A widespread alternative is the

Figure 9.8: In this series of images, the top half uses a polynomial texture map, and the bottom half a conventional texture map as the angle of incidence of incident light varies. *Source*: From Malzblender et al. [212], © 2001 ACM. Included here by permission.

use of polynomial texture maps, where the dependence on light direction is encoded as a low-order polynomial [212]. In the example shown in Figure 9.8, the bottom row shows images of a texture-mapped polygon with varying angles of illumination. The decrease in overall illumination is uniform across the texture. In the top row, a polynomial texture map lets the texture content adapt to the incident illumination angle, therefore, there is a better rendering of the contrasted shadows on the complex microstructures.

10 RENDERING APPEARANCE

Chapter 9 described several ways of encoding appearance properties. Let us now consider the process of creating images with realistic appearance. As described in Chapter 2, this necessarily involves taking into account—either explicitly or implicitly—the interaction of light with the objects in a scene. In this chapter, we survey relevant rendering techniques and discuss their interaction with material models to reproduce appearance.

We begin in Section 10.1 with a discussion of the main rendering strategies, including object-space projection techniques and sampling techniques. We also discuss the separation between local and global phenomena, and the implications in terms of rendering calculations. In Section 10.2, the simulation of global illumination is treated mostly from a stochastic/sampling perspective, with a discussion of caching mechanisms. In Section 10.3, we discuss how lighting information is processed locally at (or below) the surface of an object, and how local appearance characteristics are used for renderings. A key ingredient in controlling appearance in synthetic images is the treatment of color and tone mapping, discussed in Section 10.4. Precomputation strategies, allowing more interaction with the rendered elements, are discussed in Section 10.5.

10.1 AN OVERVIEW OF IMAGE CREATION TECHNIQUES

Rendering a digital image requires computing individual pixel colors, representing the appearance of an object as seen from the viewer. As discussed in Chapter 4, spectral radiance is the relevant physical quantity characterizing light. Therefore, each pixel should be assigned a color based on the incoming spectral radiance at a viewing location. The finite resolution of the image, as well as the great variability of object colors even for neighboring locations, make it impossible to define a pixel color as simply *the* color of *the* visible object at that pixel. Rather, all advanced rendering techniques operate by integrating a number of shading samples at each pixel. Each sample in turn expresses the spectral radiance measured at a given location in space (typically a visible object) and in a given direction (that of the observer). We can distinguish two main classes of rendering techniques, based on the mechanism used to select these samples:

- *Object-space sampling:* Samples are computed on the objects of a scene, for inst- ance, at polygon vertices or surface control points. The sample density can be adapted, using for instance primitive subdivision, to ensure adequate coverage of the image.
- *Image-space sampling:* Samples are computed at selected locations corresponding to a chosen image-space sampling scheme. Typically these locations are the visible surface points under each pixel center.

In both cases, the essential operation consists in determining how a given point in space will appear from the view point: either this determination is carried out for all ele- ments of a scene, or it is only performed for elements that are visible in the image. Since color issues in rendering are discussed in depth in Section 10.4, for now we con- sider monochromatic images for a fixed wavelength; therefore, our goal is to compute a single radiance value. This computation can be understood as a simulation of the light transfer described in Chapter 2. Locally, around a given point on the surface of an object, we can conceptually separate the calculation into two steps:

1. Estimate a distribution of incoming illumination (see Section 10.2).
2. Process the interaction of the distribution with the material and object (Section 10.3).

Our distinction between object-space and image-space sampling should not be mis- understood as a distinction between techniques operating in three-dimensional (3D) and other techniques operating in the two-dimensional (2D) image plane. Rather, it is based on the approach chosen to pick the location of appearance calculation samples.

We discuss both approaches in the following sections, and the differences they imply in terms of physical realism or computational performance, then explain the usual distinction between local and global illumination calculations.

10.1.1 OBJECT PROJECTION TECHNIQUES

Let us first focus on techniques that compute illumination for a set of sample points on the objects in a scene, and then deal with the creation of the image. Most interactive rendering systems are based on this approach, since the low-level rendering primitives of graphics libraries such as DirectX or OpenGL associate color and textures to the geometry of a scene. Thus, a simple appearance can be modeled with little or no computation, by displaying the base color (perhaps modulated by a texture) of each object. Another possibility is to precompute all shading samples using a simulation tool, and assign the results of this computation to the object color or texture, essentially "painting" illumination on the objects. Very elaborate models of appearance, such as those presented in Chapters 5, 6, and 8, can still be used to compute the color of each sample, by means of a *shader* program [6].

Image Creation from Object Samples

The calculation of appearance samples for rendering has long been closely tied to the geometric description of a scene. Indeed, the simple rendering models of common graphics software libraries rely on a two-stage process for color calculation: first, an evaluation of the shading model at geometric surface control points (polygon vertices or polynomial surface control points); second, an interpolation stage to fill the image. However, this simple sampling mechanism often fails to capture the nonlinear variations of appearance across geometric primitives. A common example is that of a glossy object with a fairly sharp bidirectional reflectance distribution function (BRDF), illuminated by a small light source: If the expected highlight falls in the middle of a polygon, it cannot be obtained by interpolating the radiance values at the vertices.

High-quality software renderers, therefore, adapt the density of shading samples by adaptively dicing object primitives until all pixels are covered. This results in a more uniform application of the shading calculations, and guarantees that no effects will be missed due to interpolation. It is also consistent with the evolution of graphics hardware toward programmable shading. Since the early 2000s, graphics hardware has integrated the ability to perform shading calculations for each image fragment. Therefore, even for interactive, GPU-based rendering, it is now possible to perform illumination computations on the objects of a scene at a rate compatible with the image projection.

After shading samples have been generated on the objects, they are projected to image space based on a simple image formation model (see Figure 10.1). In most computer graphics applications a perspective projection is used to model a simplistic pinhole camera, but more elaborate cameras can be simulated [179]. For all parallel and perspective projections the transformation to image space is computed as a linear transform. Details can be found in all computer graphics textbooks, in particular concerning the use of homogeneous coordinates to model perspective division [288].

In the case of opaque objects, at each pixel we should only consider the samples lying on the surface closest to the view point. This selection is easily performed using the

Figure 10.1: Color (radiance) is computed on each object, then the image is assembled by projecting the scene.

z-buffer technique, or some of its variations [40]. However, in computational terms this technique is not very efficient, since it amounts to discarding all samples that end up not being visible. Most software systems, and more and more hardware, therefore propose early rejection of samples, or deferred shading, to concentrate the potentially expensive shading calculations on visible samples that actually contribute to an image.

Appearance Precomputation

In the context of object-based sampling, a possible approach consists in precomputing the appearance of all samples and attaching it to the objects in a scene. At the time of image creation, the appropriate radiance value is then extracted from the precomputed data. This approach is especially interesting when complex calculations are involved, which cannot be performed in real-time for all samples. Examples include soft shadows from complex light sources, and indirect illumination effects. However, since radiance depends on the viewing direction for all but diffuse (Lambertian) objects, a full precomputation of appearance requires the storage of a complex, high-dimensional radiance field on the objects. These "surface light fields" are described in the context of measurement and capture in Chapter 7, and some lighting precomputation techniques are further discussed in Sections 10.2 and 10.3.

A lower-dimensionality problem, therefore more tractable, consists in precomputing only view-independent effects such as diffuse lighting (essentially painting illumination on the objects), or a representation of the incident radiance distribution, which incorporates soft shadow and interreflection effects. A scene can then be rendered interactively with a changing view point by subjecting this incident distribution to the appropriate reflection (BRDF). This ability to modify the viewing angle and position is extremely useful when assessing the appearance characteristics of materials, as discussed in Chapter 3. Precomputing the appearance of all objects in a scene can be a clear waste if the view point will remain fixed, and only a fraction of the scene is visible! On the other hand, it is an efficient way of trading resources (in that case memory and offline computational power for speed) to allow interactive exploration of the scene with arbitrarily complex appearance conditions.

A major difficulty in precomputing appearance is the need for an explicit link between the appearance representation and the geometry of the objects in a scene. This manifests itself as the need for a parametrization of the surfaces (in order to apply various textures and parameter maps; see Section 9.3.1), or as the need for a fine-scale description of the geometry with large numbers of points and triangles, each carrying complex appearance information such as BRDF, irradiance, or radiance distribution.

On-the-Fly Appearance Calculation

Given the difficulties of object-based precomputation, a simpler approach consists of evaluating the necessary appearance calculations on the fly, thus entirely computing each frame from scratch. Since sample projection and visibility, as well as image interpolation, are efficiently handled by the graphics hardware (or evaluated in software-based renderers), rendering performance will typically be directly related to the performance of the appearance calculations performed for each sample.

Fixed-function graphics hardware has always offered some simple models, based on point or directional light sources and parametric BRDF models such as the Blinn-Phong model. Shadows created by point and directional lights can be added using shadow map or shadow volume techniques [58]. More elaborate calculations that could be performed at display time include the incident illumination from complex light sources (linear or area lights) or the reconstruction of indirect illumination from precomputed elements such as photon maps.

Furthermore, the advent of programmable graphics hardware now allows some of these calculations to be performed on the GPU. In particular, the division of vertex and fragment shaders is well suited to a rendering architecture in which some supporting information is evaluated or retrieved at all object vertices, and much of the calculation is deferred to a later stage where it is only applied to visible fragments, thus avoiding an unnecessary expense.

10.1.2 IMAGE SAMPLING TECHNIQUES

In the image-space approach, we reverse our perspective and start from the image to be created. The atomic operation in computing an image is the determination of a pixel value, and we consider here all pixels to be independent. What needs to be computed is the incident radiance through a pixel. We shall not review here all the difficulties associated to this operation, which amounts to a discrete sampling of continuous information. These, and the related aliasing problems, are well treated in many specialized books [288]. We note, however, that for any high-quality results in practical cases, it is imperative to integrate several samples per pixel.

Without loss of generality we focus on the calculation of a single sample, therefore, we wish to compute the radiance incident on the image plane from a single direction in space. Given a view point and the geometrical model of image formation (camera parameters, distortion model, etc.), each point on the image plane can be associated to a line in 3D space, carrying light onto that point.

Ray tracing is probably the best-known technique for evaluating the incident radiance from a given direction. It proceeds by following the path of light propagation in the reverse direction, from the viewer to the scene along the line through a pixel (Figure 10.2). Assuming the visible surface point along that line can be computed,

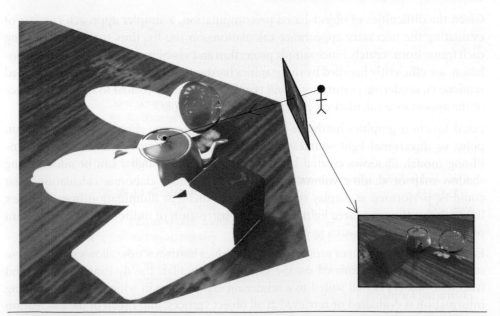

Figure 10.2: Radiance samples are gathered based on the imaging conditions, therefore focusing the calculation on relevant parts of the scene.

the sample radiance value is obtained as the radiance leaving this surface point in the direction of the viewer (see Chapter 4).

The key advantage of such image-based techniques is their clear output-sensitive character. The complexity of the calculations, hence the computational expense, is directly related to that of what is visible in the image. Therefore, there is a potential for huge computational savings in applications where we can make reasonable predictions of what is/isn't visible. For instance, the appearance of a very complex material will only be computed when and where objects made with this material come into view.

Another interesting benefit of image-space approaches is their simplicity. The ray tracing framework allows for a very modular process, where "anything that can be ray traced" can be rendered. Still, some representations, such as point-based object descriptions originating from laser scanners, can be difficult to sample with rays.

Finally, the fact that each pixel calculation is independent from all others can be considered a benefit (e.g., since it allows very easy parallel processing), or a brute-force and potentially wasteful approach since some elements may be recomputed over and over. We shall see in Section 10.2.2 that efficient caching techniques have been developed to optimize such calculations.

10.1.3 LOCAL AND GLOBAL CALCULATIONS

In most practical cases, appearance in an image is entirely determined by the light distribution leaving the visible objects. Exceptions are scenes where there is light scattering in volumes as discussed in Chapter 5 (Section 5.6, Scattering in Volume). In such "participating media," the propagation of light in a medium such as smoke, water, or mist significantly alters appearance. Since the resulting effects of haze, diffusion, and color desaturation are inherently linked to the medium rather than the objects and materials in a scene, we will treat them separately in Section 10.3.3.

For now, let us consider the typical case of objects seen from a short distance, in clear air: Atmospheric scattering and attenuation can be safely neglected[1], and the key ingredient to appearance calculation is the light leaving the surface of a visible object at a shading sample.

The light leaving a point on a surface in a given direction is the combination of two phenomena: the creation of light energy at the surface, which only occurs for

---

1   The notion of "short distance" can be clarified as a function of the absorption and scattering characteristics of the medium, which are expressed as optical thicknesses (i.e., distances that must be traveled in the medium before experiencing a significant effect; see Chapter 5). For clear air this distance is over one hundred meters.

light-emitting objects or light sources, and the scattering of light received at this point from elsewhere. We can write

$$L(x \to \Theta_o) = L_e(x \to \Theta_o) + L_r(x \to \Theta_o) \tag{10.1}$$

where $L_e(x \to \Theta_o)$ is the radiant exitance that expresses intrinsic light emission, and $L_r(x \to \Theta_o)$ is the scattered radiance.

For passive materials, the essential component is the scattered radiance, essentially the product of the reflection or transmission toward the direction of interest, of light reaching that point from all possible incident directions. Mathematically this amounts to a "convolution," or joint integration, of the bidirectional scattering distribution function and the incident radiance distribution[2], therefore:

$$L(x \to \Theta_o) = L_e(x \to \Theta_o) + \int_{\Theta_i \in \omega} f_r(x, \Theta_i \to \Theta_o) L(x \leftarrow \Theta_i) \cos(N_x, \Theta_i) d\omega_i \tag{10.2}$$

Eq. 10.2 is very difficult to evaluate, since the full distribution of incident light on the reflecting object must be known to compute the integral. In the general case, the light incident on an object can be expressed as the radiance leaving other surfaces visible from the sampling point (recall that radiance is invariant along a free path in space). In other words, if the visible point from point x in direction Θ_i is denoted by y, we have $L(x \leftarrow \Theta_i) = L(y \to -\Theta_i)$. Eq. 10.2, therefore, appears as a coupled integral equation on $L(. \to .)$, expressing the *global illumination* problem. This equation is impossible to solve analytically in the general case and requires either advanced numerical techniques and simplifications, or stochastic solutions.

A common simplification to the global illumination, Eq. 10.2, is to consider that the incoming radiance only originates from designated light sources. When considering this simplified, *local illumination* problem, radiance computation reduces to filtering a fixed (usually quite simple) direct illumination distribution from the light sources, according to the local scattering (reflection or transmission) function. This allows for much faster renderings since the set of light sources is fixed; however, in the case of complicated scattering behavior, a significant amount of calculation may still be required. Note that an intermediate formulation of the problem consists of subjecting an object to a complex, although fixed, illumination distribution called an *environment map* (see Figure 10.3). Such a map is essentially a coded representation of the incident illumination that is assumed to be independent from the location considered. It then reduces to a function of the incident direction Θ_i.

---

2   The strict mathematical definition of a "convolution" only applies for some specific cases where the BRDF depends only on the difference between incident and outgoing angles. The important fact here is that the BRDF modulates the incident radiance before integration.

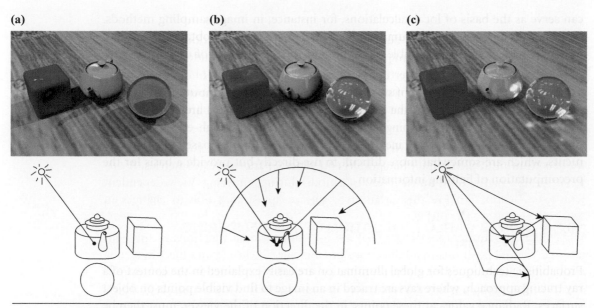

Figure 10.3: Local versus global illumination. (a) Local illumination considers incident radiance only from a set of light sources. (b) Environment map lighting allows incident light from an infinitely distant hemisphere. (c) Global illumination considers incident radiance from all other objects in the scene.

The name "environment map" refers to the fact that incident illumination is constant across the scene for a given direction, thus equivalent to the illumination coming from a distant environment (actually assumed to lie at infinite distance). The illumination function can be stored as a set of spherical samples, or more commonly as a cube map (i.e., a set of illumination textures covering the faces of a unit cube). Rendering with an environment map amounts to computing the integral in Eq. 10.2 based on the map samples, weighted by the local BRDF and optionally a visibility factor to block out portions of the distant illumination that are not "visible" from the point of interest.

10.2 SIMULATING GLOBAL ILLUMINATION

We have seen in Chapter 3 that careful consideration of the complete illumination environment of an object is required to understand or model its appearance. Therefore, realistic rendering of appearance requires a precise modeling and computation of global illumination effects. We review here the main techniques used to simulate these effects. Since global illumination involves the interaction of light with several objects in a scene, its simulation typically involves at least some amount of object-space calculations [7, 53, 83, 187, 291]. We focus in this section on these calculations, which can serve as the basis of local calculations, for instance, in image sampling methods. In such a strategy, the global illumination calculations are used to obtain the incident radiance field around each visible sample point, for the purpose of evaluating local interaction with the surface.

We begin with a presentation of stochastic approaches to the computation of global illumination, since they form the basis of most existing tools and are easiest to use. In particular, the photon mapping technique is used in several high-end commercial products. For completeness we mention deterministic techniques based on finite elements, which are somewhat more difficult to use directly but provide a basis for the precomputation of lighting information.

10.2.1 MONTE CARLO EVALUATION OF THE RENDERING EQUATION

Probabilistic techniques for global illumination are easily explained in the context of a ray tracing approach, where rays are traced in an image to find visible points on object surfaces. Radiance values at these points, in the direction of the viewer, must then be computed using Eq. 10.2. Monte Carlo integration performs this calculation in the following way: A set of random directions $\Theta_i^{(k)}$, $k = 1 \dots N$ is generated, according to a probability distribution $d(\Theta)$, and a stochastic estimator of the integral is obtained as:

$$\langle L_r(x \to \Theta_o) \rangle = \frac{1}{N} \sum_{k=1}^{N} \frac{L(x \leftarrow \Theta_i^{(k)}) f_r(x, \Theta_i^{(k)} \to \Theta_o) \cos(N_x, \Theta_i^{(k)})}{d(\Theta_i^{(k)})} \tag{10.3}$$

Since the incident radiance value in each of the chosen directions must be computed, the procedure is applied recursively by tracing a ray in the direction $\Theta_i^{(k)}$, finding the first point of intersection with the scene, and evaluating again Eq. 10.2 at this point. The sequence of evaluation points in the recursion defines a path in space, along which all reflections of light are accounted for. Note that the recursion must be controlled with an appropriate termination criterion, as discussed in Dutre et al. [83]. Several variants of this algorithm have been proposed, in particular, differing in terms of branching strategy at each reflection [168].

Monte Carlo integration in this simple form is known to numerically converge to the correct value of the integral as the number of samples goes to infinity. The approximation of Monte Carlo evaluation is due to the use of a finite number of samples, and manifests itself as noise in an image, which can be measured as variance of the estimator that is known to decrease only as $1/N$, meaning that its standard deviation, the square root of radiance, decreases as slowly as $N^{-1/2}$. Figure 10.4 shows typical

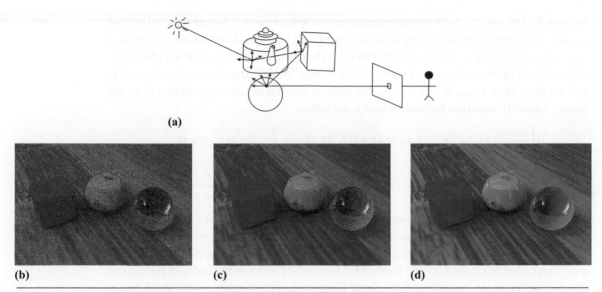

(a)

(b)   **(c)**   **(d)**

Figure 10.4: (a) A possible light path for stochastic evaluation of the reflection integral. (b–d) Images obtained with 70, 700, and 70,000 paths, respectively.

noise in the resulting images. The naive application of Monte Carlo integration to the rendering equation is particularly inefficient, because terms in the integral are computed with recursive sampling operations, and useful contributions are only obtained when sampling the light sources (with a nonzero L_e term). Since paths are generated randomly, many of them are required to obtain even a sparse sampling of the sources.

Since light sources are easily identified, as well as individual material properties, much better sampling strategies can be used resulting in more efficient use of processing power. Without diving into the details of Monte Carlo rendering, we discuss below the two main avenues for variance reduction without which no practical usage of the technique can be envisioned.

Separation of Direct and Indirect Lighting

The first important improvement to simple stochastic path tracing consists in splitting the integration into two components: one representing the integral over the directions in which a light source is found, and the other integrating over the remaining directions. These "direct" and "indirect" contributions are then evaluated separately, each with its own set of samples. In order to evaluate the direct contribution, we observe that the integral over directions hitting a light source (the set of such directions from x is denoted by ω_e) can be transformed in an integral over the surface of the light sources S_e (i.e., objects with a nonzero exitance term $L_e(x \rightarrow \Theta)$). Let us denote by y the surface point visible from a sample point x in a given incident direction Θ_i. The reflection integral from Eq. 10.2 is transformed by changing the integration variable to y. If we denote by $\Theta_{y \rightarrow x}$ the direction in which y "sees" x (it is therefore a function of y, and we have $\Theta_i = \Theta_{x \rightarrow y} = -\Theta_{y \rightarrow x}$); N_y the surface normal at point y; and $v(x, y)$ as the binary visibility function between x and y, we have:

$$\int_{\omega_e} f_r(x, \Theta_i \rightarrow \Theta_o)L(x \leftarrow \Theta_i)\cos(N_x, \Theta_i)d\omega_i = \int_{S_e} f_r(x, \Theta_{x \rightarrow y} \rightarrow \Theta_o)$$

$$L_e(y \rightarrow \Theta_{y \rightarrow x})\cos(N_x, \Theta_{x \rightarrow y})\cos(N_y, \Theta_{y \rightarrow x})\frac{v(x, y)}{\|y - x\|^2}dy \qquad (10.4)$$

In Eq. 10.5 we assume that light sources do not reflect light (i.e., their emitted radiance equals their exitance). The integral is therefore easily computed by sampling the surface of the light sources. A visibility function must be evaluated at each sample, but no recursive integration is needed. While the relative amount of noise in the indirect portion of illumination remains significant, the direct illumination is computed with much better precision than in the naive sampling approach. Since direct lighting typically dominates the content of an image, the result is a drastic reduction of overall noise (Figure 10.5).

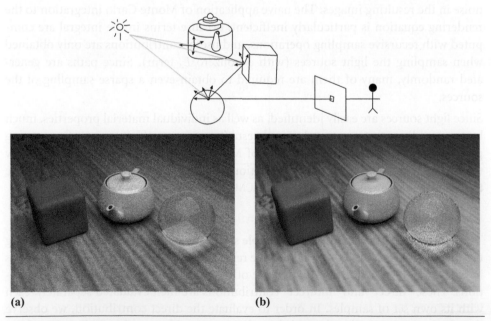

(a)   (b)

Figure 10.5: Light paths including direct lighting estimation. Note the significant reduction of noise, shown in (b), compared to Figure 10.4b, which used the same number of paths.

As for the indirect illumination integral, its computation can also be improved by using importance sampling as described in the next section.

Importance Sampling for BRDF

Importance sampling is a general principle of Monte Carlo integration techniques, whereby a well-chosen probability distribution is used to select integration samples. Looking back at Eq. 10.3 and calling $I(\Theta)$ the function to integrate

$$I(\Theta) = L(x \leftarrow \Theta)f_r(x, \Theta \rightarrow \Theta_o)\cos(N_x, \Theta)$$

the variance of the estimate is given by:

$$v\left(\frac{1}{n}\sum_{i=1}^{n}\frac{I(\Theta_i)}{d(\Theta_i)}\right) = \frac{1}{n}v\left(\frac{I}{d}\right). \tag{10.5}$$

Thus, the variance can be greatly reduced if the sampling probability distribution $d(\Theta)$ is well correlated with the integrand function $I(\Theta)$. Of course this is difficult to impose since the incident radiance at point x is generally unknown. Still, we can benefit from this idea in two main cases:

- When the BRDF at point x is strongly directional (glossy and specular materials), by using a probability distribution proportional to the BRDF (with proper normalization):

$$d(\Theta) \sim f_r(x, \Theta \rightarrow \Theta_o)$$

- When the incoming radiance distribution is known. Of course, this is rarely exactly the case, but in the particular situation of an object subjected to the illumination from an environment map, using the radiance from the environment map as an approximation to the incoming radiance amounts to only neglecting light reflection on the object itself. In this case, we choose a sample distribution according to the radiance in the map:

$$d(\Theta) \sim EnvMap(\Theta)$$

Figure 10.6 shows example angular sampling patterns based on the BRDF and on an environment map.

Note that in this case the sampling distribution is independent from the location x, which allows for consistent sampling across the object. However, in the case of time-dependent illumination, it is also very important to ensure that illumination sampling remains consistent over time.

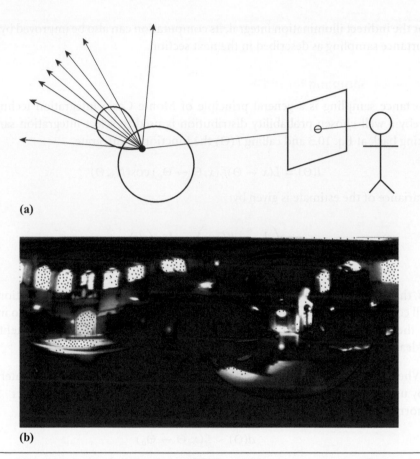

(a)

(b)

Figure 10.6: Importance sampling for (a) BRDF, and (b) environment map. *Source*: Image (b) © 2007 Zack Waters; included by permission.

10.2.2 CACHING MECHANISMS

The very slow convergence properties of Monte Carlo path tracing are due in part to the totally independent evaluation of each instance of the global illumination equation. While there may be important variations in appearance from one shading sample to the next, the following two observations can help design more efficient algorithms.

First, the local variations of incident illumination are often quite predictable and relatively smooth: small-scale, or high-frequency, variations of appearance are generally the result either of similar scale changes in material properties or of hard shadows due to neighboring objects. In the common case of a surface illuminated by fairly distant objects and light sources, incident illumination is smooth or low frequency [81].

Second, as recursive rays are traced in a scene to evaluate incident radiance, they tend to reach more and more areas in the scene, and these sampled regions for different initial image samples may overlap. The more diffuse the BRDFs are, and the deeper we proceed in the recursion, the more chance there is that we may be recomputing radiance very close to a point where that calculation has already been performed. Furthermore, when significant interreflection requires an important "diffusion" of sampling rays in the scene, one of the main benefits of image-space sampling, that is, its output-sensitive character with respect to the visible complexity of the scene, is lost.

Therefore, several caching mechanisms have been devised, where the results of previous calculations are kept for future reference, and interpolated when possible rather than performing a fresh calculation. Replacing a pure stochastic evaluation by some interpolation of previously computed samples introduces *bias* in the solution, that is, the image is no longer guaranteed to converge to the true solution as more samples are added. Care must be taken to limit the use of cached samples to situations where a good approximation can be maintained.

Irradiance Caching

The idea of reusing computed illumination samples in an image sampling approach is actually quite natural if we consider it as an effort to adapt the amount of effort to the true, object-space complexity of the distribution of light in a scene. When very complex and small-scale lighting changes occur everywhere, it is indeed useful to perform precise evaluations for each sample. However, when some areas only encounter simple, slowly varying illumination conditions, it may be sufficient to base the evaluations on a much smaller set of well-chosen samples.

The notion of *irradiance caching* was introduced in the Radiance lighting simulation system [187] to avoid the very costly calculation of irradiance for the purpose of computing diffuse interreflection in a ray tracing framework. In the case of diffuse (Lambertian) reflection, all information on the incident distribution of light is lost upon reflection, and the integral in Eq. 10.2 reduces to an integral of incident radiance. The idea is to altogether avoid the calculation of this irradiance integral when it is possible to approximate it from a number of previously computed integrals. To this end, computed irradiance integrals are stored in a spatial data structure (an octree) and are given an area of influence in which they can be reused with sufficient accuracy. The size of this area of validity is computed for each sample based on various estimates of the irradiance gradient (taking into account, for instance, object curvature). Elaborate techniques can be used to obtain a robust gradient estimate based on the actual sample points used in the Monte Carlo integration [187]. Figure 10.7 illustrates this process.

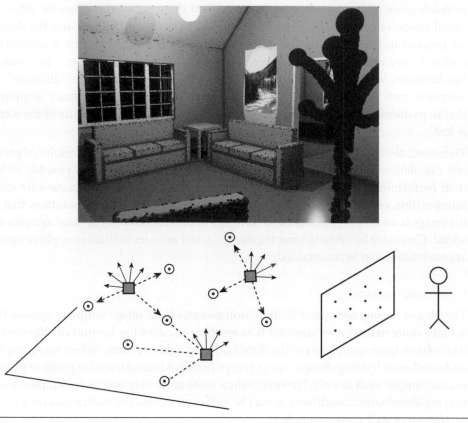

Figure 10.7: Principles of irradiance caching. The integral of incoming radiance is computed at the location of the red dots, and estimated using these cached values at all other locations. The image on the right shows the location of all cached samples. *Source*: Image courtesy of Greg Ward.

Photon Mapping

The notion of information caching has been extended and generalized to what is probably the most versatile and useful rendering technique to date—photon mapping. The idea of photon mapping consists in separating the calculation of images into two stages.

In the first stage, basic illumination samples (called photons) are generated to populate a scene, in a manner that is both efficient (in the sense that the effort is commensurate with the complexity of the actual lighting effects) and independent from either the exact geometric description of the scene, its parameterization, or the viewing conditions.

The second stage then builds an image using a ray tracing approach, where radiance values are reconstructed from the set of available photons whenever possible.

Photon Tracing Stage The first pass of a photon mapping calculation consists in recording a view-independent description of light exchanges in a scene. This is accomplished by simulating the propagation of light in a *photon tracing* phase, using a random walk algorithm.

Photons, or packets of light energy traveling in a fixed direction from a designated location, are generated on the light sources according to their relative power and spatial emission characteristics. For instance, diffuse extended emitters are sampled with a uniform distribution proportional to their emission per unit area. For directional light sources, the sampling probability distribution should also be proportional to their emissive angular characteristic.

Photons are traced by finding the first surface hit by the corresponding ray and recording the impact in a spatial data structure called the *photon map*. The photon is then reflected, and the next direction is again chosen stochastically by using the BRDF as a probability distribution function. The resulting random walk, with independent events occurring at each step, is a Markov chain and can be shown to populate the scene with a set of photon hits correctly representing the distribution of light. In a manner similar to Monte Carlo path tracing, the representation is unbiased, that is, it converges toward the actual light distribution as the number of photons goes to infinity. Naturally, appropriate termination criteria must be applied to these photon chains. In particular, the *Russian roulette* technique is used to terminate chains by conditionally reflecting photons based on the surface albedo.

Great care must be taken during this photon tracing stage to properly distribute the light energy in the scene in the forms of photons that all carry similar energy. This property cannot be strictly enforced when photons carry a spectral content to represent colored light, since reflection on different materials will modify the spectral composition of light. However, it can be approximately maintained and proves extremely useful to easily reconstruct radiance estimates.

Photon Map Storage The photon map is the sampled representation of all energy exchanges in a scene. Recall that the principle of the photon mapping technique is to conduct in the first stage all calculations that are driven by the complexity of light transport, and make the results of these calculations available to a second step that reconstructs the radiance values needed to assemble an image.

Photon hits are stored in the photon map when a photon is reflected at a surface, since radiance values always have to be generated at points on surfaces. However, the case of ideal specular (mirror) reflection is special. First, we note that many materials exhibit some level of mirror reflection, even for moderately rough surface finishes [142] (see Chapter 3). Second, mirror reflection on a surface cannot be easily reconstructed by interpolating samples that do not fall exactly in the required direction, since it may represent arbitrarily sharp detail. For this reason when a photon reaches a surface with some ideal specular reflection it should be further traced into the scene and no photon hit recorded. Since most BRDFs exhibit some nonspecular behavior in addition to mirror reflection, Russian roulette can be used to decide whether to treat the photon as specular (and propagate it further) or to store a photon hit corresponding to the nonspecular part of the BRDF (and potentially tracing a new reflected photon).

The information stored with a photon hit reduces to the location of the hit point, the direction of propagation, and the actual spectral content of the photon. Note that the photon is considered to represent incident light on the surface (i.e., before it undergoes reflection). This is important to allow further modulation of this incident radiance, for instance, due to small-scale BRDF detail or textured surfaces.

A major breakthrough introduced with the photon map idea was the decoupling between the set of photons and the actual geometry description of the scene. Rather than attaching the photons to the surfaces of the scene (and having, therefore, to consider geometric representations and parameterizations), photon hits are stored in their own spatial data structure based on a spatial subdivision scheme. A balanced k–d tree is the structure of choice for storing photon maps, because it allows efficient access to the nearest neighbors of a point in space, a useful property for radiance reconstruction as we shall see next.

Radiance Reconstruction Since each photon hit in the photon map represents a fraction of the light energy from the light sources after it has traveled in a scene, their distribution statistically models the flow of light. One possible use of the photon map is to perform density estimation to obtain irradiance values on diffuse surfaces. This is accomplished by collecting all photons in a given area around the point of interest and summing their contributions to irradiance. Better results are obtained by weighing the contributions by a spatial kernel to favor proximity. As mentioned above, this requires easy access to all photons in a spatial neighborhood, and justifies the use of a k–d tree structure for the photon map.

However, for nondiffuse surfaces, a more elaborate estimate of reflected radiance must be constructed. Recall the expression of reflected radiance from Eq. 10.2:

$$L_r(x \to \Theta_o) = \int_{\Theta_i \in \omega} f_r(x, \Theta_i \to \Theta_o) L(x \leftarrow \Theta_i) \cos(N_x, \Theta_i) d\omega_i$$

Figure 10.8: Direct reconstruction from the photon map. Note the low-frequency noise due to insufficient photon density. *Source:* Image courtesy of Cyril Soler and Laurence Boissieux.

Considering that each photon hit represents an infinitesimal contribution to the incident flux on the surface, Jensen et al. [161] proposed the following estimate for reflected radiance, where r is the radius of the sphere enclosing the n closest photon hits around point x, and a photon hit (indexed by k) transports a flux Φ_k in direction Θ_k:

$$L_r(x \to \Theta_o) \approx \frac{1}{\pi r^2} \sum_{k=1}^{n} f_r(x, -\Theta_k \to \Theta_o)\Phi_k \tag{10.6}$$

This expression essentially subjects each of the neighboring photon hits to reflection on the surface at point x, thus considering that all these photons were indeed incident at the same point. Clearly, the quality of this reconstruction is dependent on the overall density of photons (see Figure 10.8). If too few photons are available, either a high variance will result for any practical value of r, with a small number of hits found in the collection sphere, or a large value of r will be required to use enough hits, therefore combining flux estimates from very different locations.

This direct reconstruction from the photon map is hardly usable in practice, since it would require huge numbers of photons, and therefore, a very expensive photon tracing phase. A different balance of the algorithm can be found by tracing fewer photons, but using the reconstruction formula of Eq. 10.6 only for the second bounce of radiance computations. In this approach, each image sample is traced into a scene, and the

(a)   **(b)**

Figure 10.9: (a) Visualization of photons stored in the map, and (b) reconstructed image. *Source*: Image courtesy of Cyril Soler and Laurence Boissieux.

image radiance is estimated using the Monte Carlo integration of Eq. 10.3. It is only for the secondary estimation of radiance that the photon map reconstruction is used. This essentially smoothes out the reconstruction noise due to the insufficient photon density, thanks to the integration step (see Figure 10.9).

10.2.3 FINITE ELEMENTS METHODS

Despite the great conceptual simplicity of stochastic approaches to computation of global illumination, they also present a number of drawbacks, such as, elaborate sampling strategies are required to avoid computing huge numbers of samples; most of the effort is spent (for photon mapping) in a complex image reconstruction stage; and no explicit representation of the illumination in a scene is obtained, making it potentially more difficult to modify the lighting conditions or to reuse part of the calculation when creating multiple images. This aspect is particularly important in the context of evaluating the appearance of specific materials. For instance, consider what happens when we hold an object in our hand and visually inspect its appearance. We typically exploit the object's relative movement, the lighting environment, and our viewing position to build a mental model of its appearance. Therefore, in a computer graphics context, the ability to generate animations, preferably in an interactive setting, is also a crucial asset.

Finite element approaches to global illumination take a different route by computing an explicit approximation of the radiance function in a scene. The process begins with the selection of an appropriate set of *basis functions* to represent this radiance distribution. A solution is then computed as the function in the space spanned by this basis that is "closest" to the real solution of the rendering equation. Obviously the choice of an appropriate set of basis functions is a crucial step in all these methods, since it should allow a decent approximation to the real solution.

The radiance function in a scene is five-dimensional (three positional and two angular dimensions). In the absence of participating media the relevant unknown in the global illumination problem is the distribution of radiance on the surfaces, a four-dimensional function (two positional and two angular dimensions).

In very general terms, the essence of the finite element approach is to choose basis functions with limited support attached to a set of geometric elements (typically a mesh of the surfaces and/or a partition of the hemisphere of directions). Computing a solution amounts to determining the best linear combination of these basis functions to approach the real solution, or equivalently, the set of scalar coefficients of this combination. This is done by expressing a condition on these coefficients; for instance, Galerkin techniques express that the difference between the true solution and the finite element solution must be orthogonal (in the high-dimensional function space) to each of the basis functions. The computation of the combination coefficients then reduces to the solution of a matrix equation relating (in a linear fashion) the solution to the specification of input illumination (light sources).

Finite elements methods have first been applied to illumination calculations with the "radiosity" technique, originally developed in heat transfer studies. Early techniques reduced the dimensionality of the problem by limiting themselves to diffuse surfaces. Hierarchical basis functions, such as wavelets or spherical harmonics, have been used to adapt the precision of the representation to the variations of illumination, both in space and direction [121].

Figure 10.10 shows two images obtained using a finite-element hierarchical radiance algorithm. The raw, rather coarse description of radiance using piecewise constant functions is shown on the left, while a smoothed solution is shown on the right. Since the finite-element solution is an explicit representation of radiance, it can be displayed directly to obtain the image on the left at practically no cost, for any viewing conditions. This is the single major benefit of this approach, making it useful in situations of slowly varying, but significant, indirect illumination.

The most important difficulty in using the finite element radiance algorithm lies in the parametrization of the geometry and the choice of basis elements. In addition, since the calculation of the finite-element matrix is typically the dominant cost of the solution, these techniques always tend to use fairly coarse elements, requiring a final reconstruction stage (such as shown in the image on the right) to produce useful images. In this respect, they can be considered an alternative to the first stage of photon tracing (Section 10.2.2), providing a coarse solution from which to reconstruct radiance only in the integration stage of the first reflection.

Figure 10.10: Results of finite-element radiance calculation. *Source*: From Christensen et al. [47] © 1997 ACM. Included here by permission.

The need for surface parameterization, underlying the definition of finite elements, is often regarded as a drawback of these techniques, yet it can also be leveraged to create lighting solutions in the form of precomputed textures. This is typically used in the game industry to obtain lighting textures encoding static illumination patterns.

These techniques are discussed in depth in specialized documents such as Cohen and Wallace [53] and Sillion and Puech [291] and will not be presented in detail here. We note, however, the fundamental insight obtained in developing them, that is, the linear relationship between the light input in the scene (the light sources) and the global distribution of radiance. This opens the way for interactive rendering systems in which the input illumination can be modified interactively, after an appropriate transfer matrix has been precomputed.

10.3 RENDERING LOCAL APPEARANCE

The computation of global illumination, using the techniques from Section 10.2, is essentially a simulation process, involving numerical calculations to identify and follow light paths in a scene. The impact of a particular material's appearance on a given view of an object is, of course, especially noticeable at the stage of *local* calculations. In this section, we turn to the specifics of computing the radiance at a given point of a surface, and consider how the material model, or the material description, can affect the rendering process. We first consider the question of extracting information from texture maps at the relevant scale with proper filtering, and the difficulties encountered in representing nonlinear effects using textures. Then, we turn to the issue of stochastic sampling in the presence of complex BRDF or bidirectional texture function (BTF) models. Finally, we discuss the particularly challenging case of subsurface scattering, where the amount of computing resources is potentially enormous and should be adapted to the actual importance of the visual effect.

10.3.1 TEXTURE MAPPING AND DETAIL MANAGEMENT

So far we have assumed a clear separation between the geometry of an object and the description of its photometric properties using a BRDF or BTF. These photometric elements can then be represented with great detail (typically at a scale finer than that of the geometry) using texture maps. This approach is used in most high-end rendering systems, as described in Section 9.2. Color, specularity, transparency, and almost all other parameters of the appearance model can be modulated in this manner. In fact, textures can even be used as a versatile tool for representing all illumination information during rendering calculations [109].

A fundamental problem with texture-based representations, however, is that they are provided at a given resolution, which rarely corresponds to the required sampling rate for a given view. Texture filtering techniques have been devised to avoid severe aliasing artifacts. Recent GPUs and low-level graphics libraries offer tools to construct pre-filtered versions of the textures (organized in a texture pyramid, or mipmap), and to extract the needed value at the proper resolution level. Anisotropic filtering provides even better results by recognizing that the sampling rate in texture space is rarely isotropic, since it depends, for instance, on the orientation of the texture with respect to the viewing direction.

We note, however, that all texture filtering operations are based on a linearity assumption, whereby a linear filter can be applied to the information to obtain a coarse-resolution version. With the development of texture-based representations and algorithms, in high-end as well as real-time rendering situations, it becomes essential to revisit this assumption and consider its limitations.

Consider the case where a texture is used to specify the specularity (e.g., a Phong model exponent) on a surface. While the underlying optical process is linear, and the luminous power reflected by a given surface area is indeed obtained by integrating radiance across the surface, a calculation performed using a filtered version of the specularity texture will provide a completely different result, and highlights may be lost if a mipmapped texture is used.

The interdependency of geometric and photometric aspects, and the impossibility to draw a clear boundary between them, has been studied in the context of multiscale

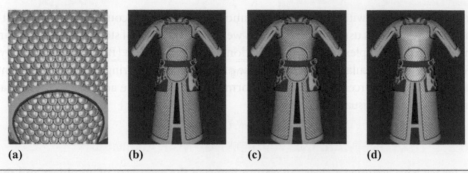

(a)   (b)   (c)   (d)

Figure 10.11: Variation of appearance with scale: (a) close-up view, (b) view from a distance computed using a filtered normal distribution, (c) ground truth image, and (d) image obtained using a fixed BRDF. Notice how the highlight is exaggerated in the last image. *Source*: From Tan et al. [311], © Eurographics Association 2005. Reproduced by kind permission of the Eurographics Association.

representations. Depending on the scale being considered, it may be advantageous to use either a geometric or photometric description to model appearance. For instance, surface detail may be represented explicitly in the geometry for close-up views, using a bump map (a simple geometry with a perturbed normal field) at intermediate distances, and a simple geometry with an appropriate reflectance function for distant views [18]. This approach is not easy to use since different representations must be maintained for the same object. Another possibility, especially interesting with the advent of programmable graphics hardware, is to identify and treat explicitly all nonlinear effects in fragment programs.

A striking example of the nonlinear behavior of shading across scales is shown in Figure 10.11. The complex geometry exhibits different characteristics, notably in terms of surface normal distribution, at different scales. If a fixed BRDF is applied in a view where each pixel covers significant geometric complexity, an incorrect shading is obtained. The solution demonstrated here consists of a multiscale representation of the normal distribution on the object [311].

10.3.2 BRDF AND BTF SAMPLING

Stochastic techniques, such as the photon mapping approach from Section 10.2.2, require that random samples be generated according to probabilistic distribution functions proportional to BRDFs or BTF. This seemingly simple operation turns out to be quite complicated in many cases, therefore accounting for a significant fraction of the global cost of these algorithms.

Drawing a random sample according to a given distribution is not a difficult operation per se, since it can always be accomplished using rejection sampling; in its simplest form, rejection sampling works as follows. If $d(x), x \in [0, 1]$ is a probability distribution function bounded by M, draw two random samples x_s and y_s uniformly in $[0, 1]$, and accept x_s if and only if $M y_s < f(x_s)$; otherwise, reject x_s and draw two new samples. However, this procedure is extremely wasteful in the case of sharply varying distribution (think of a function having a small value everywhere but in a narrow spike—in such a case most samples will be rejected).

Another common procedure for generating samples according to a distribution is to invert the cumulative distribution function $F(x) = \int_{[0,x]} f(u)du$. F being a monotonically increasing function that maps $[0, 1]$ to itself, properly distributed samples are obtained as $x_i = F^{-1}(y_i)$, where the y_i are uniformly distributed samples over $[0, 1]$. Naturally, in order for this to be usable, we must be able to compute F^{-1}. Unfortunately, this is rarely the case in practice for BRDFs. A notable exception is the Phong model and some of its derivatives such as the Phong–Blinn or Lafortune models.

More complicated models, such as the ones presented in Chapters 5, 6, and 8, cannot be sampled directly. An ever-increasing source for BRDFs is from the many efforts at gathering measured reflectance data in the research community, as described in Chapter 7. This data can be encoded and organized in many forms (see Chapter 9), some of which are particularly well suited for sampling. In particular, algorithms for sampling wavelet-encoded BRDFs have been proposed [50]; other approaches express the BRDF data as products of several factors, each being a function that is easy to sample [172, 189].

When a material exhibits small-scale, nonuniform BRDF variation, a BTF is often used to represent its surface appearance (see Section 9.3.1). Similarly to BRDFs, stochastic samples should also be generated accordingly. Figures 10.12 and 10.13 show some of the advanced effects allowed by the use of BTFs.

10.3.3 SUBSURFACE SCATTERING AND PARTICIPATING MEDIA

Many materials are not opaque to visible light, but rather allow some level of light propagation in the volume of the material. Local interactions of light and objects is then no longer restricted to reflection on their surface at a single point. When light cannot be considered to travel unaltered along a straight line of propagation, the medium is said to be "participating." (Stricly speaking, all media but those in a complete vacuum are participating!)

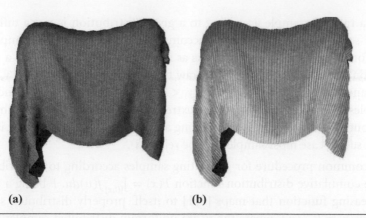

(a)   (b)

Figure 10.12: Comparison of rendering techniques for knitwear (a material exhibiting complex surface detail): (a) combination of BRDF and texture, and (b) rendering using a BTF. Note the subtle illumination details captured with the BTF. *Source*: From Müller et al. [237]. Image © 2005, used courtesy of The Eurographics Association and Blackwell Publishing, Inc.

Figure 10.13: Example rendering with complex BTFs for realistic material evaluation in digital mockups. *Source*: © 2007 Cyril Soler; included by permission.

The consideration of participating media for rendering originated largely from flight simulation, where very large distances are considered and, therefore, the effects of the atmosphere (aerial perspective, fog) cannot be ignored. The simulation of lighting in clouds introduced an added level of complexity, since these objects scatter light very strongly, requiring the consideration of multiple scattering events. The simulation of clouds, dense fog, and turbid liquids is one of the most resource-consuming rendering tasks, since it must model very long and complex light paths [72, 140, 161, 322].

When evaluating the appearance of individual objects, one typically considers much smaller spatial scales, and the most interesting visual effect is called *subsurface scattering*. While this is simply the result of the material beneath the object surface being a participating medium, the rendering techniques used are generally different: first, because the materials of interest are typically quite dense (optically speaking), resulting in fairly short light paths; and second, because they can be considered semi-local, in that the radiance leaving a surface point due to subsurface scattering is typically computed by integrating incoming radiance in a small area around that point. The effect of scattering is modeled using a BSSRDF (bidirectional scattering surface reflectance distribution function) in place of a BRDF, and actual computation techniques have been described in Chapter 5.

Rendering systems used for movie production or accurate imaging should always include at least an estimation of subsurface scattering, because its softening effect on shadows and surface texture is often a key perceptual component in the identification of partially translucent materials such as human skin or liquids. Figures 5.48, 5.49, and 5.50 in Chapter 5 focused on characteristic effects due to strong backlighting, but as shown in Figure 10.14, the inclusion of subsurface scattering also dramatically changes the appearance in very simple lighting conditions. The most common calculation techniques are based on a diffusion approximation well suited to small-distance multiple scattering [160].

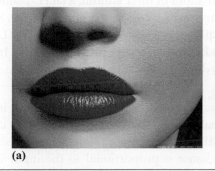 

(a)   (b)

Figure 10.14: Illustration of the softening effect of subsurface scattering: (a) this image is computed using light reflection only, while image (b) uses a BSSRDF to model internal scattering. *Source*: From Jensen et al. [162], © 2001 ACM. Included here by permission.

10.4 COLOR AND TONE

10.4.1 SPECTRAL RENDERING

We have seen in Chapter 2 that the sensation of color is produced by the spectral distribution of light energy across wavelengths. In most of the earlier discussions of rendering techniques, we have not considered this aspect, and treated radiance as purely monochromatic. Still, the careful consideration of color rendering is an absolute necessity if any fidelity is required. Note that color issues in rendering may be encountered in two different cases.

First, accurate prediction of full radiance spectra is expected when using computer simulation techniques to predict appearance or physical response to given lighting conditions. This requirement of accurate spectral calculations for faithful color rendering and appearance reproduction is perhaps best understood by considering the variety of illumination conditions that can be encountered. A given object or material may look just fine under sunlight, with a simple RGB calculation, and yet take on a totally wrong color under artificial lighting such as a fluorescent tube. Let us emphasize again that a key to proper rendering of appearance is the ability to maintain image fidelity for all possible lighting and viewing conditions.

Second, when generating images for viewing or printing, it is important to reliably generate faithful color preception, even though physical accuracy may be violated. The notion of "color balancing," well known to digital photographers, equally applies to all means of digital imagery including rendering. Therefore, each rendered image is created with respect to a chosen "white balance" reflecting the virtual viewing conditions.

Color reproduction is a very difficult task that has been studied for decades in the different contexts of photography, printing, and electronic display devices such as CRT of LCD screens. All color reproduction systems make use of the fact that most color sensations can be reproduced using linear combinations of three stimuli, a fact explained by the presence of three different types of color-sensitive cells in the human retina. Stimuli may be thought of as individual (RGB) phosphors or light-emitting diodes (LEDs) in computer screens, or different colored inks in a subtractive printing process. In this section, we refer to the screen as our display device, even though similar techniques can generally be devised for other media.

The accurate display of a given light spectrum on a given screen is done in the following way. First, the screen must be calibrated, that is, its three primary colors should be measured and expressed in the CIE XYZ color space [303]. Second, it should be linearized to ensure that its output radiance is proportional to the input value. This is easily done, at least approximately, by a gamma-correction step. The location of the three primaries in the XYZ space enclose the subspace of realizable colors on the device (gamut). Any target spectrum that falls in this area, once expressed in XYZ, can be reproduced as a linear combination of the three primaries whose coefficients are obtained as barycentric coordinates.

This suggests a possible avenue for accurate color rendering. If the result of the computation is a faithful spectrum (i.e., all radiance values are actually distributions across the visible wavelength range), then each pixel's spectrum can be transformed to the screen's RGB space for display. This approach is called *spectral rendering* and raises a number of issues.

The first issue is the availabilty of spectral data in order to conduct the necessary rendering calculations. All steps of rendering that involve interactions between spectral (wavelength-dependent) quantities should be computed in vector form for all wavelengths simultaneously. While light source spectra are relatively easy to come by for real-world illuminants, including natural ones such as the sun, spectral data for BRDFs or other appearance parameters are often missing or difficult to find. This should change in the future since there is a definite tendency toward incorporating spectral data in reflectance measurements.

Another difficulty lies in the choice of representation for spectral data. Sampling the spectrum using some number of monochromatic samples is an obvious possibility, a fairly natural extension to the common trisample RGB representation found in all graphics libraries and underlying the display technology. Unfortunately, many samples are required to cover all possible illumination cases. For instance, some artificial illuminants have discontinuous spectra with sharp spikes at precise wavelengths, which should be sampled exactly. Material properties are generally more continuous, although some special cases involving wave effects exhibit discontinuous spectra (some butterfly wings or surface coatings).

The solution to avoid multiplying the number of samples is to adapt the color representation to the contents of the scene (materials and illuminants). For instance, Peercy [261] showed how to build a set of spectral basis functions, reducing the representation to a coordinate vector on this basis. In particular, a fairly small number of bases can be used by using characteristic vector analysis with the reflectance and illuminant spectra. Figure 10.15 illustrates the use of three well-chosen bases, providing better results than nine evenly-spaced samples. This technique requires a modification of the rendering engine, since light reflection is described as a spectral matrix multiplication rather than a set of disjoint (monochromatic) multiplications. A possible alternative would be to provide specialized operations on the graphics processors to perform color vector operations with a full matrix multiplication [262].

An even simpler approach works extremely well when there exists a single dominant illuminant. In this case, Ward and Eydelberg–Vileshin [327] showed that color interactions and color balance can all be handled using standard RGB rendering by transforming all reflectance data according to the illuminant and viewing conditions.

Figure 10.15: Spectral rendering using linear decomposition, under fluorescent lighting: (a) full spectral rendering, (b) rendering with three automatically selected basis functions, and (c) rendering with nine evenly-spaced point samples. *Source*: From Peercy [261], © 1993 ACM. Included here by permission.

In essence, the RGB color of each material is transformed into the XYZ color obtained when it reflects the illuminant and is converted to the white-balanced display space. The resulting colors are then used for rendering, with the illuminant replaced by a white light source. This technique introduces approximations, first because different illuminants may be present with differing spectral characteristics, but also because only direct lighting (with a single reflection) is guaranteed to be handled correctly. The authors show, however, that in many cases this simple approach provides excellent results.

10.4.2 DYNAMIC RANGE AND TONE MAPPING

The acquisition, manipulation, and production of appearance data, that is, radiance values and spectra represented in digital form, all require consideration of dynamic range issues. Indeed, any step involving analog-to-digital conversion is likely to potentially suffer from saturation and information loss. One may conjecture that the development of high-quality rendering techniques operating from real-world appearance data in the 1990s was a main cause to the generalized perception of the dynamic range problem, and an accelerator for associated research. Film or video capture uses exposure controls to modify the adaptation of an image to lighting conditions, and the special effects industry was naturally among the first to encounter the need for similar controls on synthetic imagery.

The dynamic range of all but the simplest scenes largely exceeds that of conventional display devices, such as CRT and LCD monitors, or print (which are typically limited to two orders of magnitude in luminance). Specular highlights, for instance, are generally much brighter than their immediate surroundings, and their faithful rendering can be a key to the perception of a material (think of metals with subtle color variations in their specular reflections). A striking example of materials that cannot be correctly perceived without their true dynamic illumination is gemstones, as shown in Figure 6.26 in Chapter 6. The best approach for the realistic display of synthetic imagery is to use high-dynamic range display devices! At the time of writing, the technology is maturing, and commercial products associating several layers of semi-transparent imagery already provide contrast ratios in the ten thousands. But when only conventional displays are available, a *tone mapping* operation is needed to reduce the overall dynamic range of a scene and make it fit the display capacity. Yet, it is important that all rendering be performed before the tone mapping stage, which should be the last operation before display. An important illustration for this is motion blur, in which different areas of a scene are blended together, because either camera or object motion during exposure makes them project to the same pixel. Such blending should remain linear and must occur before tone mapping [272].

As already stated several times in this book, effective appearance rendering requires an ability to reproduce the look of an object or material under varying conditions, possibly in an interactive manner. Tone mapping, especially when it can be modified interactively, provides a very useful mechanism for the visual inspection of appearance. It lets the viewer develop a precise sense of the intensity variations in highlights and reflections, as well as subtle tone variations, especially in translucent areas. Figure 10.16 illustrates that detail may be lost in either the dark or bright areas of a scene, depending on the exposure settings (top tow). Tone-mapped images in the bottom row attempt to compress the information within the available display range. The result may be visually interesting because it provides more information in all areas, however, it does not correspond to a particular "reality."

The many approaches for tone mapping are well covered in Reinhard et al. [272] and are beyond this book's scope. However, the absolute necessity for a full dynamic range rendering calculation followed by appropriate tone mapping should be a lasting message.

10.5 PRECOMPUTED RENDERING ELEMENTS

Let us mention once again how important it is to interactively visualize an object in order to study and understand its appearance. The viewer needs to move it, change the viewpoint, or change the lighting, and immediately visualize the dynamically changing appearance. The challenge of obtaining realistic appearance (typically with global illumination and complex BRDF with subsurface scattering) while maintaining interactive response, led to the investigation of precomputed rendering. The idea is to express the result of a rendering calculation (be it an image, a set of radiance values at model vertices, a set of radiance distributions at model vertices, etc.) as the response of a linear system to a particular input. The response matrix is often very costly to compute, but this calculation is only performed once for a given object.

The simplest precomputed lighting algorithm consists in extending environment map lighting to glossy BRDFs using filtered environment maps. Recall from Section 10.1.3 that an environment map contains incident radiance values from all directions,

(a)

(b)

Figure 10.16: (a) Two renditions of a single HDR image, with different exposures. (b) Two compressed range images (using the techniques of Tumblin and Reinhard). *Source*: From Cadik et al. [38], © 2006 Martin Cadik.

representing the illumination from an infinitely distant environment. For any visible point at the surface of an object, the reflected radiance is expressed as an integral over incident directions, where the integrand combines incident radiance and the object BRDF. For diffuse reflection, the resulting radiance is simply an integral over incident radiance, since the BRDF is constant. Thus, ignoring the issue of partial hemisphere visibility due to self-occlusion by the object, the reflected radiance only depends on the surface normal direction, and can be looked up in a filtered version of the environment map storing its diffuse integral [123].

To avoid the costly integration step, an expansion of the original environment map into spherical harmonics can be used to quickly obtain the diffusely reflected integral for any direction [271]. For nondiffuse reflectors, it is still possible to prefilter an environment map to lookup values of the reflected radiance integral. However, the dimensionality of the radiance maps is increased in all but the simplest cases, such as when a simple Phong BRDF model maintains a fixed shape of the reflectance kernel across all possible orientations. When using more realistic BRDFs, they should be decomposed into sums of simple reflectance lobes, each of which yielding a prefiltered environment map [173].

The notion of precomputed radiance transfer (PRT) extends the idea of environment map lighting, by recognizing that the entire process that transforms source radiance (from an environment map) into the desired result is linear. By expressing the result as a vector (a vector of pixels in the case of an image, or a vector of radiance values at model vertices for a diffuse material), this transformation is viewed as a matrix, which can be computed once and reused at will with different sources. This approach, therefore, allows easy illumination changes, since all that is needed to obtain the new result is a matrix multiplication.

The most common application of precomputed radiance transfer is for low-frequency environment maps, because these can be expressed as a linear combination of a small number of low-order spherical harmonics basis functions. By also expressing the transfer matrix in terms of spherical harmonics, the calculation of the result radiance values reduces to a simple dot product between spherical harmonics coefficient vectors! The beauty of the precomputed approach is that a transfer matrix can actually encode all the difficult effects, such as visibility, light interreflection, and even subsurface scattering (see Figure 10.17). The original idea of PRT has been extended to glossy objects, lighting distributions with sharp variations (using wavelets rather than spherical harmonics), changing viewpoints, and so on.

Figure 10.17: Interactive rendering of an object with precomputed transport (shadows, interreflection, subsurface scattering) in two different lighting environments. *Source*: From Sloan et al. [292] © 2003 ACM. Included here by permission.

Bibliography

[1] Gregory D. Abram and Turner Whitted. Building block shaders. In *SIGGRAPH '90: Proceedings of the 17th annual conference on computer graphics and interactive techniques*, 283–288. New York: ACM Press, 1990.

[2] Neeharika Adabala, Guangzheng Fei, and Nadia Magnenat-Thalmann. Visualization of woven cloth. In Dutré et al. [84], 178–185.

[3] Tomas Akenine-Moller and Eric Haines. *Real-Time Rendering, Second Edition*. Natick, MA: A. K. Peters, 2002.

[4] T. L. Anderson, D. S. Covert, S. F. Marshall, M. L. Laucks, R. J. Charlson, A. P. Waggoner, J. A. Ogren, R. Caldow, R. L. Holm, F. R. Quant, et al. Performance characteristics of a high-sensitivity, threewavelength, total scatter/backscatter nephelometer. *J. Atmos. Oceanic Technol.*, 13(5):967–986, 1996.

[5] K. Aoki, Ngo Hai Dong, T. Kaneko, and S. Kuriyama. Physically-based simulation of cracks on drying 3D solid. In *10th Pacific graphics conference on computer graphics and applications*, 467–468. Beijing, China: IEEE, October 2002.

[6] A. A. Apodaca and L. Gritz. *Advanced RenderMan: Creating CGI for Motion Pictures*. San Francisco: Morgan Kaufmann, 1999.

[7] Ian Ashdown. *Radiosity: A Programmer's Perspective*. New York: John Wiley and Sons, 1994.

[8] Michael Ashikhmin and Peter Shirley. An anisotropic Phong BRDF model. *Journal of Graphic Tools*, 5(2):25–32, 2000.

[9] Michael Ashikmin, Simon Premoze, and Peter Shirley. A microfacet-based BRDF generator. In *Proceedings of the 27th annual conference on computer graphics and interactive techniques*, 65–74, New York: ACM Press/Addison-Wesley, 2000.

[10] Masashi Baba, Sachiko Miura, Masayuki Mukunoki, and Naoki Asada. Reflectance estimation of sparkle in metallic paints. In *SIGGRAPH '05: ACM SIGGRAPH posters*, 45. New York: ACM Press, 2005.

[11] Shaun Bangay and Judith D. Radloff. Kaleidoscope configurations for reflectance measurement. In *AFRIGRAPH '04: Proceedings of the 3rd international conference*

on computer graphics, virtual reality, visualisation and interaction in Africa, 161–170. New York: ACM Press, 2004.

[12] David C. Banks. Illumination in diverse codimensions. In *SIGGRAPH '94: Proceedings of the 21st annual conference on computer graphics and interactive techniques*, 327–334. New York: ACM Press, 1994.

[13] G. V. G. Baranoski and J. G. Rokne. An algorithmic reflectance and transmittance model for plant tissue. *Computer Graphics Forum*, 16(3):141–150, 1997.

[14] G. V. G. Baranoski and J. G. Rokne. Efficiently simulating scattering of light by leaves. *The Visual Computer*, 17(8):491–505, 2001.

[15] Rejean Baribeau, Marc Rioux, and Guy Godin. Color reflectance modeling using a polychromatic laser range sensor. *IEEE Trans. Pattern Anal. Mach. Intell.*,14(2):263–269, 1992.

[16] P. Y. Barnes, E. A. Early, and A. C. Parr. Spectral tri-function automated reference reflectometer. Technical report, National Institute of Standards and Technology, Gaithersburg, MD, 1998.

[17] A. Baumberg. Blending images for texturing 3D models. In *British Machine Vision Conference*, 404–413, 2002.

[18] Barry G. Becker and Nelson L. Max. Smooth transitions between bump rendering algorithms. In *Proceedings of the 20th annual conference on computer graphics and interactive techniques*, 183–190. New York: ACM Press, 1993.

[19] P. Beckmann and A. Spizzichino. *The Scattering of Electromagnetic Waves from Rough Surfaces*, Revised edition. Boston: Artech House, 1987.

[20] B. Berlin and P. Kay. *Basic Color Terms: Their Universality and Evolution*. Berkeley: University of California Press, 1969.

[21] Fausto Bernardini, Ioana M. Martin, and Holly Rushmeier. High-quality texture reconstruction from multiple scans. *IEEE Transactions on Visualization and Computer Graphics*, 7(4):318–332, 2001.

[22] F. Bernardini and H. Rushmeier. The 3D model acquisition pipeline. *Computer Graphics Forum*, 21(2):149–172, 2002.

[23] Francois Blais. Review of 20 years of range sensor development. *Journal of Electronic Imaging*, 13(1):231–240, 2004.

[24] F. Blais, J. Taylor, L. Cournoyer, M. Picard, L. Borgeat, L.-G. Dicaire, M. Rioux, J.-A. Beraldin, G. Godin, C. Lahnanier, and G. Aitken. Ultra-high resolution imaging at 50 m using a portable XYZRGB color laser scanner. *International workshop on recording, modeling and visualization of cultural heritage*, Ascona, 22–27, May 2005.

[25] A. A. Blazej, J. Galatik, Z. Galatik, Z. Krul, and M. Mladek. *Atlas of Microscopic Structures of Fur Skins 1*. New York: Elsevier, 1989.

[26] James F. Blinn. Models of light reflection for computer-synthesized pictures. In *Proceedings of the 4th annual conference on computer graphics and interactive techniques*, 192–198. New York: ACM Press, 1977.

[27] James F. Blinn. Light reflection functions for simulation of clouds and dusty surfaces. In *Proceedings of the 9th annual conference on computer graphics and interactive techniques*, 21–29. New York: ACM Press, 1982.

[28] James F. Blinn and Martin E. Newell. Texture and reflection in computer-generated images. In *Proceedings of the 3rd annual conference on computer graphics and interactive techniques*, 266–266. New York: ACM Press, 1976.

[29] James F. Blinn. Simulation of wrinkled surfaces. In *Proceedings of the 5th annual conference on computer graphics and interactive techniques*, 286–292. New York: ACM Press, 1978.

[30] Jules Bloomenthal. Modeling the mighty maple. In *Proceedings of the 12th annual conference on computer graphics and interactive techniques*, 305–311. New York: ACM Press, 1985.

[31] Jules Bloomenthal and Brian Wyvill. *Introduction to Implicit Surfaces*. San Francisco: Morgan Kaufmann, 1997.

[32] C. Bohren. *Clouds in a Glass of Beer*. New York: John Wiley and Sons, 1987.

[33] C. F. Bohren and D. R. Huffman. *Absorption and Scattering of Light by Small Particles*. New York: Wiley, 1983.

[34] L. Boissieux, G. Kiss, N. Magnenat-Thalmann, and P. Kalra. Simulation of skin aging and wrinkles with cosmetics insight. *Computer Animation and Simulation 2000*, 15–27, 2000.

[35] C. Bosch, X. Pueyo, S. Mérillou, and D. Ghazanfarpour. A physically-based model for rendering realistic scratches. *Computer Graphics Forum*, 23(3):361–370, 2004.

[36] John W. Buchanan. Simulating wood using a voxel approach. *Computer Graphics Forum*, 17(3):105–112, 1998.

[37] Brian Cabral, Nelson Max, and Rebecca Springmeyer. Bidirectional reflection functions from surface bump maps. In *Proceedings of the 14th annual conference on computer graphics and interactive techniques*, 273–281. New York: ACM Press, 1987.

[38] Martin Cadik, Michael Wimmer, Laszlo Neumann, and Alessandro Artusi. Image attributes and quality for evaluation of tone mapping operators. In *Proceedings of the 14th Pacific Conference on Computer Graphics and Applications*, 35–44, Taipei, Taiwan: National Taiwan University Press, 2006.

[39] Patrick Callet. Pertinent data for modeling pigmented materials in realistic rendering. *Computer Graphics Forum*, 15(2):119–128, 1996.

[40] L. Carpenter. The A-buffer, an antialiased hidden surface method. *Proceedings of the 11th annual conference on computer graphics and interactive techniques*, 103–108, 1984.

[41] Nathan A. Carr and John C. Hart. Meshed atlases for real-time procedural solid texturing. *ACM Trans. Graph.*, 21(2):106–131, 2002.

[42] J. L. Castagner and I. J. Bigio. Polar nephelometer based on a rotational confocal imaging setup. *Applied Optics*, 45(10):2232–2239, 2006.

[43] K. Cena and J. L. Monteith. Transfer processes in animal coats, I. Radiative transfer. *Proc. R. Soc. Ser. B*, 188:395–411, 1975.

[44] Yao-Xun Chang and Zen-Chung Shih. Physically-based patination for underground objects. *Computer Graphics Forum*, 19(3):109–117, 2000.

[45] Yao-Xun Chang and Zen-Chung Shih. The synthesis of rust in seawater. *The Visual Computer*, 19(1):50–66, 2003.

[46] Yanyun Chen, Yingqing Xu, Baining Guo, and Heung-Yeung Shum. Modeling and rendering of realistic feathers. In *Proceedings of the 29th annual conference on computer graphics and interactive techniques*, 630–636. New York: ACM Press, 2002.

[47] Per H. Christensen, Dani Lischinski, Eric J. Stollnitz, and David H. Salesin. Clustering for glossy global illumination. *ACM Trans. Graph.*, 16(1):3–33, 1997.

[48] Nelson S.-H. Chu and Chiew-Lan Tai. Moxi: Real-time ink dispersion in absorbent paper. *ACM Trans. Graph.*, 24(3):504–511, 2005.

[49] A. J. Chung, F. Deligianni, P. Shah, A. Wells, and Yang Guang-Zhong. Patient-specific bronchoscopy visualization through BRDF estimation and disocclusion correction. *IEEE Transactions on Medical Imaging*, 25(4):503–513, 2006.

[50] L. Claustres, M. Paulin, and Y. Boucher. BRDF measurement modelling using wavelets for efficient path tracing. *Computer Graphics Forum*, 25(4):701–716, 2003.

[51] T. Cockshott, J. Patterson, and D. England. Modelling the texture of paint. *Computer Graphics Forum*, 11(3):C217–C226, C476, 1992.

[52] Jonathan Cohen, Marc Olano, and Dinesh Manocha. Appearance-preserving simplification. In *SIGGRAPH '98: Proceedings of the 25th annual conference on computer graphics and interactive techniques*, 115–122. New York: ACM Press, 1998.

[53] Michael F. Cohen and John R. Wallace. *Radiosity and Realistic Image Synthesis*. Boston: Academic Press, 1993.

[54] Mark Colbert, Sumanta Pattanaik, and Jaroslav Krivanek. BRDF-Shop: Creating physically correct bidirectional reflectance distribution functions. *IEEE Comput. Graph. Appl.*, 26(1):30–36, 2006.

[55] Robert L. Cook. Shade trees. In *Proceedings of the 11th annual conference on computer graphics and interactive techniques*, 223–231. New York: ACM Press, 1984.

[56] R. L. Cook and K. E. Torrance. A reflectance model for computer graphics. *ACM Transactions on Graphics*, 1(1):7–24, 1982.

[57] K. M. Cooper, R. T. Hanlon, and B. U. Budelmann. Physiological color change in squid ridophores. *Cell and Tissue Research*, 259(1):15–24, 1990.

[58] Franklin C. Crow. Shadow algorithms for computer graphics. In *SIGGRAPH '77: Proceedings of the 4th annual conference on computer graphics and interactive techniques*, 242–248. New York: ACM Press, 1997.

[59] Cassidy J. Curtis, Sean E. Anderson, Joshua E. Seims, Kurt W. Fleischer, and David H. Salesin. Computer-generated watercolor. In *Proceedings of the 24th annual conference on computer graphics and interactive techniques*, 421–430. New York: ACM Press/Addison-Wesley, 1997.

[60] Barbara Cutler, Julie Dorsey, Leonard McMillan, Matthias Müller, and Robert Jagnow. A procedural approach to authoring solid models. In *Proceedings of the 29th annual conference on computer graphics and interactive techniques*, 302–311. New York: ACM Press, 2002.

[61] Wen-Kai Dai, Zen-Chung Shih, and Ruei-Chuan Chang. Synthesizing feather textures in galliformes. *Computer Graphics Forum*, 14(3):407–420, 1995.

[62] Kristin J. Dana, Bram van Ginneken, Shree K. Nayar, and Jan J. Koenderink. Reflectance and texture of real-world surfaces. *ACM Transactions on Graphics*, 18(1):1–34, 1999.

[63] Kristin J. Dana and Jing Wang. Device for convenient measurement of spatially varying bidirectional reflectance. *Journal of the Optical Society of America A*, 1–12, January 2004.

[64] Jean de Rigal, Marie-Laurence Abella, Franck Giron, Laurence Caisey, and Marc Andre Lefebvre. Development and validation of a new skin color chart. *Skin Research and Technology*, 13(1):101–109, 2007.

[65] P. Debevec and S. Gibson. In *Proceedings of the 13th Eurographics workshop on rendering*, Pisa, Italy, 2002.

[66] Paul Debevec, Tim Hawkins, Chris Tchou, Haarm-Pieter Duiker, Westley Sarokin, and Mark Sagar. Acquiring the reflectance field of a human face. In *Proceedings of the 27th annual conference on computer graphics and interactive techniques*, 145–156. New York: ACM Press/Addison-Wesley, 2000.

[67] Paul E. Debevec, Camillo J. Taylor, and Jitendra Malik. Modeling and rendering architecture from photographs: a hybrid geometry- and image-based approach. In *Proceedings of the 23rd annual conference on computer graphics and interactive techniques*, 11–20. New York: ACM Press, 1996.

[68] Paul Debevec, Chris Tchou, Andrew Gardner, Tim Hawkins, Charis Poullis, Jessi Stumpfel, Andrew Jones, Nathaniel Yun, Per Einarsson, Therese Lundgren, Marcos

Fajardo, and Philippe Martinez. Estimating surface reflectance properties of a complex scene under captured natural illumination. Technical report, USC ICT, December 2004.

[69] Brett Desbenoit, Eric Galin, and Samir Akkouche. Simulating and modeling lichen growth. *Computer Graphics Forum*, 23(3):341–350, 2004.

[70] Jean-Michel Dischler. Efficient rendering macro geometric surface structures with bidirectional texture functions. In Drettakis and Max [78], 169–180.

[71] J. M. Dischler, D. Ghazanfarpour, and R. Freydier. Anisotropic solid texture synthesis using orthogonal 2D views. *Computer Graphics Forum*, 17(3):87–96, 1998.

[72] Yoshinori Dobashi, Tsuyoshi Yamamoto, and Tomoyuki Nishita. Interactive rendering of atmospheric scattering effects using graphics hardware. In *HWWS '02: Proceedings of the ACM SIGGRAPH/Eurographics conference on graphics hardware*, 99–107. Aire-la-Ville, Switzerland: Eurographics Association, 2002.

[73] R. A. Dobbins, G. W. Mulholland, and N. P. Bryner. Comparison of a fractal smoke optics model with light extinction measurements. *Atmospheric Environment*, 28(5): 889–897, 1994.

[74] Julie Dorsey, Alan Edelman, Henrik Wann Jensen, Justin Legakis, and Hans Køhling Pedersen. Modeling and rendering of weathered stone. In *Proceedings of the 26th annual conference on computer graphics and interactive techniques*, 225–234. New York: ACM Press/Addison-Wesley, 1999.

[75] Julie Dorsey and Pat Hanrahan. Modeling and rendering of metallic patinas. In *Proceedings of the 23rd annual conference on computer graphics and interactive techniques*, 387–396. New York: ACM Press/Addison-Wesley, 1999.

[76] Julie Dorsey, Hans Køhling Pedersen, and Pat Hanrahan. Flow and changes in appearance. In *Proceedings of the 23rd annual conference on computer graphics and interactive techniques*, 411–420. New York: ACM Press, 1996.

[77] Julie Dorsey and Philipp Slusallek, editors. *Rendering Techniques '97*. In *Proceedings 8th Eurographics rendering workshop*, Saint Etienne, France, June 16–18. New York: Springer-Verlag, 1997.

[78] George Drettakis and Nelson Max, editors. *Rendering Techniques '98*. *Proceedings 9th Eurographics Rendering Workshop*, Vienna, June 29–July 1. New York: Springer-Verlag 1998.

[79] Arne Duer. An improved normalization for the Ward reflectance model. *Journal of Graphics Tools*, 11(1):51, 2006.

[80] P. Dumont-Bécle, A. Kemeny, S. Michelin, and D. Arqués. Multi-texturing approach for paint appearance simulation on virtual vehicles. *Proceedings of the driving simulation conference*, 123–133, 2001.

[81] Frédo Durand, Nicolas Holzschuch, Cyril Soler, Eric Chan, and François X. Sillion. A frequency analysis of light transport. In *SIGGRAPH '05: ACM SIGGRAPH 2005 papers*, 1115–1126. New York: ACM Press, 2005.

[82] Roman Durikovic and William L. Martens. Simulation of sparkling and depth effect in paints. In *SCCG '03: Proceedings of the 19th spring conference on computer graphics*, 193–198, New York: ACM Press, 2003.

[83] Philip Dutré, Philippe Bekaert, and Kavita Bala. *Advanced Global Illumination*. Wellesley, MA: A. K. Peters, 2003.

[84] Philip Dutré, Frank Suykens, Per H. Christensen, and Daniel Cohen-Or, editors. *Proceedings of the 14th Eurographics workshop on rendering*, Eurographics Association. Leuven, Belgium, 2003.

[85] E. A. Early, P. Y. Barnes, B. C. Johnson, J. J. Butler, C. J. Bruegge, S. F. Biggar, P. R. Spyak, and M. M. Pavlov. Bidirectional reflectance round-robin in support of the Earth observing system program. *Journal of Atmospheric and Oceanic Technology*, 17(8):1077–1091, 2000.

[86] David S. Ebert, editor. *Texturing and Modeling: A Procedural Approach, Third Edition*. San Francisco: Morgan Kaufmann, 2002.

[87] Mohamed A. Elhelw, Benny P. Lo, Ara Darzi, and Guang-Zhong Yang. Real-time photo-realistic rendering for surgical simulations with graphics hardware. *Lecture Notes in Computer Science*, 3150:346–352, 2004.

[88] E. Enderton. Computer graphics for *Jurassic Park*. In *Compcon Spring '94, Digest of Papers*, 456–457, 28 February–4 March 1994.

[89] Sergey Ershov, Roman Durikovic, Konstantin Kolchin, and Karol Myszkowski. Reverse engineering approach to appearance-based design of metallic and pearlescent paints. *Vis. Comput.*, 20(8–9):586–600, 2004.

[90] Sergey Ershov, Konstantin Kolchin, and Karol Myszkowski. Rendering pearlescent appearance based on paint-composition modelling. *Computer Graphics Forum*, 20(3), 2001.

[91] Mark Fairchild. *Color Appearance Models, 2nd Edition*. New York: John Wiley and Sons, 2005.

[92] Gerald E. Farin. *Curves and Surfaces for Computer-Aided Geometric Design: A Practical Code*. New York: Academic Press, 1996.

[93] R. J. Ferek, P. V. Hobbs, J. A. Herring, K. K. Laursen, and R. E. Weiss. Chemical composition of emissions from the Kuwait oil fires. *Journal of Geophysical Research*, 97(D13):14483–14489, 1992.

[94] Richard P. Feynman. *QED: The Strange Theory of Light and Matter*. Princeton: Princeton University Press, 1985.

[95] Frederick Fisher and Andrew Woo. R.E versus N.H specular highlights. *Graphics Gems IV*, 388–400, 1994.

[96] R. Fleming, R. Dror, and E. Adelson. Real-world illumination and the perception of surfaces. *Journal of Vision*, 3(5):347–368, 2003.

[97] Roland W. Fleming, Henrik Wann Jensen, and Heinrich H. B. lthoff. Perceiving translucent materials. In *Proceedings of the 1st symposium on applied perception in graphics and visualization*, 127–134. New York: ACM Press, 2004.

[98] Sing-Choong Foo. A gonioreflectometer for measuring the bidirectional reflectance of material for use in illumination computation. Master's thesis, Program of Computer Graphics, Cornell University, Ithaca, NY, August 1997.

[99] Deborah R. Fowler, James Hanan, and Przemyslaw Prusinkiewicz. Modeling spiral phyllotaxis. *Computers and Graphics*, 13(3):291–296, 1989.

[100] Deborah R. Fowler, Przemyslaw Prusinkiewicz, and Johannes Battjes. A collision-based model of spiral phyllotaxis. In *Proceedings of the 19th annual conference on computer graphics and interactive techniques*, 361–368. New York: ACM Press, 1992.

[101] Oliver Franzke and Oliver Deussen. Rendering plant leaves faithfully. In *Proceedings of the SIGGRAPH 2003 conference on sketches and applications*, 1–1. New York: ACM Press, 2003.

[102] Martin Fuchs, Hendrik Lensch, and Hans-Peter Seidel. Reflectance from images: A model-based approach for human faces. *IEEE Transactions on Visualization and Computer Graphics*, 11(3):296–305, 2005.

[103] Martin Führer, Henrik Wann Jensen, and Przemyslaw Prusinkiewicz. Modeling hairy plants. *Graphical Models*, 68(4):333–392, July 2006.

[104] Andrew Gardner, Chris Tchou, Tim Hawkins, and Paul Debevec. Linear light source reflectometry. *ACM Trans. Graph.*, 22(3):749–758, 2003.

[105] Athinodoros S. Georghiades. Recovering 3D shape and reflectance from a small number of photographs. In *EGRW '03: Proceedings of the 14th Eurographics workshop on rendering*, 230–240. Aire-la-Ville, Switzerland: Eurographics Association, 2003.

[106] Athinodoros S. Georghiades, Jianye Lu, Chen Xu, Julie Dorsey, and Holly Rushmeier. Observing and transferring material histories. Technical Report YALEU/DCS/TR-1329, Yale University, New Haven, CT, June 2005.

[107] H. E. Gerber and E. E. Hindman. *Light Absorption by Aerosol Particles*. New York: Spectrum Press, 1982.

[108] T. A. Germer and C. C. Asmail. Scattering and surface roughness. In Z.-H. Gu and A. A. Maradudin, editors, *Proceedings of the SPIE 3141*, 220–237, 1997.

[109] Reid Gershbein, Peter Schroeder, and Pat Hanrahan. Textures and radiosity: controlling emission and reflection with texture maps. In *SIGGRAPH '94: Proceedings of the 21st*

annual conference on computer graphics and interactive techniques, 51–58. New York: ACM Press, 1994.

[110] Djamchid Ghazanfarpour and Jean-Michel Dischler. Generation of 3D texture using multiple 2D models analysis. *Computer Graphics Forum*, 15(3):311–324, 1996.

[111] Andrew Glassner. A model of phosphorescence and fluorescence. In *5th Eurographics rendering workshop*, 57–68, 1994.

[112] S. Gobron and N. Chiba. Simulation of peeling using 3D-surface cellular automata. In *9th Pacific graphics conference on computer graphics and applications*, 338–347. Tokyo, Japan: IEEE, October 2001.

[113] Stéphane Gobron and Norishige Chiba. Crack pattern simulation based on 3D surface cellular automata. *The Visual Computer*, 17(5):287–309, 2001.

[114] Michael Goesele, Hendrik P. A. Lensch, Jochen Lang, Christian Fuchs, and Hans-Peter Seidel. Disco: Acquisition of translucent objects. *ACM Trans. Graph.*, 23(3):835–844, 2004.

[115] Frank Goetz, Ralf Borau, and Gitta Domik. An XML-based visual shading language for vertex and fragment shaders. In *Web3D '04: Proceedings of the 9th international conference on 3D Web technology*, 87–97, New York: ACM Press, 2004.

[116] Dan B. Goldman. Fake fur rendering. In *Proceedings of the 24th annual conference on computer graphics and interactive techniques*, 127–134. New York: ACM Press/ Addison-Wesley, 1997.

[117] Aleksey Golovinskiy, Wojciech Matusik, Hanspeter Pfister, Szymon Rusinkiewicz, and Thomas Funkhouser. A statistical model for synthesis of detailed facial geometry. In *SIGGRAPH '06: papers*, 1025–1034, New York: ACM Press, 2006.

[118] Jay S. Gondek, Gary W. Meyer, and Jonathan G. Newman. Wavelength-dependent reflectance functions. In *Proceedings of the 21st annual conference on computer graphics and interactive techniques*, 213–220. New York: ACM Press, 1994.

[119] Gabriele Gorla, Victoria Interrante, and Guillermo Sapiro. Texture synthesis for 3D shape representation. *IEEE Transactions on Visualization and Computer Graphics*, 9(4):512–524, 2003.

[120] Steven J. Gortler, Radek Grzeszczuk, Richard Szeliski, and Michael F. Cohen. The lumigraph. In *Proceedings of the 23rd annual conference on computer graphics and interactive techniques*, 43–54. New York: ACM Press, 1996.

[121] Steven J. Gortler, Peter Schroeder, Michael F. Cohen, and Pat Hanrahan. Wavelet radiosity. In *SIGGRAPH '93: Proceedings of the 20th annual conference on computer graphics and interactive techniques*, 221–230. New York: ACM Press, 1993.

[122] Y. M. Govaerts, S. Jacquemoud, M. M. Verstraete, and S. L. Ustin. Three-dimensional radiation transfer modeling in a dicotyledon leaf. *Applied Optics*, 35(33):6585–6598, 1996.

[123] Ned Greene and Michael Kass. Error-bounded antialiased rendering of complex environments. In *SIGGRAPH '94: Proceedings of the 21st annual conference on computer graphics and interactive techniques*, 59–66. New York: ACM Press, 1994.

[124] J. Greffet and M. Nieto-Vesperinas. Thermodynamic constraints on reflectance reciprocity and Kirchhoff's law. *J. Opt. Soc. Am.*, 15:2735–2744, 1998.

[125] Eduard Groeller, Rene T. Rau, and Wolfgang Strasser. Modeling and visualization of knitwear. *IEEE Transactions on Visualization and Computer Graphics*, 1(4):302–310, 1995.

[126] Jinwei Gu, Chien-I Tu, Ravi Ramamoorthi, Peter Belhumeur, Wojciech Matusik, and Shree Nayar. Time-varying surface appearance: acquisition, modeling and rendering. *ACM Trans. Graph.*, 25(3):762–771, 2006.

[127] Brian Guenter, Todd B. Knoblock, and Erik Ruf. Specializing shaders. In *Proceedings of the 22nd annual conference on computer graphics and interactive techniques*, 343–350. New York: ACM Press, 1995.

[128] Johannes Günther, Tongbo Chen, Michael Goesele, Ingo Wald, and Hans-Peter Seidel. Efficient acquisition and realistic rendering of car paint. In Günther Greiner, Joachim Hornegger, Heinrich Niemann, and Marc Stamminger, editors, *Proceedings of 10th international fall workshop—vision, modeling, and visualization (VMV) 2005*, 487–494. Akademische Verlagsgesellschaft Aka GmbH, November 2005.

[129] Q. Guo and T. Kunii. Modeling the diffuse painting of sumie. In *Proceedings of IFIP WG5: Modeling in computer graphics*, vol. 10:331–336, 1991.

[130] Stephane Guy and Cyril Soler. Graphics gems revisited: fast and physically-based rendering of gemstones. *ACM Trans. Graph.*, 23(3):231–238, 2004.

[131] N. Guzelsu, J. F. Federici, H. C. Lim, H. R. Chauhdry, A. B. Ritter, and T. Findley. Measurement of skin stretch via light reflection. *Journal of Biomedical Optics*, 8(1):80–86, 2003.

[132] Chet S. Haase and Gary W. Meyer. Modeling pigmented materials for realistic image synthesis. *ACM Transactions on Graphics*, 11(4):305–335, 1992.

[133] M.A.C.E. Hadley and J.M.G. Oldman. Physiological color changes in reptiles. *Integrative and Comparative Biology*, 9(2):489, 1969.

[134] David Halliday, Robert Resnick, and Jearl Walker. *Fundamentals of Physics, 6th Edition, Vol. 2/Extended*. New York: John Wiley, 2001.

[135] Jefferson Y. Han and Ken Perlin. Measuring bidirectional texture reflectance with a kaleidoscope. *ACM Trans. Graph.*, 22(3):741–748, 2003.

[136] Pat Hanrahan and Paul Haeberli. Direct WYSIWYG painting and texturing on 3D shapes. In *Proceedings of the 17th annual conference on computer graphics and interactive techniques*, 215–223. New York: ACM Press, 1990.

[137] Pat Hanrahan and Wolfgang Krueger. Reflection from layered surfaces due to sub-surface scattering. In *Proceedings of the 20th annual conference on computer graphics and interactive techniques*, 165–174. New York: ACM Press, 1993.

[138] Pat Hanrahan and Jim Lawson. A language for shading and lighting calculations. In *Proceedings of the 17th annual conference on computer graphics and interactive techniques*, 289–298. New York: ACM Press, 1990.

[139] Antonio Haro, Irfan A. Essa, and Brian K. Guenter. Real-time photo-realistic physically based rendering of fine scale human skin structure. In *Proceedings of the 12th Euro-graphics workshop on rendering techniques*, 53–62, London: Springer-Verlag, 2001.

[140] M. J. Harris and A. Lastr. Real-time cloud rendering. *Computer Graphics Forum*, 20(3):76–85, 2001.

[141] Tim Hawkins, Per Einarsson, and Paul Debevec. Acquisition of time-varying participating media. *ACM Trans. Graph.*, 24(3):812–815, 2005.

[142] Xiao D. He, Kenneth E. Torrance, François X. Sillion, and Donald P. Greenberg. A comprehensive physical model for light reflection. In *Proceedings of the 18th annual conference on computer graphics and interactive techniques*, 175–186. New York: ACM Press, 1991.

[143] David J. Heeger and James R. Bergen. Pyramid-based texture analysis/synthesis. In *SIGGRAPH '95: Proceedings of the 22nd annual conference on computer graphics and interactive techniques*, 229–238, New York: ACM Press, 1995.

[144] Wolfgang Heidrich and Hans-Peter Seidel. Realistic, hardware-accelerated shading and lighting. In *SIGGRAPH '99: Proceedings of the 26th annual conference on computer graphics and interactive techniques*, 171–178. New York: ACM Press/Addison-Wesley, 1999.

[145] T. Scott Hemphill, Ilene M. Reinitz, Mary L. Johnson, and James E. Shigley. Modeling the appearance of the round brilliant cut diamond: an analysis of brilliance. *Gems and Gemology*, 34(3):158–183, 1998.

[146] Roger D. Hersch, Fabien Collaud, and Patrick Emmel. Reproducing color images with embedded metallic patterns. *ACM Trans. Graph.*, 22(3):427–434, 2003.

[147] Brad Hiebert, Jubin Dave, Tae-Yong Kim, Ivan Neulander, Hans Rijpkema, and Will Telford. The *Chronicles of Narnia*: the lion, the crowds and rhythm and hues. In *SIGGRAPH '06: ACM courses*, 1. New York: ACM Press, 2006.

[148] H. Hirayama, K. Kaneda, H. Yamashita, and Y. Monden. An accurate illumination model for objects coated with multilayer films. *Computers and Graphics*, 25(3):391–400, 2001.

[149] Koichi Hirota, Yasuyuki Tanoue, and Toyohisa Kaneko. Generation of crack patterns with a physical model. *The Visual Computer*, 14(3):126–137, 1998.

[150] Koichi Hirota, Yasuyuki Tanoue, and Toyohisa Kaneko. Simulation of three-dimensional cracks. *The Visual Computer*, 16(7):371–378, 2000.

[151] Siu-Chi Hsu and Tien-Tsin Wong. Simulating dust accumulation. *IEEE Comput. Graphics Appl.*, 15(1):18–22, 1995.

[152] Richard S. Hunter and Richard W. Harold. *The Measurement of Appearance*. New York: John Wiley, 1987.

[153] Hayley N. Iben and James F. O'Brien. Generating surface crack patterns. In *SCA '06: Proceedings of the 2006 ACM SIGGRAPH/Eurographics symposium on computer animation*, 177–185, Aire-la-Ville, Switzerland: Eurographics Association, 2006.

[154] Isabelle Icart and Didier Arquès. An illumination model for a system of isotropic substrate—isotropic thin film with identical rough boundaries. In Lischinski and Larson, editors, In *Proceedings of the 10th Eurographics rendering workshop*, 261–272, Granada, Spain, June 21–23. New York: Springer-Verlag Wien, 1999.

[155] Isabelle Icart and Didier Arquès. Technical section—an approach to geometrical and optical simulation of soap froth. *Computers and Graphics*, 23(3):405–418, 1999.

[156] Masataka Imura, Takaaki Abe, Ichiroh Kanaya, Yoshihiro Yasumuro, Yoshitsugu Manabe, and Kunihiro Chihara. Rendering of "play of color" using stratified model based on amorphous structure of opal. In Changming Sun, Hugues Talbot, S'ebastien Ourselin, and Tony Adriaansen, editors, *DICTA*, 349–358. Collingwood, Victoria, Australia: CSIRO Publishing, 2003.

[157] Takayuki Itoh, Kazunori Miyata, and Kenji Shimada. Generating organic textures with controlled anisotropy and directionality. *IEEE Comput. Graph. Appl.*, 23(3): 38–45, 2003.

[158] Robert Jagnow, Julie Dorsey, and Holly Rushmeier. Stereological techniques for solid textures. *ACM Trans. Graph.*, 23(3):329–335, 2004.

[159] Francis Jenkins and Harvey White. *Fundamentals of Optics*. New York: McGraw-Hill, 1976.

[160] Henrik Wann Jensen and Juan Buhler. A rapid hierarchical rendering technique for translucent materials. In *SIGGRAPH '02: Proceedings of the 29th annual conference on computer graphics and interactive techniques*, 576–581. New York: ACM Press, 2002.

[161] Henrik Wann Jensen and Per H. Christensen. Efficient simulation of light transport in scences with participating media using photon maps. In *SIGGRAPH '98: Proceedings of the 25th annual conference on computer graphics and interactive techniques*, 311–320. New York: ACM Press, 1998.

[162] Henrik Wann Jensen, Justin Legakis, and Julie Dorsey. Rendering of wet material. In Lischinski and Larson, editors, 273–282. In *Proc. 10th Eurographics rendering workshop*, Granada, Spain, June 21–23. New York: Springer-Verlag Wien, 1999.

[163] Henrik Wann Jensen, Stephen R. Marschner, Marc Levoy, and Pat Hanrahan. A practical model for subsurface light transport. In *Proceedings of the 28th annual conference on computer graphics and interactive techniques*, 511–518. New York: ACM Press, 2001.

[164] Dave Jessey and Don Tarman. Igneous rock identification: Nature's fiery cauldron, at *http://geology.csupomona.edu/alert/igneous/ignrxs.htm*, 2006.

[165] Bela Julesz. Visual pattern discrimination. *IRE Trans. Inf. Theory*, IT-8:84–92, 1962.

[166] Bela Julesz. *Dialogues on Perception*. Cambridge, MA: MIT Press, 1995.

[167] James T. Kajiya. Anisotropic reflection models. In *Proceedings of the 12th annual conference on computer graphics and interactive techniques*, 15–21. New York: ACM Press, 1985.

[168] James T. Kajiya. The rendering equation. In *Proceedings of the 13th annual conference on computer graphics and interactive techniques*, 143–150. New York: ACM Press, 1986.

[169] J. T. Kajiya and T. L. Kay. Rendering fur with three-dimensional textures. In *Proceedings of the 16th annual conference on computer graphics and interactive techniques*, 271–280. New York: ACM Press, 1989.

[170] Konrad F. Karner, Heinz Mayer, and Michael Gervautz. An image-based measurement system for anisotropic reflection. *Computer Graphics Forum*, 15(3):119–128, 1996.

[171] A. Kaufman. TSLA texture synthesis language. *The Visual Computer*, 4(3):148–158, 1988.

[172] Jan Kautz and Michael D. McCool. Interactive rendering with arbitrary BRDFs using separable approximations. In *SIGGRAPH '99: ACM SIGGRAPH conference abstracts and applications*, 253. New York: ACM Press, 1999.

[173] Jan Kautz, Pere-Pau Vazquez, Wolfgang Heidrich, and Hans-Peter Seidel. Unified approach to prefiltered environment maps. In *Proceedings of the Eurographics workshop on rendering techniques*, 185–196. London: Springer-Verlag, 2000.

[174] G. Kay and T. Caelli. Inverting an illumination model from range and intensity maps. *CVGIP: Image Understanding*, (59):183–201, 1994.

[175] Kenneth E. Kidd and Martha Ann Kidd. A classification system for glass beads for the use of field archaeologists. Technical report. Ottawa: National Historic Sites Service, National and Historic Parks Branch, Department of Indian Affairs and Northern Development, 1970.

[176] A. Knüttel, S. Bonev, and W. Knaak. New method for evaluation of in vivo scattering and refractive index properties obtained with optical coherence tomography. *Journal of Biomedical Optics*, 9:265, 2004.

[177] J. Koenderink. Note. *Perception*, 32:391–394, 2003.

[178] J. Koenderink and S. Pont. The secret of velvety skin. *Machine Vision and Applications*, 14(4):260–268, 2003.

[179] Craig Kolb, Don Mitchell, and Pat Hanrahan. A realistic camera model for computer graphics. In *SIGGRAPH '95: Proceedings of the 22nd annual conference on computer graphics and interactive techniques*, 317–324. New York: ACM Press, 1995.

[180] M. L. Koudelka. *Capture, Analysis, and Synthesis of Textured Surfaces with Variation in Illumination, Viewpoint, and Time*. Ph.D. thesis, Department of Electrical Engineering, Yale University, New Haven, CT, 2004.

[181] A. Krishnaswamy and G.V.G. Baranoski. A biophysically-based spectral model of light interaction with human skin. *Computer Graphics Forum*, 23(3):331–340, 2004.

[182] P. Kubelka. New contributions to the optics of intensely light-scattering material, part I. *J. Opt. Soc. Am.*, 38:448, 1948.

[183] P. Kubelka. New contributions to the optics of intensely light-scattering material, part II. *J. Opt. Soc. Am.*, 44:330, 1954.

[184] P. Kubelka and F. Munk. Ein beitrag zur optik der farbanstriche. *Z. Tech. Physik.*, 12:330, 1931.

[185] Eric P. F. Lafortune, Sing-Choong Foo, Kenneth E. Torrance, and Donald P. Greenberg. Non-linear approximation of reflectance functions. In *Proceedings of the 24th annual conference on computer graphics and interactive techniques*, 117–126. New York: ACM Press/Addison-Wesley, 1997.

[186] Michael W. Y. Lam and Gladimir V. G. Baranoski. A predictive light transport model for the human iris. *Computer Graphics Forum*, 25(3):359–368, 2006.

[187] Greg Ward Larson and Rob Shakespeare. *Rendering with Radiance: The Art and Science of Lighting Visualization*. San Francisco: Morgan Kaufmann, 1998.

[188] Lutz Latta and Andreas Kolb. Homomorphic factorization of BRDF-based lighting computation. In *SIGGRAPH '02: Proceedings of the 29th annual conference on computer graphics and interactive techniques*, 509–516. New York: ACM Press, 2002.

[189] Jason Lawrence, Szymon Rusinkiewicz, and Ravi Ramamoorthi. Efficient BRDF importance sampling using a factored representation. In *SIGGRAPH '04: ACM SIGGRAPH 2004 papers*, 496–505. New York: ACM Press, 2004.

[190] R. L. Lee Jr. and J. Hernández-Andrés. Virtual tunnels and green glass: the colors of common mirrors. *American Journal of Physics*, 72:53–59, 2004.

[191] Laurent Lefebvre and Pierre Poulin. Analysis and synthesis of structural textures. In *Proceedings of graphics interface*, 77–86, May 2000.

[192] Sylvain Lefebvre and Fabrice Neyret. Synthesizing bark. In *13th Eurographics workshop on rendering*, 105–116, 2002.

[193] Aaron Lefohn, Brian Budge, Peter Shirley, Richard Caruso, and Erik Reinhard. An ocularist's approach to human iris synthesis. *IEEE Comput. Graphics Appl.*, 23(6):70–75, 2003.

[194] Jerome Edward Lengyel. Real-time hair. In *Proceedings of the Eurographics workshop on rendering techniques 2000*, 243–256. London: Springer-Verlag, 2000.

[195] Hendrik P. A. Lensch, Michael Goesele, Philippe Bekaert, Jan Kautz, Marcus A. Magnor, Jochen Lang, and Hans-Peter Seidel. Interactive rendering of translucent objects. In *PG '02: Proceedings of the 10th Pacific conference on computer graphics and applications*, 214–224. Washington, DC: IEEE Computer Society, 2002.

[196] Hendrik P. A. Lensch, Jan Kautz, Michael Goesele, Wolfgang Heidrich, and Hans-Peter Seidel. Image-based reconstruction of spatial appearance and geometric detail. *ACM Transactions on Graphics*, 22(2):234–257, 2003.

[197] Marc Levoy and Pat Hanrahan. Light field rendering. In *Proceedings of the 23rd annual conference on computer graphics and interactive techniques*, 31–42. New York: ACM Press, 1996.

[198] Bruno Lévy. Constrained texture mapping for polygonal meshes. In *Proceedings of the 28th annual conference on computer graphics and interactive techniques*, 417–424. New York: ACM Press, 2001.

[199] Bruno Lévy, Sylvain Petitjean, Nicolas Ray, and Jerome Maillot. Least squares conformal maps for automatic texture atlas generation. In *Proceedings of the 29th annual conference on computer graphics and interactive techniques*, 362–371. New York: ACM Press, 2002.

[200] R. R. Lewis. Making shaders more physically plausible. *Computer Graphics Forum*, 13(2):109–120, 1994.

[201] C. S. Li, F. T. Jenq, and W. H. Lin. Field characterization of submicron aerosols from indoor combustion sources. *Journal of Aerosol Science*, 23(S1):S547–S550, 1992.

[202] K. N. Liou. *Radiation and Cloud Processes in the Atmosphere*. New York: The Oxford University Press, 1992.

[203] Dani Lischinski and Greg Ward Larson, editors. *Rendering Techniques '99, Eurographics*. In *Proceedings of the 10th Eurographics rendering workshop, Granada, Spain, June 21–23*. New York: Springer-Verlag Wien, 1999.

[204] Dave Litwiller. CMOS vs. CCD: maturing technologies, maturing markets. *Photonics Spectra*, August 2005.

[205] Xinguo Liu, Yizhou Yu, and Heung-Yeung Shum. Synthesizing bidirectional texture functions for real-world surfaces. In *Proceedings of the 28th annual conference on computer graphics and interactive techniques*, 97–106. New York: ACM Press, 2001.

[206] Margaret Livingstone. *Vision and Art: The Biology of Seeing*. New York: Harry N. Abrams, 2002.

[207] Tom Lokovic and Eric Veach. Deep shadow maps. In *SIGGRAPH '00: Proceedings of the 27th annual conference on computer graphics and interactive techniques*, 385–392, New York: ACM Press/Addison-Wesley, 2000.

[208] Jianye Lu, Athinodoros S. Georghiades, Holly Rushmeier, Julie Dorsey, and Chen Xu. Synthesis of material drying history: phenomenon modeling, transferring and rendering. In *Proceedings of Eurographics workshop on natural phenomena*, 7–16, 2005.

[209] Jianye Lu, Athinodoros S. Georghiades, Andreas Glaser, Hongzhi Wu, Li-Yi Wei, Baining Guo, Julie Dorsey, and Holly Rushmeier. Context-aware textures. *ACM Trans. Graph.*, 26(1):3, 2007.

[210] Rong Lu, Jan J. Koenderink, and Astrid M. L. Kappers. Optical properties (bidirectional reflection distribution functions) of velvet. *Applied Optics*, 37(25):5974–5984, 1998.

[211] H. B. Mall Jr. and N. da Vitoria Lobo. Determining wet surfaces from dry. In *Proceedings of the 5th international conference on computer vision*, 963–968, 1995.

[212] Tom Malzbender, Dan Gelb, and Hans Wolters. Polynomial texture maps. In *Proceedings of the 28th annual conference on computer graphics and interactive techniques*, 519–528. New York: ACM Press, 2001.

[213] Stephen R. Marschner. *Inverse Rendering in Computer Graphics*. Ph.D. thesis, Program of Computer Graphics, Cornell University, Ithaca, NY, 1998.

[214] Stephen R. Marschner, Brian K. Guenter, and Sashi Raghupathy. Modeling and rendering for realistic facial animation. In *Proceedings of the Eurographics Workshop on Rendering Techniques 2000*, 231–242, London: Springer-Verlag, 2000.

[215] Stephen R. Marschner, Henrik Wann Jensen, Mike Cammarano, Steve Worley, and Pat Hanrahan. Light scattering from human hair fibers. *ACM Trans. Graph.*, 22(3):780–791, 2003.

[216] Stephen R. Marschner, Stephen H. Westin, Adam Arbree, and Jonathan T. Moon. Measuring and modeling the appearance of finished wood. *ACM Trans. Graph.*, 24(3):727–734, 2005.

[217] W. Martin and J. Aggarwal. Volumetric descriptions of objects from multiple views. *IEEE Transactions on Pattern Analysis and Machine Intelligence*, 5(2):150–174, 1983.

[218] Wojciech Matusik. *A Data-Driven Reflectance Model*. Ph.D. thesis, Department of Electrical Engineering and Computer Science, MIT, Boston, 2003.

[219] Wojciech Matusik, Hanspeter Pfister, Matt Brand, and Leonard McMillan. A data-driven reflectance model. *ACM Trans. Graph.*, 22(3):759–769, 2003.

[220] Wojciech Matusik, Hanspeter Pfister, Matthew Brand, and Leonard McMillan. Efficient isotropic BRDF measurement. In Philip Dutré, Frank Suykens, Per H. Christensen, and Daniel Cohen-Or, editors, *Proceedings of the 14th Eurographics workshop on rendering*, 241–248, Leuven, Belgium. Aire-la-Ville, Switzerland: Eurographics Association, 2003.

[221] MAXON. BodyPaint (software package).

[222] Michael D. McCool, Jason Ang, and Anis Ahmad. Homomorphic factorization of BRDFs for high-performance rendering. In *Computer Graphics Proceedings, Annual Conference Series (SIGGRAPH 2001)*, August 2001.

[223] Morgan McGuire, George Stathis, Hanspeter Pfister, and Shriram Krishnamurthi. Abstract shade trees. In *SI3D '06: Proceedings of the 2006 symposium on interactive 3D graphics and games*, 79–86. New York: ACM Press, 2006.

[224] M. P. Mengüç and P. Dutta. Scattering tomography and its application to diffusion flames. *Journal of Heat Transfer*, 144–151, February 1994.

[225] S. Merillou, J.-M. Dischler, and D. Ghazanfarpour. A BRDF postprocess to integrate porosity on rendered surface. *IEEE Transactions on Visualization and Computer Graphics*, 6(4):306–318, 2000.

[226] S. Merillou, J. M. Dischler, and D. Ghazanfarpour. Surface scratches: measuring, modeling and rendering. *The Visual Computer*, 17(1):30–45, 2001.

[227] Stephane Merillou, Jean-Michel Dischler, and Djamchid Ghazanfarpour. Corrosion: simulating and rendering. In *Proceedings of GI 2001*, 167–174, June 2001.

[228] F. Metelli. The perception of transparency. *Scientific American*, 230:90–98, 1974.

[229] Alexandre Meyer and Fabrice Neyret. Multiscale shaders for the efficient realistic rendering of pine-trees. In *Graphics Interface*, 137–144, Canadian Information Processing Society, Canadian Human–Computer Communications Society, May 2000.

[230] Gary Meyer, Clement Shimizu, Alan Eggly, David Fischer, Jim King, and Allan Rodriguez. Computer aided design of automotive finishes. In *Proceedings of 10th Congress of the international colour association*, 685–688, 2005.

[231] Gavin S. P. Miller. The motion dynamics of snakes and worms. In *SIGGRAPH '88: Proceedings of the 15th annual conference on computer graphics and interactive techniques*, 169–173. New York: ACM Press, 1988.

[232] Gavin Miller. Efficient algorithms for local and global accessibility shading. In *Proceedings of the 21st annual conference on computer graphics and interactive techniques*, 319–326. New York: ACM Press, 1994.

[233] Mike Milne. Dinosaurs before the beginning. *SIGGRAPH Comput. Graph.*, 33(2): 11–14, 1999.

[234] Joel Mobley and Tuan Vo-Dinh. Optical properties of tissue. In Tuan Vo-Dinh, editor, *Biomedical Photonics Handbook*. Boca Raton, FL: CRC Press, 2003.

[235] Jonathan T. Moon and Stephen R. Marschner. Simulating multiple scattering in hair using a photon mapping approach. In *SIGGRAPH '06: ACM SIGGRAPH papers*, 1067–1074, New York: ACM Press, 2006.

[236] G. W. Mulholland and N. P. Bryner. Radiometric model of the transmission cell-reciprocal nephelometer. *Atmospheric Environment*, 28(5):873–887, 1994.

[237] G. Müller, J. Meseth, M. Sattler, R. Sarlette, and R. Klein. Acquisition, synthesis, and rendering of bidirectional texture functions. *Computer Graphics Forum*, 24(1):83–109, 2005.

[238] Noriko Nagata, Toshimasa Dobashi, Yoshitsugu Manabe, Teruo Usami, and Seiji Inokuchi. Modeling and visualization for a pearl-quality evaluation simulator. *IEEE Transactions on Visualization and Computer Graphics*, 3(4):307–315, 1997.

[239] E. Nakamae, K. Kaneda, T. Okamoto, and T. Nishita. A lighting model aiming at drive simulators. In *Proceedings of Siggraph 1990*, pages 395–404. ACM SIGGRAPH, 1990.

[240] S. G. Narasimhan, M. Gupta, C. Donner, R. Ramamoorthi, S. K. Nayar, and H. W. Jensen. Acquiring scattering properties of participating media by dilution. *ACM Transactions on Graphics (TOG)*, 25(3):1003–1012, 2006.

[241] Kurt Nassau. *The Physics and Chemistry of Color: The Fifteen Causes of Color*. New York: Wiley-Interscience, 2001.

[242] Shree K. Nayar, Xi-Sheng Fang, and Terrance Boult. Separation of reflection components using color and polarization. *Int. J. Comput. Vision*, 21(3):163–186, 1997.

[243] Shree K. Nayar, Gurunandan Krishnan, Michael D. Grossberg, and Ramesh Raskar. Fast separation of direct and global components of a scene using high frequency illumination. *ACM Trans. Graph.*, 25(3):935–944, 2006.

[244] Diego Nehab, Szymon Rusinkiewicz, James Davis, and Ravi Ramamoorthi. Efficiently combining positions and normals for precise 3D geometry. *ACM Trans. Graph.*, 24(3):536–543, 2005.

[245] Ivan Neulander and Michiel van de Panne. Rendering generalized cylinders with paintstrokes. In *Graphics Interface*, 233–244, 1998.

[246] Sir Isaac Newton. *Opticks: Or, a Treatise of the Reflections, Refractions, Inflections and Colours of Light, Third Edition*. London: William and John Innys, 1721.

[247] Fabrice Neyret. Modeling animating and rendering complex scenes using volumetric textures. *IEEE Transactions on Visualization and Computer Graphics*, 4(1):55–70, 1998.

[248] Fabrice Neyret, Raphal Heiss, and Franck Senegas Realistic rendering of an organ surface in real-time for laparoscopic surgery simulation. *The Visual Computer*, 18(3):135–149, 2002.

[249] Addy Ngan, Frédo Durand, and Wojciech Matusik. Experimental analysis of BRDF models. In *Eurographics symposium on rendering (2005)*, 117–126, 2005.

[250] Addy Ngan, Frédo Durand, and Wojciech Matusik. Image-driven navigation of analytical BRDF models. In *Eurographics symposium on rendering*, 399–408, June 2006.

[251] F. Nicodemus, J. Richmond, J. Hsia, I. Gisberg, and T. Limperis. Geometric considerations and nomenclature for reflectance, NBS monograph 160. National Bureau of Standards, October, 1977.

[252] Ko Nishino, Yoichi Sato, and Katsushi Ikeuchi. Eigen-texture method: appearance compression based on 3D model. In *Modelling from Reality*, 117–135. Norwell, MA: Kluwer Academic, 2001.

[253] T. Nishita, H. Iwasaki, Y. Dobashi, and E. Nakamae. A modeling and rendering method for snow by using metaballs. *Computer Graphics Forum*, 16(3):357–364, 1997.

[254] Michael Oren and Shree K. Nayar. Generalization of Lambert's reflectance model. In *Proceedings of the 21st annual conference on computer graphics and interactive techniques*, 239–246. New York: ACM Press, 1994.

[255] D. Osorio and A. D. Ham. Spectral reflectance and directional properties of structural coloration in bird plumage. *J. Exp. Biol.*, 205(14):2017–2027, 2002.

[256] Edward Palik. *Handbook of Optical Solids*. New York: Academic Press, 1985.

[257] Stephen Palmer. *Vision Science: Photons to Phenomenology*. Cambridge, MA: MIT Press, 2002.

[258] Eric Paquette, Pierre Poulin, and George Drettakis. The simulation of paint cracking and peeling. In *Proceedings of the graphics interface 2002*, 59–68, May 2002.

[259] Eric Paquette, Pierre Poulin, and George Drettakis Surface aging by impacts. In *Proceedings of graphics interface 2001*, 175–182, June 2001.

[260] Darwyn R. Peachey. Solid texturing of complex surfaces. In *Proceedings of the 12th annual conference on computer graphics and interactive techniques*, 279–286. New York: ACM Press, 1985.

[261] Mark S. Peercy. Linear color representations for full speed spectral rendering. In *Proceedings of the 20th annual conference on computer graphics and interactive techniques*, 191–198. New York: ACM Press, 1993.

[262] Mark S. Peercy, Benjamin M. Zhu, and Daniel R. Baum. Interactive full spectral rendering. In *SI3D '95: Proceedings of the symposium on interactive 3D graphics*, 67–ff. New York: ACM Press, 1995.

[263] Fabio Pellacini, James A. Ferwerda, and Donald P. Greenberg. Toward a psychophysically-based light reflection model for image synthesis. In *Proceedings of the 27th annual conference on computer graphics and interactive techniques*, 55–64. New York: ACM Press/Addison-Wesley, 2000.

[264] Bui Tuong Phong. Illumination for computer generated pictures. *Commun. ACM*, 18(6):311– 317, 1975.

[265] Pixologic. Zbrush (software package).

[266] Marc Pollefeys, Luc Van Gool, Maarten Vergauwen, Frank Verbiest, Kurt Cornelis, Jan Tops, and Reinhard Koch. Visual modeling with a hand-held camera. *Int. J. Comput. Vision*, 59(3):207–232, 2004.

[267] D. Ponceleon , G.S.P. Miller, and S. M. Rubin. Lazy decompression of surface light fields for precomputed global illumination. In *Proceedings of the 9th Eurographics workshop on rendering*, 281–292, 1998.

[268] Joanna L. Power, Brad S. West, Eric J. Stollnitz, and David H. Salesin. Reproducing color images as duotones. In *Proceedings of the 23rd annual conference on computer graphics and interactive techniques*, 237–248. New York: ACM Press, 1996.

[269] R. O. Prum and R. Torres. Structural colouration of avian skin: convergent evolution of coherently scattering dermal collagen arrays. *Journal of Experimental Biology*, 206(14): 2409–2429, 2003.

[270] Przemyslaw Prusinkiewicz, Aristid Lindenmayer, and James Hanan. Development models of herbaceous plants for computer imagery purposes. In *SIGGRAPH '88: Proceedings of the 15th annual conference on computer graphics and interactive techniques*, 141–150. New York: ACM Press, 1988.

[271] Ravi Ramamoorthi and Pat Hanrahan. An efficient representation for irradiance environment maps. In *SIGGRAPH '01: Proceedings of the 28th annual conference on computer graphics and interactive techniques*, 497–500. New York: ACM Press, 2001.

[272] Erik Reinhard, Greg Ward, Sumanta Pattanaik, and Paul Debevec. *High Dynamic Range Imaging: Acquisition, Display and Image-Based Lighting*. San Francisco: Morgan Kaufmann, 2005.

[273] Ilene M. Reinitz, Mary L. Johnson, T. Scott Hemphill, Al M. Gilbertson, Ron H. Geurts, Barak D. Green, and James E. Shigley. Modeling the appearance of the round brilliant cut diamond: an analysis of fire and more about brilliance. *Gems and Gemology*, 37(3):174–197, 2001.

[274] Right Hemisphere. DeepPaint (software package).

[275] James Robertson. *Forensic Examination of Human Hair*. Boca Raton, FL: CRC Press, 1999.

[276] C. Rocchini, P. Cignoni, C. Montani, and R. Scopigno. Acquiring, stitching and blending diffuse appearance attributes on 3D models. *The Visual Computer*, 18(3):186–204, 2002.

[277] Barry Rubin. Tailored fiber cross sections. *Advanced Materials*, 10(15):1225–1227, 1998.

[278] B. Rubin, H. Kobsa, and S. M. Shearer. Prediction and verification of an iridescent synthetic fiber. *Appl. Opt.*, 36:6388–6392, 1997.

[279] D. Rudolf, D. Mould, and E. Neufeld. Simulating wax crayons. In *Proceedings of the 11th Pacific graphics conference on computer graphics and applications*, 163–172, Banff, AB, October 2003.

[280] Adam Runions, Martin Fuhrer, Brendan Lane, Pavol Federl, Anne-Gálle Rolland-Lagan, and Przemyslaw Prusinkiewicz. Modeling and visualization of leaf venation patterns. *ACM Trans. Graph.*, 24(3):702–711, 2005.

[281] Holly Rushmeier, Gabriel Taubin, and André Guéziec. Applying shape from lighting variation to bump map capture. In Julie Dorsey and Philipp Slusallek, editors, *Proceedings of the 8th Eurographics rendering workshop*, 35–44, Saint Etienne, France, June 16–18. New York: Springer-Verlag Wien, 1997.

[282] J. S. Ryu, S. G. Park, T. J. Kwak, M. Y. Chang, M. E. Park, K. H. Choi, K. H. Sung, H. J. Shin, C. K. Lee, Y. S. Kang, et al. Improving lip wrinkles: lipstick-related image analysis. *Skin Research and Technology*, 11(3):157, 2005.

[283] Yoichi Sato, Mark D. Wheeler, and Katsushi Ikeuchi. Object shape and reflectance modeling from observation. In *Proceedings of the 24th annual conference on computer graphics and interactive techniques*, 379–387. New York: ACM Press/Addison-Wesley, 1997.

[284] Christophe Schlick. A fast alternative to Phong's specular shading model. *Graphics Gems IV*, 363–366, 1994.

[285] Christophe Schlick. A customizable reflectance model for everyday rendering. In Michael Cohen, Claude Puech, and François Sillion, editors, *Rendering Techniques '93*, 73–84. Consolidation Express Bristol. *Proceedings 4th Eurographics rendering workshop*, Paris, June 14–16, 1993.

[286] Clement Shimizu and Gary Meyer. Computer-aided color appearance design using environment map-based lighting. In *Eurographics workshop on computational aesthetics in graphics, visualization, and imaging*, 223–230, 2005.

[287] Clement Shimizu, Gary W. Meyer, and Joseph P. Wingard. Interactive goniochromatic color design. In *Eleventh Color Imaging Conference*, 16–22, 2003.

[288] Peter Shirley, Michael Gleicher, Stephen R. Marschner, Erik Reinhard, Kelvin Sun, and William B. Thompson. *Fundamentals of Computer Graphics, Second Edition*. Natick, MA: A. K. Peters, 2005.

[289] R. Siegel and J. Howell. *Thermal Radiation Heat Transfer, Fourth Edition*. New York: Taylor and Francis, 2001.

[290] François X. Sillion, James R. Arvo, Stephen H. Westin, and Donald P. Greenberg. A global illumination solution for general reflectance distributions. In *SIGGRAPH '91:*

Proceedings of the 18th annual conference on computer graphics and interactive techniques, 187–196. New York: ACM Press, 1991.

[291] François X. Sillion and Claude Puech. *Radiosity and Global Illumination*. San Francisco: Morgan Kaufmann, 1994.

[292] Peter-Pike Sloan, Jesse Hall, John Hart, and John Synder. Cliustered principal components for precomputed radiance transfer. *ACM Trans. Graph*, 22(3): 382–391, 2003.

[293] David Small. Simulating watercolor by modeling diffusion, pigment, and paper fibers. In *Proceedings of SPIE—Volume 1460: image handling and reproduction systems integration*, 140–146, August 1991.

[294] Brian E. Smits and Gary W. Meyer. Newton's color: simulating interference phenomena in realistic image synthesis. In Kadi Bouatouch and Christian Bouville, editors, *Rendering techniques '90, Eurographics*, 185–194, *Proceedings of the 1st Eurographics rendering workshop*, June 11–13. Rennas, France: Imprimerie de l'université de Rennes, 1990.

[295] W. Snyder, Z. Wan, and X. Li. Thermodynamic constraints on reflectance reciprocity and Kirchhoff's law. *Applied Optics*, 37(16):3464–3470, 1998.

[296] W. C. Snyder. Definition and invariance properties of structured surface BRDF. *IEEE Trans. Geoscience and Remote Sensing*, 40:1032–1037, 2002.

[297] Jos Stam. Diffraction shaders. In *Proceedings of the 26th annual conference on computer graphics and interactive techniques*, 101–110. New York: ACM Press/Addison-Wesley, 1999.

[298] Jos Stam. An illumination model for a skin layer bounded by rough surfaces. In *Proceedings of the 12th Eurographics workshop on rendering techniques*, 39–52, London: Springer-Verlag, 2001.

[299] Jos Stam and Eugene Fiume. Depicting fire and other gaseous phenomena using diffusion processes. In *SIGGRAPH '95: Proceedings of the 22nd annual conference on computer graphics and interactive techniques*, 129–136. New York: ACM Press, 1995.

[300] G. N. Stamatas and N. Kollias. Blood stasis contributions to the perception of skin pigmentation. *Journal of Biomedical Optics*, 9(2):315–322, 2006.

[301] A. James Stewart. Vicinity shading for enhanced perception of volumetric data. In *Proceedings of IEEE visualization*, 355–362, October 2003.

[302] Eric J. Stollnitz, Victor Ostromoukhov, and David H. Salesin. Reproducing color images using custom inks. In *Proceedings of the 25th annual conference on computer graphics and interactive techniques*, 267–274. New York: ACM Press, 1998.

[303] Maureen Stone. *A Field Guide to Digital Color*. Natick, MA: A. K. Peters, 2003.

[304] L. Streit and W. Heidrich. A biologically-parameterized feather model. *Computer Graphics Forum*, 21(3):565–565, 2002.

[305] Yinlong Sun. Rendering biological iridescences with RGB-based renderers. *ACM Trans. Graph.*, 25(1):100–129, 2006.

[306] Yinlong Sun, F. David Fracchia, Thomas W. Calvert, and Mark S. Drew. Deriving spectra from colors and rendering light interference. *IEEE Comput. Graph. Appl.*, 19(4):61–67, 1999.

[307] Yinlong Sun, F. David Fracchia, Mark S. Drew, and Thomas W. Calvert. Rendering iridescent colors of optical disks. In *Proceedings of the Eurographics workshop on rendering techniques*, 341–352, London: Springer-Verlag, 2000.

[308] Yinlong Sun, F. David Fracchia, Mark S. Drew, and Thomas W. Calvert. A spectrally based framework for realistic image synthesis. *The Visual Computer*, 17(7):429–444, 2001.

[309] Atsushi Takagi, Hitoshi Takaoka, Tetsuya Oshima, and Yoshinori Ogata. Accurate rendering technique based on colorimetric conception. In *SIGGRAPH '90: Proceedings of the 17th annual conference on computer graphics and interactive techniques*, 263–272. New York: ACM Press, 1990.

[310] A. Takagi, A. Watanabe, and G. Baba. Prediction of spectral reflectance factor distribution of automotive paint finishes. *Color Research and Application*, 30(4): 275–282, 2005.

[311] P. Tan, S. Lin, L. Quan, B. Guo, and H. Y. Shum. Multiresolution reflectance filtering. *Proceedings Eurographics symposium on rendering 2005*, 111–116, 2005.

[312] David C. Tannenbaum, Peter Tannenbaum, and Michael J. Wozny. Polarization and birefringency considerations in rendering. In *Proceedings of the 21st annual conference on computer graphics and interactive techniques*, 221–222. New York: ACM Press, 1994.

[313] K. E. Torrance and E. M. Sparrow. Theory for off-specular reflection from rough surfaces. *Journal of the Optical Society of America*, 57(9):1105–1114, 1967.

[314] T. S. Trowbridge and K. P. Reitz. Average irregularity representation of a roughened surface for ray reflection. *J. Opt. Soc. America*, 65:531–536, 1975.

[315] Roger Y. Tsai. An efficient and accurate camera calibration technique for 3D machine vision. In *Proceedings of IEEE conference on computer vision and pattern recognition*, 364–374, 1986.

[316] Greg Turk. Texture synthesis on surfaces. In *SIGGRAPH '01: Proceedings of the 28th annual conference on computer graphics and interactive techniques*, 347–354. New York: ACM Press, 2001.

[317] Kazunori Umeda, Megumi Shinozaki, Guy Godin, and Marc Rioux. Correction of color information of a 3D model using a range intensity image. In *3DIM '05: Proceedings of the fifth international conference on 3D digital imaging and modeling*, 229–236, 2005.

[318] Steve Upstill. *The Renderman Companion: A Programmer's Guide to Realistic Computer Graphics*. Boston: Addison-Wesley, 1990.

[319] H. C. van de Hulst. *Light Scattering by Small Particles*. New York: Dover, 1981.

[320] C. Vogelmann. Plant tissue optics. *Annual Review of Plant Physiol. Plant Mol. Biol.*, 44:231–251, 1993.

[321] Pete Vukusic and J. Roy Sambles. Photonic structures in biology. *Nature*, 424:852–855, 2003.

[322] Bruce Walter, Adam Arbree, Kavita Bala, and Donald P. Greenberg. Multi-dimensional lightcuts. In *SIGGRAPH '06: ACM SIGGRAPH papers*, 1081–1088. New York: ACM Press, 2006.

[323] Kenneth A. Walters. *Dermatological and Transdermal Formulations*. New York: Marcel Dekker, 177–124, 2002.

[324] Jiaping Wang, Xin Tong, Stephen Lin, Minghao Pan, Chao Wang, Hujun Bao, Baining Guo, and Heung-Yeung Shum. Appearance manifolds for modeling time-variant appearance of materials. *ACM Trans. Graph.*, 25(3):754–761, 2006.

[325] Lifeng Wang, Wenle Wang, Julie Dorsey, Xu Yang, Baining Guo, and Heung-Yeung Shum. Real-time rendering of plant leaves. In *SIGGRAPH '05: ACM SIGGRAPH papers*, 712–719. New York: ACM Press, 2005.

[326] Gregory J. Ward. Measuring and modeling anisotropic reflection. In *Proceedings of the 19th annual conference on computer graphics and interactive techniques*, 265–272. New York: ACM Press, 1992.

[327] Greg Ward and Elena Eydelberg-Vileshin. Picture perfect RGB rendering using spectral prefiltering and sharp color primaries. In *Proceedings of the 13th Eurographics workshop on rendering*, 117–124, 2002.

[328] Kelly Ward, Florence Bertails, Tae-Yong Kim, Marie-Paule Cani Stephen R. Marschner, and Ming C. Lin. A survey on hair modeling: styling, simulation, and rendering. *IEEE Transactions on Visualization and Computer Graphics*, 13(2):213–234, 2007.

[329] C. Ware. *Information Visualization*. San Francisco: Morgan Kaufmann, 2004.

[330] Joseph D. Warren and Henrik Weimer. *Subdivision Methods for Geometric Design: A Constructive Approach*. San Francisco: Morgan Kaufmann, 2001.

[331] Li-Yi Wei and Marc Levoy. Texture synthesis over arbitrary manifold surfaces. In *SIGGRAPH '01: Proceedings of the 28th annual conference on computer graphics and interactive techniques*, 355–360. New York: ACM Press, 2001.

[332] Frederick M. Weinhaus and Venkat Devarajan. Texture mapping 3D models of real-world scenes. *ACM Comput. Surv.*, 29(4):325–365, 1997.

[333] Stephen H. Westin, James R. Arvo, and Kenneth E. Torrance. Predicting reflectance functions from complex surfaces. In *Proceedings of the 19th annual conference on computer graphics and interactive techniques*, 255–264. New York: ACM Press, 1992.

[334] Harold B. Westlund and Gary W. Meyer. Applying appearance standards to light reflection models. In *Proceedings of the 28th annual conference on computer graphics and interactive techniques*, 501–551. New York: ACM Press, 2001.

[335] Harold Westlund and Gary Meyer. A BRDF database employing the Beard–Maxwell reflection model. In *Proc. Graphics Interface*, 189–201, May 2002.

[336] Tim Weyrich, Wojciech Matusik, Hanspeter Pfister, Bernd Bickel, Craig Donner, Chien Tu, Janet McAndless, Jinho Lee, Addy Ngan, Henrik Wann Jensen, and Markus Gross. Analysis of human faces using a measurement-based skin reflectance model. In *SIGGRAPH '06: ACM SIGGRAPH papers*, 1013–1024. New York: ACM Press, 2006.

[337] Alexander Wilkie, Robert F. Tobler, and Werner Purgathofer. Combined rendering of polarization and fluorescence effects. In *Proceedings of the 12th Eurographics workshop on rendering*, 197–204, 2001.

[338] R. J. Wolfe. *3D Graphics: A Visual Approach*. New York: Oxford University Press, 2000.

[339] Lawrence B. Wolff and David J. Kurlander. Ray tracing with polarization parameters. *IEEE Comput. Graph. Appl.*, 10(6):44–55, 1990.

[340] Tien-Tsin Wong, Wai-Yin Ng, and Pheng-Ann Heng. A geometry dependent texture generation framework for simulating surface imperfections. In Julie Dorsey and Philipp Slusallek, editors, *Proceedings 8th Eurographics rendering workshop*, 139–150, Saint Etienne, France, June 16–18. New York: Springer-Verlag Wein, 1997.

[341] Daniel N. Wood, Daniel I. Azuma, Ken Aldinger, Brian Curless, Tom Duchamp, David H. Salesin, and Werner Stuetzle. Surface light fields for 3D photography. In *Proceedings of the 27th annual conference on computer graphics and interactive techniques*, 287–296. New York: ACM Press/Addison-Wesley, 2000.

[342] R. J. Woodham. Photometric method for determining surface orientation from multiple images. *Optical Engineering*, 19:139–144, 1980.

[343] Steven Worley. A cellular texture basis function. In *SIGGRAPH '96: Proceedings of the 23rd annual conference on computer graphics and interactive techniques*, 291–294. New York: ACM Press, 1996.

[344] Chen Xu, Athinodoros Georghiades, Holly Rushmeier, and Julie Dorsey. A system for reconstructing integrated texture maps for large structures. In *Proceedings of the 3rd international symposium on 3D data processing, visualization and transmission*, 2006.

[345] Chris I. Yessios. Computer drafting of stones, wood, plant and ground materials. In *SIGGRAPH '79: Proceedings of the 6th annual conference on computer graphics and interactive techniques*, 190–198. New York: ACM Press, 1979.

[346] Shigeki Yokoi, Kosuke Kurashige, and Jun Ichiro Toriwaki. Rendering gems with aterism or chatoyancy. *The Visual Computer*, 2(5):307–312, September 1986.

[347] Yizhou Yu, Paul Debevec, Jitendra Malik, and Tim Hawkins. Inverse global illumination: recovering reflectance models of real scenes from photographs. In *Proceedings of SIGGRAPH '99*, Annual Conference Series, 215–224, August 1999.

[348] Ying-Qing Xu, Yanyun Chen, Stephen Lin, Hua Zhong, Enhua Wu, Baining Guo, and Heung-Yeung Shum. Photorealistic rendering of knitwear using the lumislice. In *Proceedings of the 28th annual conference on computer graphics and interactive techniques*, 391–398. New York: ACM Press, 2001.

[349] Ying Yuan, Tosiyasu L. Kunii, Naota Inamato, and Lining Sun. Gemstone fire: Adaptive dispersive ray tracing of polyhedrons. *The Visual Computer*, 4(5):259–270, November 1988.

[350] Z. Zhang. A flexible new technique for camera calibration. *IEEE Transactions on Pattern Analysis and Machine Intelligence*, 22(11):1330–1334, 2000.

[351] S. Zhukov, A. Iones, and G. Kronin. An ambient light illumination model. In *Rendering Techniques '98*, Eurographics, 45–56. New York: Springer-Verlag, 1998.

[352] Todd E. Zickler, Peter N. Belhumeur, and David J. Kriegman. Helmholtz stereopsis: exploiting reciprocity for surface reconstruction. *Int. J. Comput. Vision*, 49(2–3): 215–227, 2002.

[353] Arno Zinke and Andreas Weber. Light scattering from filaments. *IEEE Trans. on Vis. and Comp. Graphics*, 13(2):342–356, 2007.

Index

Printed and bound by CPI Group (UK) Ltd, Croydon, CR0 4YY

03/10/2024

01040299-0001